TECHNOLOGY, WAR AND FASCISM

COLLECTED PAPERS OF HERBERT MARCUSE
EDITED BY DOUGLAS KELLNER

Volume One
TECHNOLOGY, WAR AND FASCISM

Volume Two
TOWARDS A CRITICAL THEORY OF SOCIETY

Volume Three
FOUNDATIONS OF THE NEW LEFT

Volume Four
ART AND LIBERATION

Volume Five
PHILOSOPHY, PSYCHOANALYSIS AND EMANCIPATION

Volume Six
MARXISM, REVOLUTION AND UTOPIA

TECHNOLOGY, WAR AND FASCISM

HERBERT MARCUSE

COLLECTED PAPERS
OF HERBERT MARCUSE

Volume One

Edited by
Douglas Kellner

London and New York

First published 1998 by Routledge
11 New Fetter Lane, London EC4P 4EE

Simultaneously published in the USA and Canada
by Routledge
29 West 35th Street, New York, NY 10001

Typeset in Sabon by Keystroke, Jacaranda Lodge, Wolverhampton
Printed and bound in Great Britain by Biddles Ltd,
Guildford and King's Lynn

British Library Cataloguing in Publication Data
A catalogue record for this book is available from the British Library

Library of Congress Cataloguing in Publication Data
Marcuse, Herbert, 1898–
Technology, war, and fascism / Herbert Marcuse; edited by Douglas
Kellner.
(Collected papers of Herbert Marcuse; v. 1)
Includes bibliographical references and index.
1. Technology—Philosophy. 2. War (Philosophy) 3. Fascism.
4. National socialism—Germany. 5. Political science—Philosophy.
I. Kellner, Douglas. II. Title. III. Series: Marcuse,
Herbert, 1898– Collected papers of Herbert Marcuse; v. 1
B945.M2983T43 1988
[T14]
191—dc21 97-14885

ISBN 0–415–13780–2

In remembrance of the victims of fascism

CONTENTS

FOREWORD

━━━━━━━━━━

Peter Marcuse

I am very pleased that these papers from my father's unpublished works are finally seeing the light of day, in a fashion accessible both to the general interested reader and to scholars. They are, I think, remarkably relevant today. Their historical interest is indisputable: the contribution of the Frankfurt School in shaping critical social theory, and my father's role in both the intellectual and the political (he always saw them together) history of the new left and the diverse movements of our time are important in any attempt to assess the possibilities of progressive social change.

But the interest of the pieces collected in this volume goes beyond the historical. They speak to issues at the cutting edge of social debate today. One will find here:

- striking examples of discourse analysis (in pieces dealing both with fascist propaganda and the means of combating it);
- contributions to clarity in the "culture wars" (in pieces dealing with anti-Semitism, with the German personality and with the cultural conditions in the West that permitted the rise of fascism);
- notes on social change provocative in the context of the defeat of real existing socialism and the re-examination of social democracy.

And one will find a deeply troubling question raised: Is fascism a foreign (in both senses of the word) excrescence grafted on the main body of Western liberal democracy, made possible only by the weakness of the Weimar Republic and the Great Depression, rejected and combated tooth and nail by the Western democracies, or might it be an outgrowth of tendencies internal to those democracies? There is even an undercurrent in the analysis which suggests fascism as the logical further development of democracies within the prevailing social and economic systems. Those hints, of course, arose with the context of the fall of Weimar, the strong fascist tendencies in Italy, France, Spain, even Britain, the ambiguities of the war and the incipient cold war, and McCarthyism in the United States. My father always strongly rejected any suggestion that conditions in the United States, at their political worst, should be labeled "fascist" or compared to Nazism. Yet the question of whether authoritarian tendencies (or chaotic tendencies as in Neumann's *Behemoth*) are integrally linked to other aspects of existing Western-style democracies remains an open and troubling one today.

Personal history is interwoven with intellectual and political events in these papers. We debated whether letters belonged here: whether some should be published at all. My father had a deep sense of personal privacy, both as a character trait and as a political expression of resistance to the commodification of the private. Yet the letters contain substantive discussions also. We could have edited out, expurgated some of the material. While not publishing every letter my father wrote (most, indeed, are no longer extant; he did not squirrel away no longer needed papers), our selection was based on interest, and every letter that is included is printed in full.

That decision was in part painful for me personally. The juxtaposition of the letters to Horkheimer and the exchange with Heidegger highlights the point. I was only in my early teens when most of the correspondence published here was written, but I remember certain things very well. I remember that the personal relationships between several members of the Institute and its leadership were quite different from their intellectual relationship. Horkheimer lived in Scarsdale when the Institute was in New York City, and in Pacific Palisades when it was in Los Angeles, in high-class enclaves of the well-to-do. The lifestyle was formal, with servants. Children visiting were expected to be (when they were brought along at all) quiet and inconspicuous. Members "siezt" each other, addressed each other with the formal "you," although they had been working together (and through tremendous turmoil) for over ten years. The affairs of the Institute were not run democratically: Horkheimer, with Pollock's advice, made all the administrative (including financial) decisions. Both my mother and the Neumanns were desperate (I do not think I exaggerate, although I was young and only occasionally privy to the discussions) to escape from the dependence on the Institute. Franz Neumann aggressively sought a position in Washington, not because the money for him at the

Institute ran out, but because he wanted out. My mother wanted my father to do the same. I remember I once wrote a P.S. on a letter from my mother in Santa Monica to my father in Washington, after he had gone out there to look for a position, in which I said we all looked forward to going there too, and how pleased my mother was. I think they had arguments about it; between my mother's (and the Neumanns') pull, and Horkheimer and Pollock's push, the decision was made.

Yet the letters from my father to Horkheimer show a deep ambivalence about the move, and reflect none of the personal tensions that I experienced on a family level. In the letters to Heidegger, my father speaks of the inseparability of the personal and the political, and in his relations with others he always put the criterion of decency ("Anständigkeit") first when making an assessment. Yet, in this one case, with the leadership of the Institute, it was different. Later on, after Horkheimer and Adorno had returned to Germany, and particularly when they both ended up supporting the U.S. position on Vietnam and proved entirely unsympathetic, indeed uncomprehending, about the student movement, there did indeed come a break. Whether that break was foreshadowed in the 1940s in their respective intellectual directions I am not in a position to say; the material in this volume sheds some light on the question. In what was not said as well as what was said, the letters published here were in part painful for me to read.

This is the first volume in a projected six-volume edition of the most interesting writings that were found in my father's files after his death. If we had published everything, it would have been some sixteen volumes. What has been left out is of much less interest: repetitive drafts of papers, business correspondence, reading notes, etc. They will all be available to interested scholars at the Marcuse archives and the Stadt-und-Universitäts-Bibliothek in Frankfurt. The material published will be organized both by theme and by period; Doug Kellner's Preface sketches the plan. We expect they will appear at the rate of one a year until completed. We are grateful to Routledge for their willingness to undertake this large project and for their helpfulness in bringing it to fruition.

I am personally delighted that Doug Kellner was willing to undertake the task. Doug Kellner participated in the student movement influenced by my father and met him first when he was a philosophy student at Columbia University in the 1960s. He and other young student activists of the period were deeply influenced by my father's thought, and Doug began the research in the 1960s that produced his book *Herbert Marcuse and the Crisis of Marxism*,[1] eventually published in 1984. Kellner has also been one of the major contributors to preserving and developing the Frankfurt

School tradition in the English-speaking countries with his book *Critical Theory, Marxism and Modernity*,[2] his *Critical Theory and Society: A Reader*,[3] his many articles on critical theory, and the Frankfurt School website that he is developing. I am therefore happy that he has agreed to participate in the publishing of my father's writings.

Santa Monica, 1940: Peter, Sophie and Herbert Marcuse

1 London and Berkeley: Macmillan and University of California Press
2 Cambridge and Baltimore: Polity Press and Johns Hopkins University Press, 1989
3 London and New York: Routledge, 1989

PREFACE

The Unknown Marcuse: New Archival Discoveries

Douglas Kellner

During the late 1960s and early 1970s, Herbert Marcuse was considered one of the world's most important living theorists. Acclaimed throughout the world as a philosopher of liberation and revolution, Marcuse was a prominent figure in the Zeitgeist of the times, deeply influencing the New Left and oppositional movements. His work was passionately debated by individuals of every political and theoretical persuasion, and he deeply influenced a generation of radical intellectuals and activists. Indeed, his books even reached a general public and he was discussed, attacked and celebrated in the mass media, as well as scholarly publications.

Since his death in 1979, however, Herbert Marcuse's influence has been steadily waning. There has been, to be sure, a steady stream of books on Marcuse,[1] and the publication of his unpublished texts could lead to new

---

1 Significant texts on Marcuse since his death include Morton Schoolman, *The Imaginary Witness*. New York: Free Press, 1980; Vincent Geoghegan, *Reason and Eros: The Social Theory of Herbert Marcuse*. London: Pluto Press, 1981; Barry Katz, *Herbert Marcuse and the Art of Liberation*. London: New Left Books, 1982; Douglas Kellner, *Herbert Marcuse and the Crisis of Marxism*. London and Berkeley: Macmillan Press and University of California Press, 1984; C. Fred

interest in his work. While the waning of the revolutionary movements with which he was involved helps explain Marcuse's slip in popularity, the lack of new texts and publications has also contributed. For while there have been a large number of new translations of works by Benjamin, Adorno and Habermas during the past decade, little untranslated or un-collected material by Marcuse has appeared. In addition, while there has been great interest in recent years in the writings of French "postmodern," or "poststructuralist," theorists, such as Foucault, Derrida, Baudrillard, Lyotard and others, Marcuse did not fit into the fashionable debates concerning modern and postmodern thought.[2] Unlike Adorno, Marcuse did not anticipate the postmodern attacks on reason and enlightenment, and his dialectics were not "negative." Rather, Marcuse subscribed to the project of reconstructing reason and of positing utopian alternatives to the existing society – a dialectical imagination that has fallen out of favor in an era that rejects revolutionary thought and grand visions of liberation and social reconstruction.

Alford, *Science and the Revenge of Nature: Marcuse and Habermas*. Gainesville: University of Florida Press, 1985; Roland Roth, *Rebellische Subjektivität: Herbert Marcuse und die neuen Protestbewegungen*. Frankfurt: Campus Press, 1985; Timothy J. Lukes, *The Flight Into Inwardness: An Exposition and Critique of Herbert Marcuse's Theory of Liberative Aesthetics*. Cranbury, N.J., London, and Toronto: Associated University Presses, 1986; Alain Martineau, *Herbert Marcuse's Utopia*. Montreal: Harvest House, 1986; Hauke Brunkhorst and Gertrud Koch, *Herbert Marcuse zur Einführung*. Hamburg: Junius Verlag, 1987; *Herbert Marcuse, Text + Kritik* 98 (April 1988); Robert Pippin, *et al.*, editors, *Marcuse: Critical Theory and the Promise of Utopia*. South Hadley, Mass.: Bergin & Garvey Publishers, 1988; *Faut-il Oublier Marcuse?*, *Archives de Philosophie*, Tome 52, Cahier 3 (Juillet–Septembre 1989); *Politik und Asthetik am Ende der Industriegesellschaft: Zur Aktualität von Herbert Marcuse*, *Tüte*, Sonderheft (September 1989); Peter-Erwin Jansen, editor, *Befreiung denken – Ein politischer Imperative*. Offenbach: Verlag 2000, 1990; Bernard Görlich, *Die Wette mit Freud: Drei Studien zu Herbert Marcuse*. Frankfurt: Nexus, 1991; Institut für Sozialforschung, *Kritik und Utopie im Werk von Herbert Marcuse*. Frankfurt: Suhrkamp, 1992; Gérard Raulet, *Herbert Marcuse. Philosophie de l'émancipation*. Paris: Presses Universitaires de France, 1992; and John Bokina and Timothy J. Lukes, editors, *Marcuse: From the New Left to the Next Left*. Lawrence, Kansas: University of Kansas Press, 1994.

2 In the Marcuse archives, I found an ad for one of Derrida's books with a contemptuous scrawl over it in Marcuse's handwriting: "This is what passes for philosophy today!" There are no references that I have found in Marcuse's texts, letters or other manuscripts to the major French theorists who I just noted. Although Marcuse spent some years in France, which he frequently visited, and kept up with many currents of French thought, he seemed to have little interest in the trends eventually identified with poststructuralist or postmodern theory. On these trends, see Steven Best and Douglas Kellner, *Postmodern Theory: Critical Interrogations* (London and New York: Macmillan Press and Guilford Press, 1991) and *The Postmodern Turn* (New York: Guilford Press, 1997).

The neglect of Marcuse may be altered through the publication of a wealth of material, much of it unpublished and unknown, that is found in the Herbert Marcuse archives in Frankfurt.[3] The present volume – the first of six planned collections from the Marcuse archives which will be published by Routledge – contains some extremely interesting material from the 1940s, when Marcuse was engaged in collaborative work with the Institute for Social Research, and then working for the U.S. government in Washington as his contribution to the war against German fascism. Our reader opens with essays on modern technology, National Socialism and theories of social change that Marcuse composed during his collaboration with the Institute for Social Research. This material is followed by analyses of German fascism drafted just before and during his work with the U.S. government. Next, we provide some unpublished post-war 1940s essays that anticipate Marcuse's later theoretical, political and aesthetic perspectives. And the volume concludes with letters to Max Horkheimer and Martin Heidegger which are of historical and theoretical interest, illuminating Marcuse's life and thought during a momentous historical epoch that shaped the contours of the second half of the twentieth century.

The work collected in this volume should make clear the continuing relevance of Marcuse's thought to contemporary issues. The texts published here exhibit his penetrating critiques of technology and analyses of the ways that modern technology is producing novel forms of society and culture with new modes of social control. His analyses of fascism reveal the connections between totalitarianism, capitalism, technology and potent forms of cultural domination. Several essays demonstrate the abiding importance of philosophy, social theory and art for the emancipatory project. Indeed, much of the material collected provides exemplary attempts to link theory with practice, to develop ideas that can be used to grasp and transform existing social reality.

The texts that we have assembled should thus provide fresh insight into Marcuse's work and indicate his enduring significance in the contemporary moment. Succeeding collections from the archives will be published at one-year intervals and will also provide inaccessible and unpublished material that should demonstrate Marcuse's contemporary relevance and abiding interest. The collections will be organized thematically around topics such as Marcuse's aesthetics, philosophical work, critical theory of society, engagement with Marxism and interventions in the 1960s. Each

---

3 Information on the origin, genesis and significance of the essays will be found in my Introduction, and bibliographical notes will precede each essay.

volume will contain unpublished manuscripts, or texts difficult to access, letters and notes, plus introductory essays which contextualize the works and indicate the persisting importance of Marcuse's thought as we prepare for the next millennium.

ACKNOWLEDGMENTS

I am especially indebted to Peter Marcuse, who chose me to edit these manuscripts, made his father's unpublished writings available to me, and discussed and commented on each stage of this work. I would also like to thank Adrian Driscoll, Emma Davis, Anna Gerber and Barbara Duke for help in bringing the manuscripts to publication and to Sandra Dykstra for negotiating the contract with Routledge.

Thanks are due to AKG London for the photograph on page 261, to Rowohlt Verlag for those on pages 39 and 229 which are from *Max Horkheimer* by Helmut Gumnior and Rudolf Ringuth (1973), and to Peter Marcuse for all other photographs, which he made available from his private collection.

The Frankfurt School in exile: Franz Neumann, Inge Neumann, Golde
Löwenthal, Leo Löwenthal, Herbert Marcuse, Sophie Marcuse (c. 1937)

INTRODUCTION

Technology, War and Fascism: Marcuse in the 1940s

Douglas Kellner

From 1942–1951, Herbert Marcuse worked for various agencies of the United States government, including World War Two intelligence agencies and the State Department. During this period, Marcuse wrote some important essays on German fascism and carried out historical and theoretical studies that shaped his subsequent oeuvre. His 1940s work provides substantive historical insight into German fascism and a strong historico-empirical grounding for his later thought and writings, which would continue to engage the most important issues and events of his times. The insights into fascism, the trends of advanced industrial societies and the emancipatory potential of critical social theory and art present in Marcuse's 1940s work continues to be of importance today, as new technologies transform every aspect of life and various fascist and rightwing movements persistently prey on the insecurities and fears of our epoch.

In this Introduction, I provide some contextual analysis of the genesis of Marcuse's texts of the 1940s and indicate why I think this work is of continued significance in helping us to understand technology, war, fascism and various forms of totalitarianism which continue to threaten our future.

I argue that the 1940s were extremely important for Herbert Marcuse's own life and work, and that his unknown writings both illuminate a vitally important historical epoch and provide theoretical and political resources for the present age.[1]

MARCUSE AND THE INSTITUTE FOR SOCIAL RESEARCH

The Institute for Social Research was founded in Frankfurt, Germany, during the 1920s as the first Marxist-oriented research institute in Europe.[2] Under the directorship of Max Horkheimer, who assumed his position in 1930, the Institute developed a conception of critical social theory which they contrasted with "traditional theory." In addition, members of the Institute produced critiques of dominant theories and concepts of bourgeois ideology, philosophy and social science, and carried out analyses of the transition from liberal and market capitalism to state and monopoly capitalism, including analysis of German fascism. Marcuse participated in all of these projects and was one of the central and most productive members in the Institute along with Horkheimer, T.W. Adorno, Erich Fromm, Leo Löwenthal, Franz Neumann and Friedrich Pollock.

Yet it was Horkheimer who was the central and ruling figure of the Institute. Letters and other documents from the Horkheimer and Marcuse archives reveal the deference of the associates of the Institute toward Horkheimer and the intense competition for his favors and friendship during the insecure situation of exile when the various members were dependent on the Institute for financial support, and academic positions in America were scarce for the German exiles.[3] Horkheimer controlled

---

1 For material helpful in writing this introduction and producing this volume I am grateful to John Abroweit, Barbara Brick, Stephan Brundshuh, Helmut Dubiel, Benjamin Gregg, Martin Jay, Gunzelin Schmid Noerr and Alfons Söllner.

2 On the history and projects of the Institute for Social Research, also known as the "Frankfurt School," see Martin Jay, *The Dialectical Imagination*. Boston: Little, Brown and Company, 1973 (new edition, University of California Press, 1996); Helmut Dubiel, *Theory and Politics*. Cambridge, Mass.: MIT Press, 1985; Douglas Kellner, *Critical Theory, Marxism, and Modernity*. Cambridge and Baltimore: Polity Press and Johns Hopkins University Press, 1989; and Rolf Wiggershaus, *The Frankfurt School*. Cambridge and Cambridge, Mass.: Polity Press and MIT Press, 1995.

3 See the collections of letters and documents in Max Horkheimer, *Gesammelte Schriften*, Volumes 1–19, edited by Gunzelin Schmid Noerr and published by Fischer Verlag. These texts are an indispensable aid in understanding the vicissitudes of the Institute work and relationships during the difficult period of

the Institute purse-strings and doled out monthly stipends to the various members and associates. He also supervised publications and projects, and the Institute members contended for his approval and assignments.

Marcuse joined the Institute in 1933, fleeing from Frankfurt to work in their Geneva Branch after Hitler's rise to power. He emigrated to the United States on July 4, 1934, and soon took out naturalization papers, becoming an American citizen in 1940. In July 1934, Columbia University invited the Institute to affiliate with them and placed a building at their disposal, enabling them to organize an "International Institute for Social Research" to continue their projects. Marcuse was one of the first of the members to arrive in New York and help set up the Institute. During the 1930s, the group continued to publish their studies in German in the *Zeitschrift für Sozialforschung*, which they began publishing in Europe in 1932, though the final 1941 volumes were published in English.

H. Stuart Hughes has described the migration of European intellectual scholars to the United States fleeing fascism "as the most important cultural event – or series of events – of the second quarter of the twentieth century."[4] The German émigré scholars organized around the International Institute focused intently from the late 1930s through the 1940s on the genesis, structure and effects of German fascism, producing important insights into it and into the broader features of new forms of totalitarianism, different aspects of which were appearing in both capitalist and communist countries. Marcuse was one of the first critical theorists of the new forms of technological and political domination in the advanced industrial societies. He thus emerges from this era as an important theorist of technology, fascism and the vicissitudes of advanced industrial society – themes that he would develop in his post-World War Two writings.

While working with the Institute, Marcuse was their philosophy specialist who prepared a book *Reason and Revolution* which would introduce Hegel, Marx and social theory to English-speaking audiences and would delineate the origins and perspectives of the sort of critical social theory being developed by the Institute, which itself had strong Hegelian and Marxian roots.[5] Marcuse sought to demonstrate the incompatibility of

---

exile. Volume 12 contains many documents concerning Institute projects, including protocol descriptions of seminars, and Volumes 15–18 contain the voluminous correspondence between Horkheimer and various members of the Institute during the period of exile.

4 H. Stuart Hughes, *The Sea Change*. New York: McGraw-Hill, 1975: 1.

5 Herbert Marcuse, *Reason and Revolution*. New York: Oxford University Press, 1941. The 1954 edition published by Columbia University Press contains an important Afterword which delineates the emerging theoretical-political

Hegelian philosophy with German fascism, and how Hegel's philosophy and dialectical method contained socially critical and emancipatory motifs that were taken up in Marx and a later tradition of critical thought. Strong emphasis was put on the categories of critique, negation, contradiction and the relation of theory to practice – motifs central to Frankfurt School critical theory.

In the context in which it was written and published, *Reason and Revolution* demonstrated an anti-fascist potential in the German tradition and the continued relevance and indeed increasing importance of the need for critical social theory in the current conjuncture. In the early 1940s, when Hitler's armies were taking over Europe and marching on the Soviet Union, it appeared that German fascism would conquer the world and that vestiges of freedom, democracy and the progressive heritage of Western civilization would be eliminated. Another of Marcuse's texts of the period contained passages and pathos which articulated the dire threat to human freedom and well-being at the time. In one poignant passage, Marcuse wrote: "Under the terror that now threatens the world the ideal constricts itself to one single and at the same time common issue. Faced with fascist barbarism, everyone knows what freedom means."[6]

Our collection opens with several important texts written in the context of Marcuse's work with the Institute. An extremely significant 1941 article, "Some Social Implications of Modern Technology," published in English in the Institute's journal, contains Marcuse's first sketch of the role of technology in modern industrial societies and anticipates his later analysis in *One-Dimensional Man*.[7] In this article, Marcuse delineates the historical decline of individualism from the time of the bourgeois revolutions to the rise of the modern technological society. Individual rationality, he claims, was won in the struggle against regnant superstitions, irrationality and

---

perspectives that would inform Marcuse's *One-Dimensional Man* (Boston: Beacon Press, 1964). The 1960 Beacon Press paperback edition of *Reason and Revolution* contains a new Preface that delineates the continuing importance of Hegel's dialectical thought for Marcuse's critical theory.

6 Herbert Marcuse, "Some Social Implications of Modern Technology," *Studies in Philosophy and Social Science*, Vol. 9, Nr. 3 (1941): 435f.

7 Marcuse, "Some Social Implications." Most of the first eight volumes of the *Zeitschrift für Sozialforschung* (1932–1940) were published in German, while beginning with Volume VIII, Nr. 3 (1940) and through Volume IX (1940–1941) the Institute journal was published in English because of conditions of war and to connect more vitally with English-language scholars. Horkheimer's introduction to the volume which contains Marcuse's essay on technology indicates that: "The present issue is made up exclusively of articles written in the Institute alongside the pursuit of larger bodies of research. Dr. Pollock's article and that of Dr. Kirchheimer originated from lectures aiming at a fundamental economic and social critique of National Socialism, delivered at Columbia University as a part of a

domination, and posed the individual in a critical stance against society. Critical rationality was thus a creative principle which was both the source of the individual's liberation and society's advancement. In the emerging bourgeois ideology of the eighteenth and nineteenth centuries, the nascent liberal-democratic society was deemed the social arrangement in which the individual could pursue its own self-interest and at the same time contribute to social progress. The development of modern industry and technological rationality, however, undermined the basis of the critical rationality and submitted the individual to increasing domination by the technical–social apparatus. As capitalism and technology developed, advanced industrial society demanded increasing adjustment to the economic and social apparatus, and submission to increasingly total domination and administration. Hence, a "mechanics of conformity" spread throughout the society. The efficiency and power of technological/industrial society overwhelmed the individual, who gradually lost the earlier traits of critical rationality (i.e. autonomy, dissent, the power of negation, etc.), thus producing a decline of individuality and what Marcuse would later call a "one-dimensional society" and "one-dimensional man."

In the light of the Frankfurt School tendency to posit technology primarily as an instrument of domination and industrial society as an apparatus of social control and standardization, it is interesting to note that Marcuse presents a more dialectical theory of society and technology in his 1941 study collected in this volume (see page 41f.). He distinguishes between "technology" (defined "as a mode of production, as the totality of instruments, devices and contrivances which characterize the machine age") and "technics" (defined as the instruments and practices "of industry, transportation, communication") to distinguish the system of technological domination from technical devices and their uses. Marcuse thus distinguishes between *technology* as an entire "mode of organizing and perpetuating (or changing) social relationships, a manifestation of prevalent thought and behavior patterns, an instrument for control and domination", contrasted to *technics* which refers to techniques of production and such instruments as cars or computers. Whereas the former constitutes for

---

series by the Institute. Dr. Marcuse's article expands his paper for the same occasion into a more comprehensive discussion of the problem of the individual in present day society" (p. 365). This is not completely accurate in Marcuse's case, as examination of his lecture on National Socialism, which follows the study of technology in this volume, indicates that "Some Social Implications" pursues for the first time Marcuse's interrogations of the role of technology in modern societies, while his lecture on National Socialism focused more on the themes of state and individual under German fascism.

Marcuse a system of technological domination, he claims that the latter can themselves "promote authoritarianism as well as liberty, scarcity as well as abundance, the extension as well as the abolition of toil."

Marcuse's critique focuses on technology as a system of domination and he presents National Socialism as an example in which technology and a rationalized society and economy can serve as instruments of totalitarian domination, describing the Third Reich as a form of "technocracy" dedicated to the greatest technological efficiency – a trait shared in his analysis with industrial democracies, but which perhaps underplays the obvious irrationality of National Socialism. Yet after documenting in detail the ways that technology and technological rationality promote conformity and erode individuality, Marcuse concludes his study with a vision of how technics might produce abundance for all, eliminate the necessity for excessive toil and alienated labor, and increase the realm of freedom. Building on Marx's sketch on automation in the *Grundrisse* without citing it,[8] Marcuse writes:

> Technics hampers individual development only insofar as they are tied to a social apparatus which perpetuates scarcity, and this same apparatus has released forces which may shatter the special historical form in which technics is utilized. For this reason, all programs of an anti-technological character, all propaganda for an anti-industrial revolution serve only those who regard human needs as a by-product of the utilization of technics. The enemies of technics readily join forces with a terroristic technocracy.

The latter reference is to those German theorists like Heidegger who sharply criticized technology, yet embraced National Socialism, which in Marcuse's vision combined a terrorist technocracy with irrationalist ideology. Unlike the wholly negative critics of technology, with whom he is sometimes identified, Marcuse sketches out a dialectical theory that avoids both its technocratic celebration as inherently an instrument of liberation and progress, as well as its technophobic denunciation as solely an instrument of domination. In the concluding pages, he points to the "possible democratization of functions which technics may promote and which may facilitate complete human development in all branches of work and administration." In addition, "mechanization and standardization may one day help to shift the center of gravity from the necessities of material production to the arena of free human realization."

---

8 See Karl Marx, *Grundrisse*. London: Penguin Books, 1973: 704 ff. Later, Marcuse would explicitly and repeatedly call attention to these Marxian analyses of technology as eliminating labor and a world of want, creating the basis for a new realm of freedom.

This dialectical model is important for studying specific technologies and the technological society of the present era since contemporary discourses on technology tend to dichotomize into either technophilic celebrations of the arrival of new technologies upon which they predicate a golden future, or technophobic discourses which demonize technology as an instrument of destruction and domination. Marcuse's critical theory of technics/technology by contrast differentiates negative features with positive potentials that could be used to democratize and enhance human life. Following Marx's classical positions, Marcuse envisages the possibility that new technologies could significantly reduce the working day and increase the realm of freedom: "The less time and energy man has to expend in maintaining his life and that of society, the greater the possibility that he can 'individualize' the sphere of his human realization." The essay thus concludes with Marcusean utopian speculations on how a new technological society of abundance and wealth could allow the full realization of individual potentials and produce a new realm of freedom and happiness.

One notes the great number of American and English-language sources in Marcuse's article on technology, including Thorstein Veblen, Lewis Mumford, Thurman Arnold, Henry Wallace and others, as well as government documents and monographs on technology. Throughout the 1940s, Marcuse immersed himself in a vast variety of academic literature and primary documents, belying the image that he was merely a speculative philosopher. Indeed, Marcuse was engaging the central ideas and events of his period during the 1940s in line with the Institute project of developing a theory of the present age. This concern and the exigencies of history necessitated a serious engagement with National Socialism.

NATIONAL SOCIALISM AND A THEORY OF SOCIAL CHANGE

Throughout the early 1940s, Marcuse hoped for a more secure position with the Institute for Social Research and in particular a more formalized working relationship with Horkheimer. In April 1941, Horkheimer moved to southern California, advised by his doctor to seek a better climate, and Marcuse followed in May 1941. Indeed, part of Horkheimer's motivation to move to California was to leave behind his Institute responsibilities so that he could devote himself full time to theoretical work, especially to a long-announced project on dialectics.[9] In the Fall, however, Marcuse returned to New York to work on Institute projects and to inquire into the possibility of paid lectures for Institute members with Columbia University. In an October 15, 1941 letter to Horkheimer (see page 231), Marcuse reports a "thorough discussion" with Robert Lynd, a distinguished member of the Columbia University sociology department with which the Institute was attempting to develop closer relations and to get teaching positions for its members. This letter notes Lynd's disappointment that the Institute did not more fully integrate itself in the American cultural and academic scene, and reveals some of the tensions between the Institute and American intellectuals.

Marcuse tells Horkheimer in his October 1941 letter of a lecture that he was planning on "State and Individual under National Socialism." The lecture was part of a series of Fall 1941 lectures that the Institute was offering on German fascism at Columbia University and this volume publishes the text for the first time (see page 67f.). Marcuse opened his lecture, stating:

> Today, we need no longer refute the opinion that National Socialism signifies a *revolution*. If we understand by revolution a change in the very structure of society, that is to say, the transfer of the predominant power to a new social group, the introduction of new standards for the production and distribution of wealth, etc., then National Socialism is nothing of that sort. The following lectures will attempt to show that the same forces and interests which determined German society at least since the first World War still hold sway over the National Socialist state.[10]

Marcuse's conception of National Socialism was deeply influenced by Franz Neumann's *Behemoth*.[11] Neumann's title refers to Hobbes' contrast between the "Leviathan" – a mythical figure he deployed to describe an absolutist state – and "Behemoth," a figure of anarchy and chaos. Neumann used this figure to describe the Nazi state as a "non-state, a chaos, a situation of lawlessness, disorder, and anarchy" (xii). For Neumann, National Socialism was "a form of society in which the ruling groups control the rest of the population directly, without the mediation

---

9 See the discussion of the project to write a book on dialectics, which preoccupied Horkheimer, Marcuse and other Institute members during the early 1940s, in Wiggershaus, *The Frankfurt School*: 248ff., 302ff., passim.

10 The opening of the lecture text, from which I cite here, is slightly different from the text Marcuse prepared for publication which we include in this volume (see page 69f.). We also include the interesting concluding remarks in the lecture on sex and art under National Socialism which were excluded from the version prepared for publication (see page 89f.).

11 Franz Neumann, *Behemoth*. New York: Oxford University Press, 1942 and 1944 (page references in text). Neumann was a distinguished legal scholar and political activist who was closely associated in Weimar Germany with the German trade

of that rational though coercive apparatus hitherto known as the state"
(470). Marcuse follows Neumann in his lecture on National Socialism by
stating:

> The proposition which we are going to develop is that National Socialism has
> done away with the essential features which characterized the modern state.
> It tends to abolish any separation between state and society by transfering the
> political functions to the social groups actually in power. In other words,
> National Socialism tends toward direct and immediate selfgovernment by the
> prevailing social groups over the rest of the population. And it manipulates
> the masses by unleashing the most brutal and selfish instincts of the
> individual.

For Marcuse and Neumann, National Socialism puts aside the rule of
law and separation of powers which was the defining form of the modern
liberal state. Its ruling cliques reject the forms of parliamentary democracy
and use a combination of force and ideology to keep the masses in line.
The state itself, therefore, is not "totalitarian," but rather the Nazi party
attempts to control political, social and cultural life, while, however,
leaving ownership of the means of production in the hands of the capitalist
class. Yet National Socialism is also characterized by a tremendous degree
of societal organization, rationalization and administration. Indeed, in
"Some Social Implications of Modern Technology," Marcuse argues:
"National Socialism is a striking example of the ways in which a highly
rationalized and mechanized economy with the utmost efficiency in
production can operate in the interest of totalitarian oppression and
continued scarcity. The Third Reich is indeed a form of 'technocracy': the
technical considerations of imperialistic efficiency and rationality supersede
the traditional standards of profitability and general welfare."

Although this conception of German fascism seems contradictory,
Marcuse would consistently argue that it was characterized by tensions
between lawlessness and disorder contrasted to extreme rationalization
and order, thus seeing it both as an anarchic gangster state that systematically violated both internal and international law *and* a highly
rationalized system of social organization and domination. Marcuse also
saw National Socialism as a new kind of state in which it was difficult to

---

union movement and Social Democratic Party, both of which he represented as
lawyer. After arrest and internment in 1933, he left Germany and studied
economics in London with Harold Laski. In 1936, he emigrated to New York
and joined the Institute, becoming their most successful lecturer at Columbia
University and best-known figure in the 1940s after the publication of *Behemoth*.
Marcuse was especially close to Neumann, with whom he worked in Washington
during the war and collaborated on several projects. The two families were best
friends and Neumann helped to get his job in Washington.

say whether economic or political factors were primary. There was, in fact, a significant debate within the Institute as to whether National Socialism was or was not a new kind of post-capitalist social formation which was governed by politics more than economics. The Institute economic theorist Frederick Pollock openly argued for the "primacy of the political," arguing that National Socialism was a new form of "state capitalism" in which capital accumulation and the profit motive were secondary to fascist political objectives and goals.[12] Neumann, by contrast, argued that German fascism preserved central features of the capitalist economy and should be interpreted as a form of "Totalitarian Monopoly Capitalism," preserving the primacy of economic relations stressed by Marx.[13]

Marcuse's passage cited above describing National Socialism as a "form of technocracy" would seem to side with Pollock's account of the primacy of the political, yet in the same article Marcuse situates the analysis of the new functions of technology in contemporary societies within the context of an analysis of capitalist development, and attempts to demonstrate how "Business, technics, human needs, and nature are welded together into one rational and expedient mechanism. . . . Expediency in terms of technological reason is, at the same time, monopolistic standardization and concentration." Marcuse thus mediates between the two competing Institute positions, arguing that economic and political factors are integrally related in the construction of the fascist society. Instead of arguing for the primacy of the economic or the political, Marcuse thus claims that they are interrelated, pointing to the various connections "between private, semi-private (party) and public (governmental) bureaucracies. The efficient realization of the interests of large scale enterprise was one of the strongest motives for the transformation of economic into totalitarian political control, and efficiency is one of the main reasons for the Fascist regime's hold over its regimented population."

---

12 Pollock was a childhood friend of Horkheimer's who remained close to the Director for his entire life. He managed the Institute's funds and was their resident economist. For Pollock's position, see "State Capitalism," *Studies in Philosophy and Social Science*, Vol. IX/1941, pp. 200–225; reprinted in Bronner and Kellner 1989: 95–118. On Pollock, see Barbara Brick and Moishe Postone, "Friedrich Pollock and the 'Primacy of the Political': A Critical Examination," *International Journal of Politics*, Vol. VI, No. 3 (Fall 1976), pp. 3–28, and "Critical Pessimism and the Limits of Traditional Marxism," *Theory and Society*, Vol. 11, Nr. 5 (Sept. 1982), pp. 617–58.

13 On the Institute debates over fascism, see the sources in note 2 and Alfons Söllner, *Geschichte und Herrschaft*. Frankfurt: Suhrkamp, 1979, pp. 139ff., and the introduction by Söllner and Helmut Dubiel to their collection of Institute essays on fascism, *Wirtschaft, Recht, und Staat im Nationalsozialismus*. Frankfurt: Europäische Verlagsanstalt, 1981.

On this analysis, although German fascism involves political control over the economy and populace, economic factors continue to play an autonomous role in the constitution of fascist society and, as with Neumann, National Socialism should be interpreted in its relationship to the dynamics of monopoly capitalism. For Marcuse and Neumann, fascism represented a historical stage that followed liberal capitalism and which negated the progressive aspects of the democratic tradition (i.e. human rights, individual freedoms, parliamentary democracy, etc.). In addition, Marcuse, like Neumann, tended to stress the political tensions within National Socialism that could be used to destroy the system, whereas Pollock's pessimistic analysis seemed to posit National Socialism as a new social formation which solved the problems of the crisis-tendencies of capitalism, while preserving intact capitalist relations of production and generating a new system of domination.

In "State and Individual Under National Socialism," Marcuse discusses the structure of German fascism, its differences from the liberal state, and the relationship between its three major powers – industry, the army, and the National Socialist party. The "unity" of the fascist state is in part produced by veneration for the *Führer*, but Marcuse stresses that it is the bureaucracy which creates a systemic apparatus governed by efficiency and a form of technological rationality that really holds the system together. The resultant fascist "state-machine" is geared toward imperialist expansion and promises booty and prestige to those who submit to its dictates and pursue its aims.

The masses, who are the objects of administration and domination, are atomized individuals pursuing their self-interests, and their need for self-preservation binds them to the whole. Marcuse claims that German fascism "is not the reversal but the consummation of competitive individualism," which unleashes forces of aggression, desubliminated erotic impulses and various sado-masochistic impulses. This analysis of how the loosening of sexual taboos and moral restraints helps bind individuals to fascist society anticipates Marcuse's later concept of "repressive desublimation" in which instinctual gratification binds individuals more closely to a repressive order.

Thus, National Socialism for Marcuse both unleashes the bourgeois individual and provides gratification for individual submersion in the masses. Marcuse continued his interrogations of National Socialism in some studies for the U.S. government which I discuss in the next section. Yet a hitherto unknown set of manuscripts by Marcuse and Neumann devoted to the theory of social change, which was evidently produced during their work with the Institute for Social Research, was also found in the Marcuse archives. In this project, Marcuse and Neumann sketch out their perspectives on social transformation and indicate a more political and activist orientation than many of the other Institute members. This series of manuscripts, published here for the first time, is extremely interesting and suggests a revision of the received history of the Frankfurt School. The manuscripts on theories of social change provide fascinating material that mitigates the widespread opinion that the entire group was turning away from social practice and political action in the 1940s and reveal a quite distinct difference in political orientation between Horkheimer and Adorno in contrast to Marcuse and Neumann.[14]

Manuscripts found in the Marcuse archives suggest that Marcuse was collaborating with Neumann on a project on the "history of the doctrine on social change." Two texts, published in this volume (see pages 94f. and 107f.), indicate that Marcuse and Neumann were working together to produce a systematic treatise on theories of social change in the Western tradition of political and social thought. These comprise a longer and shorter manuscript which present overviews of the project that indicate its scope, content, method and goals. There is also a document in the Marcuse archives which appears to be proposals for a lecture or seminar course on theories of social change, along with a letter commenting on the course and a list of readings. The description of the proposed university course on the topic provides a short precis of the project:

> A historical and theoretical approach to the development of a positive theory of social change for contemporary society.
>
> The major historical changes of social systems, and the theories associated with them will be discussed. Particular attention will be paid to such transitions as those from feudalism to capitalism, from laissez-faire to organized industrial society, from capitalism to socialism and communism.[15]

A note in Marcuse's handwriting on the themes of the study indicates that he and Neumann intended to analyze conflicting tendencies toward social change and social cohesion; forces of freedom and necessity in social

---

14 Claims that the Frankfurt School was abandoning radical politics in the 1940s are made in Jay's *The Dialectical Imagination* and most other standard accounts of the Institute for Social Research, as well as polemics against the Institute for abandoning or neglecting politics. Marcuse and Neumann's work during the late 1930s and 1940s puts in question this interpretation by showing that some of the Institute members were attempting to politicize their theory and to link theory to practice. Indeed, more differentiated readings of the Frankfurt School are necessary to indicate the range of positions on theory and politics within the Institute.

15 The course description and Marcuse's notes are found in a folder in his archives marked #118.01.

change; subjective and objective factors that produce social change; patterns of social change, such as evolution and revolution; and directions of social change, such as progress, regression and cycles. The project would culminate in a "theory of social change for our society." Curiously, no one seems to know anything about the genesis, nature and fate of this project. There are no references to this work within Institute documents, no extant letters discussing the enterprise, and no surviving associate of the Institute, or scholar of critical theory that I consulted, had any information about the project.[16] And yet the manuscripts exist. They are especially interesting because they develop a theory of social change oriented toward contemporary conditions, thus seeking to fill precisely the gap that its critics had always pointed to at the Institute.

A seventeen-page typed manuscript in the Marcuse archives, entitled "A History of the Doctrine of Social Change," by Marcuse and Neumann, opens:

> Since sociology as an independent science was not established before the 19th century, the theory of society up to that time was an integral part of philosophy or of those sciences (such as the economic or juristic), the conceptual structure of which was to a large extent based upon specific philosophical doctrines. This intrinsic connection between philosophy and the theory of society (a connection which will be explained in the text) formulates the pattern of all particular theories of social change occurring in the ancient world, in the middle ages, and on the commencement of modern times. One decisive result is the emphasis on the fact that social change cannot be interpreted within a particular social science, but must be understood within the social and natural totality of human life. This conception uses, to a large extent, psychological factors in the theories of social change. However, the derivation of social and political concepts from the "psyche" of man is not a psychological method in the modern sense but rather involves the negation of psychology as a special science. For the Greeks, psychological concepts were essentially ethical, social and political ones, to be integrated into the ultimate science of philosophy.

This passage clearly reveals the typically Marcusean tendency – shared by other members of the Frankfurt School – to integrate philosophy, social

---

16 Part of the problem is that there is no correspondence extant between Marcuse and Neumann, possibly because their close association, first, in New York on Institute work and, then, in Washington on government projects precluded correspondence. Yet it is somewhat mysterious that no Neumann/Marcuse correspondence whatsoever remains and that there is no reference to this text in any Institute documents, letters or discussion. Possibly, Marcuse and Neumann, totally dependent on Horkheimer for Institute support, feared that Horkheimer and others might find their project too "political," and even "Marxist" (since they seemed to privilege Marxian conceptions of social change) in an era when Horkheimer was concerned to cover over the Institute's Marxian roots.

theory, psychology and politics. While standard academic practice tended to separate these fields, Marcuse and his colleagues perceived their interrelation. Thus, Marcuse and Neumann read ancient philosophy as containing a theory of social change which was defined by a search for the conditions that would produce the highest fulfillment of the individual. This project begins, they claim, with the Sophists and proceeds through Plato, Aristotle and the later Greek and Roman schools via medieval to modern philosophy.

Marcuse and Neumann contrasted conservative and progressive theories of social change, thus presenting theories of society as a contested terrain between opposing tendencies attempting to conserve or transform existing societies, rather than, say, as a monolithic bloc of ideological legitimation of the existing social order. Generally, Marcuse and Neumann contrasted critical, materialist and progressivist theories with more idealist and conservative ones.[17] They also championed a synthesis of philosophy, politics and social theory in developing a theory of social change, noting that modern sociology "has severed the intrinsic connection between the theory of society and philosophy which is still operative in Marxism and has treated the problem of social change as a particular sociological question." Marcuse and Neumann, by contrast, argued for the importance of transdisciplinary perspectives in the spirit of critical theory.

This project is extremely interesting within the history of the Frankfurt School since it shows that in the 1940s there were two tendencies within critical theory: 1) the more pessimistic philosophical-cultural analysis of the trends of Western civilization being developed by Horkheimer and Adorno in *Dialectic of Enlightenment*; and 2) the more practical-political development of critical theory as a theory of social change anticipated by Marcuse and Neumann. For Marcuse and Neumann, critical theory was conceptualized as a theory of social change that would connect philosophy, social theory and radical politics – precisely the project of 1930s critical theory that Horkheimer and Adorno were abandoning in the early 1940s in their turn toward philosophical and cultural criticism divorced from social theory and radical politics.

Yet the texts remain a curiosity within the history of the Frankfurt School, delineating an uncompleted project that would have filled a substantial lacuna in Institute perspectives, but which was apparently never

---

17 This was precisely Marcuse's own way of conceptualizing different philosophical tendencies during the 1930s and thereafter, so the text fits into his work during that era; see the discussion of Marcuse's 1930s work in Kellner, *Herbert Marcuse*: 92ff.

completed.[18] Their work on this enterprise seems to have been interrupted by their wartime activity, and although both lectured on the topic in succeeding years in their university work, they seemed not to have returned to the venture of producing a co-authored book on the topic.

THE FRANKFURT SCHOOL IN WASHINGTON

In early 1942, Marcuse returned to Los Angeles hoping to resume collaborative work with Horkheimer on the dialectics project. He now appeared to have no prospects for a university professorship and his continued support by the Institute was problematical. After the Japanese attack on Pearl Harbor in December 1941, the United States entered the war and the prospects for university employment for emigrants were poor, with the rigors of wartime conditions and cutting back on academic funds. Institute resources were also dwindling, partly as a result of Pollock's bad investments,[19] and Horkheimer and Pollock wanted to cut back on the members to whom they were responsible for financial support. The Institute had already cut off their distinguished social psychologist Erich Fromm in 1939 and told Neumann that they would no longer be able to fund him in 1941;[20] Neumann vigorously protested and they agreed to support him temporarily with a reduced stipend. However, in 1941, both Marcuse and Neumann received decreased support and were forced to apply to outside sources to supplement their income.[21]

In the meantime, Horkheimer began closer work with T.W. Adorno, who had moved to California in November 1941, and who would henceforth be Horkheimer's major collaborator. Marcuse was thus in a very insecure situation in California, without guarantee of a continued position with the Institute and seeing himself surpassed by Adorno as Horkheimer's

---

18 In *The Origins of Negative Dialectics* (New York: The Free Press, 1977), Susan Buck-Morss argues that in the 1930s there were two distinct tendencies of critical theory: the attempt by Marcuse, Horkheimer and others to develop a critical theory of contemporary society and the attempts to develop a radical cultural criticism by T.W. Adorno and Walter Benjamin. The discovery of the manuscripts by Marcuse and Neumann on theories of social change suggest that there were also two distinct tendencies within critical theory in the 1940s.

19 Wiggershaus, *Frankfurt School*: 249.

20 See Wiggershaus, *Frankfurt School*: 262–3; 271; and 293–4.

21 Archives of the New York Public Library, Papers of the Emergency Aid of Displaced Foreign Scholars: "Correspondence with Scholars Receiving Grants or Fellowships, 1933–1945." See also, *Ten Years on Morningside Heights: A Report on the Institute's History, 1934–1944*. New York: Institute for Social Research, 1944: 6.

preferred writing partner.[22] Consequently, both Neumann and Marcuse began to consider the possibilities of U.S. government jobs. Neumann received an appointment as chief consultant at the Board of Economic Warfare in July 1942, and in autumn 1942, Marcuse travelled to Washington to investigate the possibility of a U.S. government position. In a handwritten letter dated November 11, 1942 from Washington (see page 234), Marcuse told Horkheimer that he was negotiating for a position in the intelligence bureau of the Office of War Information: "My function would be to make suggestions on 'how to present the enemy to the American people,' in the press, movies propaganda, etc." The job would require, however, that he live in Washington where all the source materials were. But, still hoping to be able to continue to work with Horkheimer, Marcuse states: "As I told you, I would not accept it [i.e. the government job]." However, Marcuse claims that Pollock told him not to be hasty in turning down the position, that "the Institute's budget will not last longer than 2 to 3 years, and that my future is at stake. I think he is over-pessimistic."

In a succeeding letter, Horkheimer, in effect, encouraged Marcuse to take the job – which he was indeed to do. A December 2, 1942 letter from Marcuse to Horkheimer indicates that he had been invited to attend a meeting at the Office of War Information "to determine which groups, persons and institutions of Nazi Germany should be actually branded as The Enemy. During the conference, I received the message that my appointment has been approved and that I should take the oath of office tomorrow." Expressing regrets to Horkheimer that they would not be able to continue their work together, Marcuse indicates that he is inclined to take the position. But, holding out against hope the prospect that

---

22 Horkheimer notoriously played off potential collaborators against each other,
    making the various Institute members think that they would be major
    contributors to the envisaged book on dialectics which turned out to be *Dialectic
    of Enlightenment*, eventually co-authored with Adorno. See Horkheimer's letters
    in *Gesammelte Schriften*, Volumes 15–17, which document his discussions with
    various members of the Institute concerning collaboration on the book on
    dialectics. In one of the low points of Institute in-fighting and back-stabbing,
    Adorno, while in Oxford working on a book on Husserl, wrote to Horkheimer,
    describing Marcuse, then one of Horkheimer's close collaborators, as a man only
    "hindered by Judaism from being a fascist." Adorno complained that Marcuse
    "had such illusions of Herr Heidegger, whom he thanked all-too-heartily in the
    foreword to his Hegel book," and that he published his Hegel book with
    Klostermann, also Heidegger's publisher. Adorno went on to suggest that he
    should himself replace Marcuse! Adorno to Horkheimer, May 13, 1935 in Max
    Horkheimer, *Gesammelte Schriften*, Volume 15: 347–8. Horkheimer tactfully
    replied (July 5, 1935) that he could not engage all of the issues in Adorno's letter
    in written form, glossing over his attack on Marcuse.

Horkheimer would convince him to stay in California to work on Institute projects, Marcuse adds: "I would not hesitate to reject the position if you have any bad feelings about it, and if you would no longer consider me as belonging to you."[23]

In December 4 and 19, 1942 letters to Marcuse, Horkheimer assures him that it is best that he take the position, that they can continue to collaborate, and that Marcuse can use his government position to advance Institute projects. Indeed, Marcuse had already submitted to the Office of Strategic Services (OSS) a manuscript prepared by the Institute on "The Elimination of German Chauvinism." A December 7, 1942 letter from OSS official Edward Hartshorne to Marcuse indicates his appreciation for the manuscript and proposes the lines along which key aspects of the proposed Institute project should be elaborated. Marcuse informed Horkheimer of OSS interest in the project in a December 4, 1942 letter and Horkheimer responded positively in a December 19, 1942 letter, indicating a desire to develop the project as suggested, although nothing seems to have come out of this exchange.

In December 1942, Marcuse therefore joined the Office of War Information as a senior analyst in the Bureau of Intelligence. An extremely interesting manuscript on "The New German Mentality," found in the Marcuse archives, developed his analysis of the current situation in Germany and how the U.S. could best produce propaganda that would turn the Germans against fascism.[24] The manuscript, published here for the first time (see page 139), is dated June 1942, and was probably written in California during the period when Marcuse worked on the study of "State and Individual Under National Socialism." The perspectives on German fascism are indeed quite similar to the earlier manuscript,

---

23 In a November 15, 1942, letter written to Horkheimer on Institute stationery (see page 236), Marcuse pays his respects to the Institute director, indicating: "In spite of my opposition to some of your conceptions, I have never and nowhere concealed my conviction that I know of no intellectual efforts today which are closer to the truth, and of no other place where one is still allowed and encouraged to think. It might be good to say this at this moment, and to tell you that I shall not forget what I learned with you."

24 Herbert Marcuse, "The New German Mentality" (#119.01, see page 139f.). In his history of the German exiles' activity with American intelligence and government agencies during World War Two, Barry Katz claims that "members of the antifascist emigration bombarded the OSS with applications, manuscripts, and research proposals calculated, they insisted, to help win the war. . . . Marcuse sent to the Chief of the Psychology Division manuscripts he had written on 'The New German Mentality' and 'Private Morale in Germany.'" *Foreign Intelligence: Research and Analysis in the Office of Strategic Services 1942–1945.* Cambridge, Mass.: Harvard University Press, 1989: 11. The text "Private Morale in Germany," however, is not by Marcuse and is referred to in note 1 of "New

though the analysis in "The New German Mentality" is much more comprehensive and detailed. Evidently, Marcuse prepared this manuscript before entering government service and, as it turned out, it helped get him a job with U.S. intelligence agencies. The analysis was closely connected to his Institute work on German fascism and presents original and penetrating insights into "the New German mentality."

The title page describes the text as a "Memorandum on a Study in the Psychological Foundations of National Socialism and the Chances for their Destruction." "The New German Mentality" is an extremely rich 63-page text that analyzes the psychological components of the new fascist ideology and mentality. It dissects the linguistic components of German fascism, while offering an interesting concept of "counter-propaganda." Marcuse indicates that the "new German mentality" is split between a "matter-of-factness," or "pragmatic layer," and a "mythological layer" which includes paganism, mysticism, racism and biologism. This bifurcation replicates the tensions between technological rationality and irrationalism in the fascist state and society.

In this study, Marcuse provides a detailed analysis of the logic and language of National Socialism, the psychological foundations of the new mentality, its attack on conventional religion and its cult of efficiency and strength. He also provides some proposals for "counter-propaganda" and ways to exploit the weakness of National Socialism. In particular, Marcuse proposes using the "matter-of-factness" against the fascists themselves, urging counter-propaganda which would make primary use of facts and avoid ideology, especially ideological uses of Western concepts that National Socialism seems to have successfully undermined (such as appeals to democracy or rights). Marcuse's discussions of what forms of language, art and other modes of culture might be mobilized against German fascism contain penetrating insights into the politics of language and the specific ways that discourse and culture functioned in Nazi Germany. He also provides an interesting analysis of how different forms of propaganda should be aimed at varying groups within German society.

Germany Mentality" as a text "submitted to the Office of the Coordinator of Information (April 1942) by the Institute of Social Research." Yet "Private Morale in Germany" is neither in the Marcuse archives, nor the Horkheimer or Adorno archives and I could also not find it in the National archives. In any case, the OSS had not even been founded in April of 1942, and, as noted above, Marcuse stated he sent "The New German Mentality" to the Coordinator of Information (COI) which was the initial government agency set up to coordinate war information, out of which emerged the Office of War Information (OWI) and Office of Strategic Services (OSS), both of which Marcuse worked for.

"The New German Mentality" circulated during his work with the Office of War Information, as there are three later reports found in the Marcuse archives that mention the text and which we include in this volume as addenda. In one report (see page 174f.), Marcuse elaborates his conception of what might be effective "counter-propaganda" aimed at the German people, arguing that "the language of facts" should be the crux of U.S. propaganda efforts.[25] He criticizes allied propaganda which deploys excessively moralistic or bombastic language and provides some examples of what he considers successful anti-Nazi propaganda based on more factual discourse.

Another report (see page 179f.) presents suggestions on the presentation of the enemy to the U.S. and allied public.[26] In it, Marcuse examines ways that the mass media and official government discourse within the allied countries could present images of German fascism to the American public. Marcuse argues that the terms "Nazi" and "Nazism" present the most vivid image of a threatening German enemy, but stresses also the need to present a more differentiated image of the German public, based on factual analysis of the social and economic structure of Nazi Germany and a delineation of the differing groups and organizations, highlighting which groups, such as big business and the Nazi inner circles, are most directly implicated in German war crimes and are thus the main "enemy" of the allies.

Marcuse's government texts which analyze German fascism are important because they provide original analyses of the psychological, cultural and technological conditions of totalitarian societies and the way that these societies dominate individuals, as well as discussions about how counter-propaganda can be produced. Yet Marcuse only spent a few months as a propaganda specialist with the Office of War Information and in March 1943 he transferred to the Office of Strategic Services (OSS), working until the end of the war in the Central European Section of the Research and Analysis Branch. While the Office of War Information

---

25 No title, no date. Herbert Marcuse archives #110.02. The manuscript begins, "The following remarks are based upon the assumptions outlined in my memorandum on the New German Mentality," so we can assume that the author is Marcuse because of this reference and the analysis which follows that is compatible with his other work of the period.

26 Untitled and undated manuscript, Marcuse archives #129.00. The references to Marcuse's other reports in the text, the fact that it was collected in his archive, and the similarities of positions to his other work of the period again suggest that this report was written by Marcuse. The same criteria hold for a third report "On Psychological Neutrality" (#129.01) which we are also publishing in this volume (see page 187f.).

primarily focused on producing propaganda for the American, allied, and German public, the OSS was more deeply involved in European operations, ranging from research into conditions in Germany to active propaganda and resistance measures against the Nazis.[27]

The members of the Institute of Social Research who found themselves in government service were highly regarded members of the Central European Branch. As a later report by their Section head Eugene Anderson put it: "About the time I took charge of the Section the two leading analysts were appointed – Dr Neumann, who quickly became the research director of the Section, and Dr Marcuse, who at once became the leading analyst on Germany." Anderson also called attention to the interdisciplinary spirit of cooperation and the practice of contextualizing analysis within critical social theory, typical of the Institute of Social Research: "The spirit of cooperation among the members has been remarkably effective. Much credit in this respect is owing to Dr Neumann and Dr Marcuse, who both believe in and practice this approach in their work. . . . The uniqueness of our work, however, consists in the background analysis in terms of the total social setting and the value of the future work of the Section may well lie in the continuation of this method."[28]

Marcuse and his colleagues wrote reports for the Research and Analysis Branch of the OSS attempting to identify Nazi and anti-Nazi groups and individuals in Germany, and they drafted a *Civil Affairs Handbook Germany* that dealt with de-Nazification. No manuscripts were found in the Marcuse archive from his OSS period, although a prospectus titled "Description of Three Major Projects" summarizes what Marcuse evidently thought was his most important work.[29] Because this is the

---

27 In an April 18, 1943 letter to Max Horkheimer (see page 243), Marcuse notes that "I have decided to go to the OSS. The latest reorganization has furthermore weakened the position of the OWI, and this agency seems increasingly bound to become the prey of newspapermen and advertising agents. Apart from this fact, I have seen that the OSS has infinitely better material, and that I could do much more useful work there." On the different U.S. intelligence agencies during the war, see Bradley Smith, *The Shadow Warriors*. New York: Basic Books, 1983. On the OSS, see R. Harris Smith, *OSS: The Secret History of America's First Central Intelligence Agency*. Berkeley: University of California Press, 1972.

28 Eugene N. Anderson, *History of the European Section*, February 17, 1945, National Archives Record Group 226; cited in Alfons Söllner, editor, *Zur Archäologie der Demokratie, Volume 1*. Frankfurt: Fischer, 1986: 30. See also Söllner's interviews with Anderson, Herz and Hughes who worked in the European Section with Marcuse and Neumann, *Zur Archäologie*, Volume 2: 22–58.

29 Marcuse told me that he had not taken any of his OSS or State Department reports with him because of national security concerns and government guidelines

only document pertaining to Marcuse's OSS work found in his archives and because it provides the fullest and most accurate description of his major projects, we are including the document in full in this volume (see page 193f.).

The first project refers to the 1944 *Civil Affairs Handbook Germany*, involving the "Dissolution of the Nazi Party and its Affiliated Organizations," and "Policy toward Revival of Old Parties and Establishment of New Parties in Germany." Marcuse describes in detail his own participation in the assignment as "major," involving taking part "in the discussions, organization, and implementation of the entire project," in which he "completed several parts of it independently." This enterprise was related to the work Marcuse and his colleagues had been doing since early 1943. The three Institute members who had been working for the OSS – Marcuse, Neumann and Otto Kirchheimer – had been assembling documents providing a detailed account of the economic, political and cultural conditions in Nazi Germany, including studies of German morale, anti-Nazi jokes, Nazi propaganda, tensions between the ruling military, political and economic elites, war profiteers, and the like. Their de-Nazification studies in turn attempted to specify which forces in Germany could or could not be worked with to provide democratization, and they proposed measures to eliminate the root causes that had produced fascism.

The second project Marcuse described concerned a December 1, 1945 report on "The Social Democratic Party of Germany." Marcuse indicated that he "wrote the entire project" and "was responsible for drawing conclusions, which were then discussed with the staff." This report concerned the extent to which the German Social Democrats could be trusted to promote democracy and it evidently produced a bitter debate. Marcuse and his colleagues argued that Communist forces in the labor movement after the war would confine themselves to a "minimum program" and that Social Democrats would continue their tradition of liberal-democratic reformism.[30] Critics of the report questioned whether it

---

(December 28, 1978 interview in La Jolla, California), although the existence of some earlier OWI reports in his archives suggests restrictions were not so strict with this agency.

30 Katz, *Foreign Intelligence*: 49. Katz's study is the most detailed and comprehensive study of Marcuse's involvement with the U.S. government, although it contains mistakes, as did his earlier biography of Marcuse; see my review in *Telos* 56 (Summer 1983): 223–9. For instance, Katz is unaware of the reluctance with which Marcuse entered government service and the depth of his desire to continue working with Horkheimer on Institute projects, since he

reflected "objectivity and maturity in political research,"[31] but obviously there were political debates within the U.S. government concerning the future of Germany and the role of socialist and other leftist groups. Marcuse and his colleagues constantly fought for greater democratization of Germany and the incorporation of leftist parties, labor unions and all progressive forces in a reinvigorated German democracy. Political scientist John Herz, who worked with the Institute members in the OSS, said that Marcuse and his associates "advocated a social democratic-reformist position and not so much a Marxist one. They inclined toward a democratic (in the broad sense) constitution in Germany, which was first of all to eliminate the effects of authoritarian, illiberal tradition at all levels in German life. It was a position with which I, as a non-Marxist, could agree: a kind of Anglo-Saxon democracy, but one from which socialist measures could arise when conditions were right."[32]

Marcuse and his colleagues also argued for strong measures against the ex-Nazis, with Marcuse recommending close supervision of all rightwing organizations, as well as tolerance of public attacks against Nazi criminals: "To treat these equally with the anti-Nazi groupings (for example to grant them equal protection from interference by hostile parties) would be tantamount to perpetuating the greatest threat to the security of the occupying forces and to the restoration of a peaceful order."[33] Marcuse and his colleagues also recommended that some 220,000 Nazi officials be arrested immediately, that 1,800 business leaders who were considered "active Nazis" be incarcerated, and that once prisons were filled, Nazi concentration camps should be used to detain suspected Nazi war criminals.[34]

---

seemed not to have examined the correspondence in the Marcuse or Horkheimer archives, or Wiggershaus' account (op. cit.) which drew on this material. Katz also attributes a text to Marcuse's authorship ("Private Morale in Germany"), whereas in footnote 1 of "New German Mentality," Marcuse ascribes authorship of "Private Morale" to the Institute for Social Research and this manuscript was not found in Marcuse's *Nachlass*. And, as I point out below, Katz exaggerates Marcuse's role in drafting the de-Nazification report. Yet there are useful quotes from Marcuse's reports which I shall draw upon in the following pages.

31 Memorandum from Richard Hartshorne to William Langer, July 23, 1945, cited in Katz: 43. The OSS demanded from their Research and Analysis Branch that the reports should be: "Strictly impartial, designed to inform rather than to persuade; they should avoid all recommendations, whether explicit or veiled." "Draft of Proposed Guide to Preparation of Political Reports," cited in Katz: 43. It appears, however, that Marcuse and his colleagues on occasion attempted to persuade and that their persuasions clashed with those of more conservative colleagues.

32 Herz, in Söllner, *Zur Archäologie*, Volume 2: 37.

33 Marcuse, Projects Committee Correspondence, December 10, 1943, cited in Katz: 211.

34 R&A 1655.5a, *Civil Affairs Guide*, November 27, 1944 and Herbert Marcuse,

After the war, Neumann played a central role in the prosecution of Nazi war criminals and he and Marcuse worked on de-Nazification policy, including the abolition of the Nazi party, the prosecution of war criminals and efforts to democratize Germany.[35] Marcuse continued to make policy recommendations concerning which groups and individuals could help democratize Germany and which individuals and groups were war criminals, though he later doubted whether his recommendations had much influence. In an interview with Habermas, Marcuse indicated that his recommendations were ignored:

> MARCUSE: My main task was to identify groups in Germany with which one could work towards reconstruction after the war; and to identify groups which were to be taken to task as Nazis. There was a major de-Nazification program at the time. Based on exact research, reports, newspaper reading and whatever, lists were made up of those Nazis who were supposed to assume responsibility for their activity. . . .
>
> HABERMAS: . . . . Are you of the impression that what you did then was of any consequence?
>
> MARCUSE: On the contrary. Those whom we had listed first as 'economic war criminals' were very quickly back in the decisive positions of responsibility in the German economy. It would be very easy to name names here.[36]

Perhaps Marcuse's eulogy to Franz Neumann after his friend's untimely death in an auto accident in 1954 provides the best account of the goals

---

assisted by Francis Williamson and Louis Wiesner (RG 226, Entry 60, Box 1: Projects Committee Correspondence, Central Europe File, September 10, 1943); in Katz: 47.

35 Katz claims that Marcuse "drafted the order that formally abolished the Nazi Party" (Katz: 35), but this seems to be an exaggeration. Their government colleague and friend H. Stuart Hughes recalls that Neumann and Marcuse worked together "in the last months of the war drafting de-Nazificiation orders" and a list of Nazis and anti-Nazis; in Rainer Erd, editor, *Reform und Resignation: Gespräche über Franz L. Neumann*. Frankfurt: Suhrkamp, 1985: 161. From what we know about O.S.S. reports, orders and documents, authorship was largely collective and therefore it is a mistake to attribute specific authorship to such documents; see the discussion in Erd, pp. 161 ff. and in Söllner, *Zur Archäologie*, Volume 2, pp. 34–5, passim. Indeed, no one who knew Marcuse well whom I have interviewed ever heard Herbert mention that he had himself drafted the order abolishing the Nazi party as Katz claims, though he did work on it.

36 Herbert Marcuse, Conversation with Habermas and others, *Telos* 38 (Winter 1978–79: 130–131. Marcuse's opinion concurs with his colleague John Herz in "The Fiasco of Denazification," *Political Science Quarterly*, Vol. 63, No. 4 (December 1948): 569–594; see also Söllner, *Zur Archäologie*, Vol. 2, pp. 39ff, passim.

of the Institute members during their government work. Describing Neumann's activity, Marcuse writes:

> He devoted most of his efforts to plans for a democratization of Germany which would avoid the failures of the Weimar Republic; he tried to demonstrate that de-Nazification, in order to be effective, must be more than a purge of personnel and an abolition of Nazi legislation – that it must strike at the roots of German fascism by eliminating the economic foundation of the anti-democratic policy of German big industry. Neumann saw that the efforts to attain this objective failed, but he continued to work for strengthening the genuinely democratic forces in Germany in the narrow field still open for such efforts.[37]

Although Marcuse's 1940s work with the government has generally been considered an interruption of his theoretical work, this view needs revision. To some extent, the working conditions during his government service were not all that different from Institute activity. Marcuse worked in an office and read enormous amounts of historical and empirical material. He wrote up reports and discussed them in detail with his staff and superiors. He revised the texts accordingly and circulated them for further discussion. Moreover, his co-workers were to a large extent distinguished academics and they frequently socialized and discussed theoretical as well as political issues. H. Stuart Hughes, who worked with Marcuse and his colleagues, tells how he and other, younger would-be academics received, in effect, a free "second graduate education" from Marcuse, Neumann, Hajo Holborn, Walter Langer and other distinguished scholars who worked with the OSS.[38]

Marcuse's government work thus provided important knowledge and experiences that he would draw upon in his later work and which gave his theory empirical and historical grounding and substance. His government service, supplementing his work with the Institute for Social Research, provided him with yet another experience of interdisciplinary work that dramatized the need to integrate historical, economic, political, sociological and cultural perspectives. Consequently, his government work supported the Institute view of the value of interdisciplinary perspectives, collaborative work and critical social theory to provide a context for analysis and interpretation.

---

37 "Preface," Franz Neumann, *The Democratic and the Authoritarian State*, editor, Herbert Marcuse. New York: The Free Press, 1957: viii.
38 H. Stuart Hughes, "Social Theory in a New Context," in Jarrell C. Jackmann and Carla M. Borden, editors, *The Muses Flee Hitler*. Washington, D.C.: Smithsonian Institution Press, 1983: 118.

Decades later, when Marcuse achieved world renown as a radical guru in the 1960s, he was accused by Marxist and far-left critics of being an American intelligence agent, since the OSS was a forerunner of the CIA.[39] Marcuse responded in a conversation with Habermas that such critics "seem to have forgotten that the war then was a war against fascism and that, consequently, I haven't the slightest reason for being ashamed of having assisted in it."[40] In addition, the OSS had a much broader range of individuals working for it, including many who shared Marcuse's leftist perspectives, whereas the CIA from the beginning served narrow U.S. Cold War interests and was dominated by conservatives and anti-communist liberals.

In September 1945, after the dissolution of the OSS, Marcuse moved over to the State Department, becoming head of the Central European bureau. He remained at State until 1951 when he left government service. Marcuse's third project in his description of "Three Major Projects" involved a May 27, 1946 State Department report on the "status and prospects of German Trade Unions and Works Councils." In the summary he indicates that he wrote most of the report and "was responsible for drawing conclusions and incorporating suggestions made by members of the section's staff." Marcuse and his colleagues consistently argued that German Trade Unions were an important part of democratization and should be supported by the allied forces.

Marcuse's continued work with the State Department was incongruous in view of the purges taking place in the Cold War era that emerged soon after the end of the war. Studies of the OSS describe how various agencies within it were dispersed among other government agencies after the war. Marcuse's Research and Analysis Branch was transferred to the State Department. Under the leadership of Alfred McCormack, "a New York corporation lawyer credited with revitalizing Army intelligence during the war,"[41] there was an attempt to develop a major intelligence agency within the State Department. But Congressional critics and State Department bureaucrats teamed up against the concept and the Branch's budget was decimated. In an April 6, 1946 letter to Horkheimer (see page 250) Marcuse writes:

> You will have heard that the State Department's Research and Intelligence Division has come under fierce attack for alleged communist tendencies.

---

39 See, for example, the anonymous article, "Marcuse: Cop-out or Cop?" *Progressive Labor*, vol. 6, no. 6 (February 1969): 61–6.
40 Marcuse, in *Revolution or Reform?*, ed. A.T. Ferguson. Chicago: New University Press: 59.
41 Smith, *OSS*: 364 and Smith, *Shadow Warriors*: 386f.

With this justification the Appropriations Committee has, for the time being, rejected new funding. Now the general horse-trading over the usual compromise begins, but quite possibly the Division will be dissolved on June 30. Actually I wouldn't exactly be sad were that to happen.

Meanwhile, McCormack and Secretary of State Dean Acheson struggled to get more funds for the Research unit. As historian R. Harris Smith describes it:

> The chairman of the House Military Affairs Committee charged that persons with 'strong Soviet leanings' had joined the State Department intelligence group. McCormack denied the charge and demanded a retraction. Instead, Congress cut the entire appropriation for his unit. Conservative State Department administrators had convinced influential legislators that the ex-OSS analysts were ideologically 'far to the left of the views held by the President and his Secretary of State,' and committed to 'a socialized America in a world commonwealth of Communist and Socialist states dedicated to peace through collective security, political, economic, and social reform; and the redistribution of national wealth on a global basis.'[42]

Marcuse's Research and Analysis group was disbanded soon after the April 23 resignation of Colonel McCormack, and, on Smith's account, those who remained "floated in limbo, distrusted by the State Department professionals and seldom listened to."[43] According to H. Stuart Hughes, the R&A group "took sharp issue with the Cold War mentality of their diplomatic superiors," but "felt most of the time as though we were firing our memoranda off into a void. The atmosphere was that of Kafka's *Castle*, in which one never knew who would answer the telephone or even whether it would be answered at all" (ibid.). In Smith's summary: "A few dauntless academicians languished at State for a year or two, but they knew that the Department had already abdicated its potential role in the production of foreign intelligence" (ibid.).

Marcuse was one of the academics who languished at State for several more years. He and his remaining colleagues attempted to counter the trend toward Cold War anti-communism which had begun. In Henry Pachter's words: "Franz Neumann and Herbert Marcuse bombarded Secretary of War Stimson with plans for a post-war Germany that would give democratic socialism a chance; they probably prevented the worst stupidities an occupation regime is capable of."[44] Given the Cold War

---

42 Smith, *OSS*: 365.
43 The quotes in this paragraph are all from Smith, *OSS*: 365.
44 Henry Pachter, "On Being an Exile," *The Legacy of the German Refugee Intellectuals*, *Salmagundi* 10/11 (Fall 1969/Winter 1970): 36.

atmosphere, however, Marcuse and his friends had less and less influence as the years went by.

With the spread of anti-communist witch-hunts, Marcuse's position became increasingly perilous. As H. Stuart Hughes notes: "It has seemed deliciously incongruous that at the end of the 1940s, with an official purge of real or suspected leftists in full swing, the State Department's leading authority on Central Europe should have been a revolutionary socialist who hated the Cold War and all its works."[45] When I asked Marcuse in 1978 whether he himself suffered any government persecution because of his political convictions, he shook his head and simply stated, "No."[46] But he was increasingly frustrated that his efforts and those of his colleagues were coming to naught. Moreover, he was feeling more and more isolated as one after another of his colleagues left the government for university teaching positions.

Marcuse evidently stayed on at State because, unlike Neumann, he was not offered a university professorship and because his wife Sophie was dying of cancer, so he remained in Washington to take care of her. This could not have been a happy period for Marcuse as his former colleagues got university positions, while he worked in an increasingly conservative State Department environment in which he and his few remaining friends were increasingly isolated and without influence. Marcuse's situation is poignantly described by Hughes:

> Let me distinguish three dimensions that explain the lack of influence [i.e. of Marcuse, Hughes and their remaining progressive colleagues in the State Department]; an organizational, a personal and an ideological dimension.
>
> I will begin with *organization*: the long-time officials of the State Department could absolutely not reconcile themselves to the fact that such a large number of people had come over from the OSS; we did not come from the diplomatic corps, but from an academic background, and we just happened to land in the State Department. At that time, the official units of the State Department for the then current areas were fairly small – there were maybe three or four people working on Middle Europe. We, however, arrived

---

45 Hughes, *The Sea Change*: 175.
46 Interview in La Jolla, California, December 28, 1978. Lawrence C. Soley indicated that several of Marcuse's leftist colleagues at OSS who went to State "attracted the attention of HUAC [House Committee on Un-American Activities]. The investigation that the House committee launched was ruthless. As a result of the investigation, Maurice Halperin went into exile, and Carl Marzani was sentenced to prison for lying under oath about his Communist affiliations. The committee's investigation suggested that OSS was the most 'thoroughly infiltrated' of any wartime government agency" *Radio Warfare*. New York: Praeger, 1989: 218. Kirchheimer's widow told Barry Katz (*Foreign Intelligence*: 242) that her husband was investigated by the FBI after the war.

with 15 or 20 people and represented an organizational threat, at least for the traditional diplomatic service. . . .

The *personal* question concerned problems of ethnic and class origin. The people in the foreign service normally came, to put it bluntly, from the WASP upper class. . . . Their knowledge of Europe and foreign languages came from Swiss boarding schools – I am talking about a kind of ideal type. They found the specialists from the R. and A. Branch exotic, peculiar, probably threatening, because they were foreign, had an accent and were in large part Jewish. In the diplomatic service, it was the other way around: very few were Jewish . . .

And with this, I come to the *third dimension*. . . . From the beginning, the problem was that my friends and I did not think in national interest categories – I still cannot today, I just do not know what it would be; to us, the important thing was the well-being of the people in the country we were researching . . . it was completely obvious to us that we had to see the country we were to understand through the eyes of its inhabitants. That was already enough to violate conventions. Added to that was the fact that we were on the left, in the sense of socialism.[47]

The main work that Marcuse undertook in his State Department years was detailed studies of "World Communism". In 1949, Marcuse and his associates submitted a 532-page intelligence report on "The Potentials of World Communism" describing its appeal, prospects and strategies, as well as its limitations and integration into the existing order. After leaving U.S. government service, in fact, Marcuse received positions with the Russian Institutes at Columbia and Harvard and he published a book on *Soviet Marxism* in 1958.[48] Yet in addition to his government work, manuscripts in the Marcuse archive indicate that he had not given up his fundamental theoretical interests and several manuscripts were found which anticipated his later key ideas.

TOTALITARIANISM, THE FATE OF SOCIALISM AND THE ERA OF ONE-DIMENSIONALITY

During his years of government service – from 1942 to 1951 – Marcuse continued to develop his own perspectives on contemporary society and

---

47 Hughes in Söllner, *Zur Archäologie*, Vol. 2: 48–49.
48 See the March 30, 1949 letter to Horkheimer (see page 259) where Marcuse describes his offer of a Senior Fellowship at the Columbia University Russian Institute. Marcuse remained in Washington, however, until his wife's death from cancer in 1951 and then went to the Columbia and Harvard University Russian Institutes, doing the work that resulted in his 1958 book *Soviet Marxism*, republished in 1985 by Columbia University Press with an introduction by Douglas Kellner.

culture. The themes that would become central to *One-Dimensional Man* and his later work are adumbrated in unpublished papers collected in this volume. One of the most intriguing manuscripts found in the Marcuse archives is a text dated "September 1945" and titled "Some Remarks on Aragon: Art and Politics in the Totalitarian Era"[49] (see page 199f.). This document discloses that Marcuse was continuing his interest in art and aesthetics that was present in his earlier writings and arguably central to his later work during his years of government service.

In a world dominated by totalitarianism, Marcuse suggests, aesthetic opposition and love are the most radical oppositional forces since they produce an alternative reality completely at odds with an oppressive social reality. Art transcends everyday life by virtue of its form, by its ability to produce another world which projects images of a better life and reveals the deficiencies and horrors of existing reality. Marcuse notes the attempts of the surrealists to create alternative worlds through art, but their revolt was easily absorbed as aesthetic fashion and the terror in surrealist art "was surpassed by the real terror." The question, then, is how to produce a genuinely oppositional art. Marcuse believes that French resistance writers represent "a new stage of the solution." The political in their work is not directly represented, but intrudes to destroy a world of potential love, beauty and harmony. It shatters the ideal world projected in great poetry and art, and thus appears as that which is to be negated and destroyed, as that which stands in the way of freedom and happiness.

Authentic art thus represents for Marcuse a "great refusal" of existing reality and the postulating of another world. Authentic art preserves visions of emancipation and is thus part of the radical project. In the work of French resistance writing which he discusses, love and beauty are negated by the forces of totalitarianism that themselves appear as negations of human freedom and happiness which must in turn be negated. In the latter half of his study, Marcuse provides a detailed reading of Aragon's novel *Aurélien* which presents the story of two star-crossed lovers who reunite after a long separation only for the beloved to be shot in the arms of the hero by fascists. As with the images in Picasso's *Guernica*, Aragon's novel brings "darkness, terror and utter destruction" to life "by grace of the artistic creation and in the artistic form; they are therefore incomparable to the fascist reality."

---

49 This text is especially fascinating because it is the most detailed reading of concrete aesthetic artifacts since Marcuse's 1922 dissertation on *The German Artist-Novel*; for discussion of his dissertation and Marcuse's aesthetics, see Kellner, *Herbert Marcuse*: 18ff., passim.

Marcuse thus sketches here an early version of his unique valorization of the aesthetic and erotic dimensions of existence as preserving the possibility of another reality, a higher condition of transcendence to the existing world. In the realms of art and love, Marcuse suggests, one transcends the banality and oppressiveness of everyday life and exists in a higher dimension. But oppressive forces in existing reality negate the higher possibilities for human freedom and happiness and thus must in turn be negated. Authentic art refuses existing reality, promotes estrangement from this world, and projects images of a better world. Marcuse would spend the next thirty-five years elaborating these aesthetic ideals and fleshing out his ideal of liberation.

In fact, Marcuse seemed to turn to the consolations of aesthetics after or during extremely difficult periods of his life.[50] After the failure of the German revolution in 1919, he left Berlin and went to the University of Freiburg to write a doctoral dissertation on *The German Artist-Novel*. During a period in the early to mid-1950s when he was experiencing the pressures of McCarthyism and mourning the death of his wife Sophie, Marcuse sketched out the perspectives on liberation in *Eros and Civilization*, which assigned the aesthetic dimension a key role in both portraying alternatives to existing reality and in delineating potential routes to liberation through aesthetic and erotic experience. At the end of his life, after the failures of the movements of the 1960s, Marcuse also turned to aesthetics in his final book *The Aesthetic Dimension* (1978). And, as we see with the study of "Art and Politics in the Totalitarian Era," he turned to the consolations of art and the aesthetic dimension during the dark days of World War Two as he labored in government service.[51]

One of the most interesting finds in the Marcuse archives involves a manuscript containing thirty-three theses on the contemporary era, which forecasts the themes of *One-Dimensional Man* (see page 215f.). Although the Marcuse/Neumann project on "theories of social change" was never completed, archive material shows a continual commitment on Marcuse's part to theorize the relations between critical social theory and practice. In

---

50 See the discussion in Kellner, *Herbert Marcuse*: 347ff. which provides documentation for the claims asserted here.

51 In an April 18, 1943 letter to Horkheimer, published in this volume, Marcuse indicates that he just read Georges Bernanos' *Lettre aux Anglais*, that it "is a great book, and it comes closer to the truth than any other I have seen in many years. It gave me the only encouragement I have found here." Marcuse's essay on "Art and Politics in the Totalitarian Age" indicates that he was also reading French poetry and novels during the period, thus turning to aesthetic consolation and beginning to theorize the emancipatory potential of art, a theme that would characterize his later work.

this 1947 manuscript Marcuse sketched what he saw as the major social and political tendencies of the time.[52] The text suggests that Marcuse was still engaging in the sort of broad philosophical and political theorizing which had characterized his earlier work with the Institute for Social Research and which would come to distinguish his later work. The theses were prepared for a possible relaunching of the Institute for Social Research journal, *Zeitschrift für Sozialforschung*. In fact, Marcuse's letters to Horkheimer after the war indicate a strong desire to begin republication of the journal. In an October 18, 1946 letter to Horkheimer, Marcuse tells of visits to London and Paris where major intellectuals told him of their admiration for the Institute journal and desire for it to come out again. In a November 15, 1946 letter to Horkheimer (see page 253) Marcuse suggests some possible material for a special issue on Germany and in a February 9, 1947 letter he notes that:

> I've done my own small part toward preparation: I (and, I fear, I alone) have prepared the reports we agreed on at our last meeting. These are really nothing but notes. But I am working on them further, and since their completion is still not in sight, I'll send you the first part as soon as it is typed up. Perhaps that will at the least get a discussion going.

The plan was for Marcuse, Horkheimer, Neumann, Adorno and others to write articles on contemporary philosophy, art, social theory, politics, and so on, but this project also failed to come to fruition – perhaps because of growing philosophical and political differences between the members of the Institute. It appears that indeed Marcuse was the only one to prepare a manuscript with his perspectives on the present world situation, the text that we have published here with the title "33 Theses." In any case, the Institute journal was never relaunched and with the return of Horkheimer, Adorno and Pollock to Germany to re-establish the Institut für Sozialforschung in Frankfurt, Marcuse's connection with the Institute was further severed.[53]

---

52 For a discussion of the manuscript's history, see Wiggershaus, *Frankfurt School*: 386ff. and the letters to Horkheimer of February 9, 1947 (see page 254) and October 17, 1947 (see page 257).

53 In an October 17, 1947 letter to Horkheimer, included in this volume, Marcuse notes that after their meeting in Los Angeles: "I immediately began to work through and add to the theses, in the spirit of our discussion. Other works, inspired by our discussion, will follow." But the supposedly revised theses were not found in the Marcuse archive, so we are publishing the February 1947 version, found in the Horkheimer archive. Thanks to Gunzelin Schmid Noerr and the Horkheimer archive for making this text available. Marcuse's letters continue to mention his hope of restarting publication of the Institute journal, but his hopes came to naught as, with their return to Frankfurt, Adorno and Horkheimer decided not to take up further publication of the *Zeitschrift*.

Marcuse's "Theses," like his later *One-Dimensional Man* (1964), contain an Hegelian-Marxian overview of the contemporary world situation that was deeply influenced by classical Marxism. It provides a sketch of the obstacles to social change that projects of radical social transformation, such as were conceived in his work with Neumann, would face. In the theses, Marcuse anticipates many of the defining positions of *One-Dimensional Man*, including the integration of the proletariat, the stabilization of capitalism, the bureaucratization of socialism, the demise of the revolutionary left and the absence of genuine forces of progressive social change. In the first thesis, Marcuse writes:

> After the military defeat of Hitler-Fascism (which was a premature and isolated form of capitalist reorganization) the world is dividing into a neo-fascist and a Soviet camp. What still remains of democratic–liberal forms will be crushed between the two camps or absorbed by them. The states in which the old ruling class survived the war economically and politically will become fascistized in the foreseeable future, while the others will enter the Soviet camp.
>
> (thesis 1)

At this time, Marcuse saw a system of totalitarian controls and domination emerging that would come to encompass, in his view, the forms of both Soviet communist and advanced capitalist societies after the defeat of German fascism. He was evidently disturbed by the return to power of former Nazi officials shortly after the war and the resurgence of rightwing conservatism in the post-war period in the United States. Indeed, he seemed to fear a revival of fascism and even a war between neo-fascist capitalist countries and the Soviet Union, thus foreseeing the burgeoning Cold War rivalries between the major superpowers, while exaggerating the neo-fascist tendencies in Western democracies. Anticipating *One-Dimensional Man*, he presented both blocs as being essentially anti-revolutionary forms of domination and "hostile to socialist development." Following a position which he had argued in essays in the 1930s and in *Reason and Revolution* (1941), Marcuse claimed that liberal-democratic forms were being destroyed or absorbed into systems of domination. Anticipating his later analyses of the militarization of the capitalist and socialist blocs, he suggested that war between the Cold War antagonists was probable.

Producing one of his first comprehensive critiques of Soviet Marxism,[54] Marcuse criticized the failure to create an emancipatory socialism in the

---

54 This critique is interesting because, as Helmut Dubiel argues in *Theory and Politics*, the Institute members had previously eschewed criticizing the Soviet

Soviet Union and urged the defense of classical Marxist teaching against all compromises and deformations (thesis 3). Previewing the analysis of the integration of the working class in *One-Dimensional Man*, Marcuse argued that the working class was becoming ever more integrated into capitalist society and there were no apparent forces of revolutionary opposition to the system. With the development of new war technologies, it is hopeless to project armed struggle against forces with powerful weapons at their disposal (thesis 6). In addition, the *Verbürgerlichung* (bourgeoisification) of the working class corresponds to deep structural changes in the capitalist economy and needs to be comprehensively theorized (theses 11 and 12) – a task that Marcuse would undertake in succeeding years.

Despite the difficulties in envisaging concrete revolutionary tendencies or movements, Marcuse continued to insist that the construction of social- ism was a key goal for contemporary radical politics (thesis 21) and he himself holds onto the revolutionary tradition of Marxian theory, as he would indeed continue to do for the rest of his life. He conceived of the socialization of the means of production and their administration by the "immediate producers" as the key task of constructing socialism (thesis 25), and although he supports economic democracy and the development of a classless society as part of his conception of socialism (thesis 26), he does not sketch out a model of a democratic socialism – an omission that represents a deficit in his thought as a whole. Marcuse concludes with a view that only a revitalization of the revolutionary heritage of communist parties could reinvigorate revolutionary theory and practice and that this appears impossible:

> The political task then would consist in reconstructing revolutionary theory within the communist parties and working for the praxis appropriate to it. The task seems impossible today. But perhaps the relative independence from Soviet dictates, which this task demands, is present as a possibility in Western Europe's and West Germany's communist parties.
>
> (thesis 33)

Thus, the "33 Theses" concretize in the contemporary era the revolutionary perspectives of *Reason and Revolution* and the project of "theories of social change," but in a rather pessimistic vein that anticipates *One-Dimensional Man*. The key argument is that: "Under these circum- stances there is only one alternative for revolutionary theory: to ruthlessly and openly criticize both systems and to uphold without compromise

---

Union. Thus, Marcuse presents here the first sustained critical analysis of the Soviet Union from the perspective of Frankfurt School critical theory. These perspectives were elaborated in his 1958 book on *Soviet Marxism.*, op. cit.

orthodox marxist theory against both" (thesis 3). Later, there would be fierce debates as to whether Marcuse himself did or did not uphold "orthodox marxist theory". In any case, he posits art and radical theory during the 1940s as two forces of opposition to existing social reality – a position which he would maintain for the rest of his life. And unlike Adorno and Horkheimer, who were turning away from classical Marxism, Marcuse continued to affirm the revolutionary potential of original Marxian theory against its subsequent deformations.

Wiggershaus claims that Horkheimer never responded to Marcuse's theses,[55] and one imagines that the theoretical and political differences between them were now unbridgeable. And, in fact, the *Zeitschrift für Sozialforschung* was never again to be relaunched, and Horkheimer and Adorno were soon to return to Germany to resurrect the Institute for Social Research, while Marcuse would remain in the United States.

Marcuse's only published article during the late 1940s contains a study of "Sartre's Existentialism" which criticizes existentialist individualism and ontology, arguing: "In so far as Existentialism is a philosophical doctrine, it remains an idealistic doctrine: it hypostatizes specific historical conditions of human existence into ontological and metaphysical characteristics. Existentialism thus becomes part of the very ideology which it attacks and its radicalism is illusory."[56] In the spirit of critical theory, Marcuse argues that it is social theory and not philosophy which conceptualizes the concrete historical conditions of human existence:

> The activities, attitudes and efforts which circumscribe his concrete existence are, in the last analysis, not his but those of his class, profession, position, society. In this sense is the life of the individual indeed the life of the universal, but this universal is a configuration of specific historical forces, made up by the various groups, interests, institutions, etc., which form the social reality. The concepts which actually reach the concrete existence must therefore derive from a theory of society.
>
> (p. 335)

Hegel, Marcuse suggests, comes "close to the structure of human existence" because "he interprets it in terms of the historical universal,"

---

55 Wiggershaus, *The Frankfurt School*: 436ff. This claim is not exactly accurate as Horkheimer referred to them in several letters and in a December 29, 1948 letter claimed that he and Adorno were writing "an outline in the form of your theses." Yet such a manuscript never materialized and it is probable that Adorno and Horkheimer were put off by the aggressively Marxian-revolutionary form and tone of Marcuse's "theses."

56 Herbert Marcuse, "Existentialism: Remarks on Jean-Paul Sartre's *L'Etre et le néant*," *Philosophy and Phenomenological Research*, VIII, 3 (March 1948): 309–36 (pagination in text).

but interprets this in terms of Spirit, thus remaining within the realm of "philosophical abstraction." Kierkegaard turns to theology to grasp the concreteness of the existing individual, while Marx deploys political economy and social theory, both pronouncing "the essential inadequacy of philosophy in the face of the concrete human existence." Heidegger and Sartre, however, attempt to develop an existential philosophy to grasp the situation of the concrete individual. But Marcuse argues:

> No philosophy can possibly comprehend the prevailing concreteness. Heidegger's existential ontology remains intentionally 'transcendental': his category of *Dasein* is neutral toward all concretization. Nor does he attempt to elaborate a *Weltanschauung* and ethics. In contrast, Sartre attempts such concretization with the methods and terms of philosophy – and the concrete existence remains 'outside' the philosophical conception, as a mere example or illustration. His political radicalism lies outside his philosophy, extraneous to its essence and content.
>
> (p. 335)[57]

Existentialism was a major fad, widely discovered in the media and intellectual circles after World War Two, and in light of his own lifelong involvement with the philosophy of Martin Heidegger, Marcuse was no doubt attracted to engage Sartre's existentialism. Having studied with Heidegger in Freiburg in the late 1920s, Marcuse continued to respect and be influenced by his thought despite their growing political and philosophical differences. Indeed, Marcuse frequently said that Heidegger was the greatest philosopher of the era, as well as the most impressive interpreter of philosophical texts, the best teacher and the most original thinker that he had ever encountered. In his early work, Marcuse attempted syntheses of Marxism and Heidegger and continued to be influenced by Heideggerian thought.[58] Yet Heidegger's support of National Socialism, including becoming Rector of the University of Freiburg in 1933, was deeply shocking to Marcuse and he had difficulty understanding how Heidegger could so blatantly betray Western philosophy.

Consequently, after the end of the war Marcuse exchanged the letters with Heidegger which we include in this volume (see pages 263–7). Marcuse visited Heidegger in 1946 during a State Department trip where he was investigating conditions in Germany and the danger of anti-

---

57 This passage was left out of the 1972 reprint of the Sartre essay in *Studies in Critical Philosophy* (Boston and London: Beacon Press and New Left Books) which added as "Postscript" a more positive evaluation based on Sartre's attempts to synthesize his philosophy and politics during the period following Marcuse's first publication of his essay.

58 Kellner, *Herbert Marcuse*: 38ff.

democratic tendencies and groups. After the encounter, an obviously disturbed Marcuse wrote to Heidegger, asking him to clarify his position towards National Socialism and his own actions during the fascist regime. Heidegger answered in typically evasive fashion and Marcuse sent him a final letter and broke off relations with his former teacher, never contacting him again.

CONCLUDING REMARKS

During the 1940s, Herbert Marcuse engaged in an enormous amount of empirical and historical research which provided material that enabled him to eventually develop a more substantive theory of the present age than his Institute colleagues Horkheimer and Adorno were able to produce in their more philosophical endeavors. Marcuse's attempts to link theory with practice in his collaboration with Neumann to develop a theory of social change for the present age helped generate a more activist orientation in comparison to his Institute colleagues. I would therefore argue that, in retrospect, both Marcuse's later theoretical perspectives and his attempts to link theory and practice in the 1960s and 1970s in regard to the New Left, National Liberation movements and so-called new social movements were grounded in his work in the 1940s which attempted to link his theoretical work with political practice.

Marcuse felt that the efforts of him and his colleagues to produce a more democratic and socialist society after World War Two failed in the dismal atmosphere of the Cold War, but nonetheless his 1940s work should be read as an attempt to politicize critical theory, to link theory with politics, and thus to make theory an instrument of practice and social change. Marcuse never really abandoned the revolutionary perspectives of his youth and pushed his political positions as far as he could during his work with the U.S. government in the 1940s. He attempted to preserve radical vision and imagination during an extremely difficult historical period when many fell prey to metaphysical pessimism and/or extreme disillusion with "the god that failed," turning away from politics altogether or moving toward more conservative positions.

Marcuse, by contrast, held onto his radical vision and did the most he could to link his theoretical perspectives to actual politics. Moreover, despite the exigencies of government work, Marcuse continued his theoretical studies throughout the 1940s and sketched out the perspectives that he would enrich and develop during the next three decades. The 1940s thus emerge as a pivotal and hitherto largely unknown episode in

Marcuse's theoretical itinerary. I believe that his government service gave him a better sense of concrete history than most social theorists, as well as a tremendous amount of empirical knowledge of fascist, communist and capitalist societies that nourished his theory in the years to come. Marcuse – more than most of his Institute colleagues – was therefore able to ground his theoretical labors in real history and existing social struggles.

The 1940s were therefore an extremely important decade for Herbert Marcuse and his generation. The 1940s witnessed the rise to global prominence of German fascism and its defeat in World War Two. It was also the period of the emergence of the Cold War and the division of the world into two camps led by the two competing superpowers, the United States and the Soviet Union. Marcuse was able to acquire a privileged vantage point to analyze these events, reading and writing secret government reports, making policy recommendations, and participating in debates within the government, and then the university and public spheres. Such work contributed to Marcuse's theoretical and political labors of the following decades and enabled him to produce his own distinct perspectives.

Finally, I believe that Marcuse's 1940s work provides us with resources to engage in our own theoretical and political projects today. Marcuse's work calls for the need to ground theoretical labor in concrete historical studies and to draw upon the most advanced sciences and knowledge of the day. Marcuse was able to continue the sort of interdisciplinary work that he began with the Institute for Social Research in his government work in the 1940s and these interdisciplinary projects and perspectives enrich his thought. Moreover, he provides substantive insight into the role of technology in contemporary societies and provides critical perspectives on society and technology that challenge us to distinguish between emancipatory and oppressive forces and tendencies, rather than simply seeing all technology and society as a vast apparatus of domination, or seeing all science, technology and industry as progressive per se.

His insights into fascism illuminate the ways that political and economic elites can manipulate groups of individuals into submitting to a social order that is against their own interests. With the continuing threat of rightwing forces throughout the world today, Marcuse's studies of fascism continue to provide insights into contemporary political dynamics. Likewise, his vision of emancipation that postulates art, technology and critical theory as potentially emancipatory forces continues to be relevant. The Marcusean vision which theorizes the most oppressive forces of domination contrasted to the most exciting possibilities for emancipation is particularly significant during the present period of the global restructuring of capitalism, whereby the advent of new technologies, a global reorganization of the capitalist system and unpredictable political turbulence have been producing dramatic change and upheaval. Precisely the sort of broad theoretical and political theorizing that Marcuse undertook throughout his life is needed today to analyze the momentous changes that we are currently undergoing. Marcuse thus provides models of a dialectical social theory that can inspire us to similar efforts today in the challenging task of charting the social-historical developments and delineating progressive politics for the present age.

I

Marcuse, c. 1935

† Marcuse's 'Some Social Implications of Modern Technology' was the only text in this collection published during Marcuse's lifetime. The essay first appeared in the Institute journal, *Studies in Philosophy and Social Science*, Vol. 9, Nr. 3 (1941): 414–39. Marcuse worked on this text in both New York and California during 1940–1 when he was concluding his first book in English, *Reason and Revolution* (New York: Oxford University Press, 1941), and when he was deeply involved in the projects of the Institute for Social Research.

SOME SOCIAL
IMPLICATIONS OF MODERN
TECHNOLOGY †

In this article, technology is taken as a social process in which technics proper (that is, the technical apparatus of industry, transportation, communication) is but a partial factor. We do not ask for the influence or effect of technology on the human individuals. For they are themselves an integral part and factor of technology, not only as the men who invent or attend to machinery but also as the social groups which direct its application and utilization. Technology, as a mode of production, as the totality of instruments, devices and contrivances which characterize the machine age is thus at the same time a mode of organizing and perpetuating (or changing) social relationships, a manifestation of prevalent thought and behavior patterns, an instrument for control and domination.[1]

Technics by itself can promote authoritarianism as well as liberty, scarcity as well as abundance, the extension as well as the abolition of toil. National Socialism is a striking example of the ways in which a highly rationalized and mechanized economy with the utmost efficiency in production can also operate in the interest of totalitarian oppression and continued scarcity. The Third Reich is indeed a form of "technocracy": the technical considerations of imperialistic efficiency and rationality supersede the traditional standards of profitability and general welfare. In National Socialist Germany, the reign of terror is sustained not only by brute force which is foreign to technology but also by the ingenious manipulation of the power inherent in technology: the intensification of labor, propaganda, the training of youths and workers, the organization of the governmental,

---

1 Cf. Lewis Mumford, *Technics and Civilization*, New York 1936, p. 364: The motive in back of "mechanical discipline and many of the primary inventions . . . was not technical efficiency but business, or power over other men. In the course of their development machines have extended these aims and provided a vehicle for their fulfillment."

industrial and party bureaucracy – all of which constitute the daily implements of terror – follow the lines of greatest technological efficiency. This terroristic technocracy cannot be attributed to the exceptional requirements of "war economy"; war economy is rather the normal state of the National Socialist ordering of the social and economic process, and technology is one of the chief stimuli of this ordering.[2]

In the course of the technological process a new rationality and new standards of individuality have spread over society, different from and even opposed to those which initiated the march of technology. These changes are not the (direct or derivative) effect of machinery on its users or of mass production on its consumers; they are rather themselves determining factors in the development of machinery and mass production. In order to understand their full import, it is necessary to survey briefly the traditional rationality and standards of individuality which are being dissolved by the present stage of the machine age.

The human individual whom the exponents of the middle class revolution had made the ultimate unit as well as the end of society stood for values which strikingly contradict those holding sway over society today. If we try to assemble in one guiding concept the various religious, political and economic tendencies which shaped the idea of the individual in the sixteenth and seventeenth century, we may define the individual as the subject of certain fundamental standards and values which no external authority was supposed to encroach upon. These standards and values pertained to the forms of life, social as well as personal, which were most adequate to the full development of man's faculties and abilities. By the same token, they were the "truth" of his individual and social existence. The individual, as a rational being, was deemed capable of finding these forms by his own thinking and, once he had acquired freedom of thought, pursuing the course of action which would actualize them. Society's task was to grant him such freedom and to remove all restrictions upon his rational course of action.

The principle of individualism, the pursuit of self-interest, was conditioned upon the proposition that self-interest was rational, that is to say, that it resulted from and was constantly guided and controlled by autonomous thinking. The rational self-interest did not coincide with the individual's immediate self-interest, for the latter depended upon the standards and requirements of the prevailing social order, placed there not

2 Cf. A.R.L. Gurland, "Technological Trends and Economic Structure under National Socialism," in this journal [*Studies in Philosophy and Social Science*], IX (1941), No. 2, pp. 226ff.

by his autonomous thought and conscience but by external authorities. In the context of radical Puritanism, the principle of individualism thus set the individual against his society. Men had to break through the whole system of ideas and values imposed upon them, and to find and seize the ideas and values that conformed to their rational interest. They had to live in a state of constant vigilance, apprehension, and criticism, to reject everything that was not true, not justified by free reason. This, in a society which was not yet rational, constituted a principle of permanent unrest and opposition. For false standards still governed the life of men, and the free individual was therefore he who criticized these standards, searched for the true ones and advanced their realization. The theme has nowhere been more fittingly expressed than in Milton's image of a "wicked race of deceivers, who . . . took the virgin Truth, hewd her lovely form into a thousand peeces, and scatter'd them to the four winds. From that time ever since, the sad friends of Truth, such as durst appear, imitating the careful search that Isis made for the mangl'd body of Osiris, went up and down gathering up limb by limb still as they could find them. We have not yet found them all, . . . nor ever shall do, till her Master's second coming . . . – To be still searching what we know not, by what we know, still closing up truth to truth as we find it (for all her body is homogeneal and proportional)," this was the principle of individualistic rationality.[3]

To fulfill this rationality presupposed an adequate social and economic setting, one that would appeal to individuals whose social performance was, at least to a large extent, their own work. Liberalist society was held to be the adequate setting for individualistic rationality. In the sphere of free competition, the tangible achievements of the individual which made his products and performances a part of society's need, were the marks of his individuality. In the course of time, however, the process of commodity production undermined the economic basis on which individualistic rationality was built. Mechanization and rationalization forced the weaker competitor under the dominion of the giant enterprises of machine industry which, in establishing society's dominion over nature, abolished the free economic subject.

The principle of competitive efficiency favors the enterprises with the most highly mechanized and rationalized industrial equipment. Technological power tends to the concentration of economic power, to "large units of production, of vast corporate enterprises producing large quantities and often a striking variety of goods, of industrial empires owning and controlling materials, equipment, and processes from the extraction of raw

---

3 *Areopagitia*, in *Works*, New York 1931, 4, pp. 338–339.

materials to the distribution of finished products, of dominance over an entire industry by a small number of giant concerns. . . . " And technology "steadily increases the power at the command of giant concerns by creating new tools, processes and products."[4] Efficiency here called for integral unification and simplification, for the removal of all "waste," the avoidance of all detours, it called for radical coordination. A contradiction exists, however, between the profit incentive that keeps the apparatus moving and the rise of the standard of living which this same apparatus has made possible. "Since control of production is in the hands of enterprisers working for a profit, they will have at their disposal whatever emerges as surplus after rent, interest, labor, and other costs are met. These costs will be kept at the lowest possible minimum as a matter of course."[5] Under these circumstances, profitable employment of the apparatus dictates to a great extent the quantity, form and kind of commodities to be produced, and through this mode of production and distribution, the technological power of the apparatus affects the entire rationality of those whom it serves.

Under the impact of this apparatus,[6] individualistic rationality has been transformed into technological rationality. It is by no means confined to the subjects and objects of large scale enterprises but characterizes the pervasive mode of thought and even the manifold forms of protest and rebellion. This rationality establishes standards of judgment and fosters attitudes which make men ready to accept and even to introcept the dictates of the apparatus.

Lewis Mumford has characterized man in the machine age as an "objective personality," one who has learned to transfer all subjective spontaneity to the machinery which he serves, to subordinate his life to the "matter-of-factness" of a world in which the machine is the factor and he the factum.[7] Individual distinctions in the aptitude, insight and knowledge are transformed into different quanta of skill and training, to be coordinated at any time within the common framework of standardized performances.

Individuality, however, has not disappeared. The free economic subject rather has developed into the object of large-scale organization and

---

4 *Temporary National Committee*, Monograph No. 22, "Technology in Our Economy," Washington 1941, p. 195.

5 *Temporary National Economic Committee, Final Report of the Executive Secretary*, Washington 1941, p. 140.

6 The term "apparatus" denotes the institutions, devices and organizations of industry in their prevailing social setting.

7 L. Mumford, *Technics and Civilization*, pp. 361ff.

coordination, and individual achievement has been transformed into standardized efficiency. The latter is characterized by the fact that the individual's performance is motivated, guided and measured by standards external to him, standards pertaining to predetermined tasks and functions. The efficient individual is the one whose performance is an action only insofar as it is the proper reaction to the objective requirements of the apparatus, and his liberty is confined to the selection of the most adequate means for reaching a goal which he did not set. Whereas individual achievement is independent of recognition and consummated in the work itself, efficiency is a rewarded performance and consummated only in its value for the apparatus.

With the majority of the population, the former freedom of the economic subject was gradually submerged in the efficiency with which he performed services assigned to him. The world had been rationalized to such an extent, and this rationality had become such a social power that the individual could do no better than adjust himself without reservation. Veblen was among the first to derive the new matter-of-factness from the machine process, from which it spread over the whole society: "The share of the operative workman in the machine industry is (typically) that of an attendant, an assistant, whose duty it is to keep pace with the machine process and to help out with workmanlike manipulation at points where the machine process engaged is incomplete. His work supplements the machine process rather than makes use of it. On the contrary the machine process makes use of the workman. The ideal mechanical contrivance in this technological system is the automatic machine."[8] The machine process requires a knowledge oriented to "a ready apprehension of opaque facts, in passably exact quantitative terms. This class of knowledge presumes a certain intellectual or spiritual attitude on the part of the workman, such an attitude as will readily apprehend and appreciate matter of fact and will guard against the suffusion of this knowledge with putative animistic or anthropomorphic subtleties, quasi-personal interpretations of the observed phenomena and of their relations to one another."[9]

As an attitude, matter-of-factness is not bound to the machine process. Under all forms of social production men have taken and justified their motives and goals from the facts that made up their reality, and in doing so they have arrived at the most diverging philosophies. Matter-of-factness

---

8 Veblen, *The Instinct of Workmanship*, New York 1922, p. 306f.
9 *Ibid.*, p. 310. This training in "matter of factness" applies not only to the factory worker but also to those who direct rather than attend the machine.

animated ancient materialism and hedonism, it was responsible in the struggle of modern physical science against spiritual oppression, and in the revolutionary rationalism of the enlightenment. The new attitude differs from all these in the highly rational compliance which typifies it. The facts directing man's thought and action are not those of nature which must be accepted in order to be mastered, or those of society which must be changed because they no longer correspond to human needs and potentialities. Rather are they those of the machine process, which itself appears as the embodiment of rationality and expediency.

Let us take a simple example. A man who travels by automobile to a distant place chooses his route from the highway maps. Towns, lakes and mountains appear as obstacles to be bypassed. The countryside is shaped and organized by the highway: what one finds en route is a byproduct or annex of the highway. Numerous signs and posters tell the traveler what to do and think; they even request his attention to the beauties of nature or the hallmarks of history. Others have done the thinking for him, and perhaps for the better. Convenient parking spaces have been constructed where the broadest and most surprising view is open. Giant advertisements tell him when to stop and find the pause that refreshes. And all of this is indeed for his benefit, safety and comfort; he receives what he wants. Business, technics, human needs and nature are welded together into one rational and expedient mechanism. He will fare best who follows its directions, subordinating his spontaneity to the anonymous wisdom which ordered everything for him.

The decisive point is that this attitude – which dissolves all actions into a sequence of semi-spontaneous reactions to prescribed mechanical norms – is not only perfectly rational but also perfectly reasonable. All protest is senseless, and the individual who would insist on his freedom of action would become a crank. There is no personal escape from the apparatus which has mechanized and standardized the world. It is a rational apparatus, combining utmost expediency with utmost convenience, saving time and energy, removing waste, adapting all means to the end, anticipating consequences, sustaining calculability and security.

In manipulating the machine, man learns that obedience to the directions is the only way to obtain desired results. Getting along is identical with adjustment to the apparatus. There is no room for autonomy. Individualistic rationality has developed into efficient compliance with the pregiven continuum of means and ends. The latter absorbs the liberating efforts of thought, and the various functions of reason converge upon the unconditional maintenance of the apparatus. It has been frequently stressed that scientific discoveries and inventions are shelved as soon as they seem to interfere with the requirements of profitable marketing.[10] The necessity which is the mother of inventions is to a great extent the necessity of maintaining and expanding the apparatus. Inventions have "their chief use . . . in the service of business, not of industry, and their great further use is in the furtherance, or rather the acceleration, of obligatory social amenities." They are mostly of a competitive nature, and "any techno-logical advantage gained by one competitor forthwith becomes a necessity to all the rest, on pain of defeat," so that one might as well say that, in the monopolistic system, "invention is the mother of necessity."[11]

Everything cooperates to turn human instincts, desires and thoughts into channels that feed the apparatus. Dominant economic and social organizations "do not maintain their power by force . . . They do it by identifying themselves with the faiths and loyalties of the people,"[12] and the people have been trained to identify their faiths and loyalties with them. The relationships among men are increasingly mediated by the machine process. But the mechanical contrivances which facilitate intercourse among individuals also intercept and absorb their libido, thereby diverting it from the all too dangerous realm in which the individual is free of society. The average man hardly cares for any living being with the intensity and persistence he shows for his automobile. The machine that is adored is no longer dead matter but becomes something like a human being. And it gives back to man what it possesses: the life of the social apparatus to which it belongs. Human behavior is outfitted with the rationality of the machine process, and this rationality has a definite social content. The machine process operates according to the laws of physical science, but it likewise operates according to the laws of mass production. Expediency in terms of technological reason is, at the same time, expediency in terms of profitable efficiency, and rationalisation is, at the same time, monopolistic standard-ization and concentration. The more rationally the individual behaves and the more lovingly he attends to his rationalized work, the more he succumbs to the frustrating aspects of this rationality. He is losing his ability to abstract from the special form in which rationalization is carried through and is losing his faith in its unfulfilled potentialities. His matter-of-factness, his distrust of all values which transcend the facts of observation, his resentment against all quasi-personal and metaphysical interpretations,

---

10 Florian Znaniecki, *The Social Role of the Man of Knowledge*, New York 1940, p. 54f. – Bernard J. Stern, *Society and Medical Progress*, Princeton 1941, Chapter IX, and the same author's contribution to *Technological Trends and National Policy*, U.S. National Resources Committee, Washington 1937.
11 Veblen, *The Instinct of Workmanship*, p. 315f.
12 Thurman Arnold, *The Folklore of Capitalism*, New York 1941, p. 193f.

his suspicion of all standards which relate the observable order of things, the rationality of the apparatus, to the rationality of freedom – this whole attitude serves all too well those who are interested in perpetuating the prevailing form of matters of fact. The machine process requires a "consistent training in the mechanical apprehension of things," and this training, in turn, promotes "conformity to the schedule of living," a "degree of trained insight and a facile strategy in all manner of quantitative adjustments and adaptations . . . "[13] The "mechanics of conformity" spread from the technological to the social order; they govern performance not only in the factories and shops, but also in the offices, schools, assemblies and, finally, in the realm of relaxation and entertainment.

Individuals are stripped of their individuality, not by external compulsion, but by the very rationality under which they live. Industrial psychology correctly assumes that "the dispositions of men are fixed emotional habits and as such they are quite dependable reaction patterns."[14] True, the force which transforms human performance into a series of dependable reactions is an external force: the machine process imposes upon men the patterns of mechanical behavior, and the standards of competitive efficiency are the more enforced from outside the less independent the individual competitor becomes. But man does not experience this loss of his freedom as the work of some hostile and foreign force; he relinquishes his liberty to the dictum of reason itself. The point is that today the apparatus to which the individual is to adjust and adapt himself is so rational that individual protest and liberation appear not only as hopeless but as utterly irrational. The system of life created by modern industry is one of the highest expediency, convenience and efficiency. Reason, once defined in these terms, becomes equivalent to an activity which perpetuates this world. Rational behavior becomes identical with a matter-of-factness which teaches reasonable submissiveness and thus guarantees getting along in the prevailing order.

At first glance, the technological attitude rather seems to imply the opposite of resignation. Teleological and theological dogmas no longer interfere with man's struggle with matter; he develops his experimental energies without inhibition. There is no constellation of matter which he does not try to break up, to manipulate and to change according to his will and interest. This experimentalism, however, frequently serves the effort to develop a higher efficiency of hierarchical control over men. Technological rationality may easily be placed into the service of such control: in the

13 Thorstein Veblen, p. 314.
14 Albert Walton, *Fundamentals of Industrial Psychology*, New York 1941, p. 24.

form of "scientific management," it has become one of the most profitable means for streamlined autocracy. F. W. Taylor's exposition of Scientific Management shows within it the union of exact science, matter-of-factness and big industry: "Scientific management attempts to substitute, in the relation between employers and workers, the government of fact and law for the rule of force and opinion. It substitutes exact knowledge for guesswork, and seeks to establish a code of natural laws equally binding upon employers and workmen. Scientific management thus seeks to substitute in the shop discipline, natural law in place of a code of discipline based upon the caprice and arbitrary power of men. No such democracy has ever existed in industry before. Every protest of every workman must be handled by those on the management side and the right and wrong of the complaint must be settled, not by the opinion either of the management or the workman but by the great code of laws which has been developed and which must satisfy both sides."[15] The scientific effort aims at eliminating waste, intensifying production and standardizing the product. And this whole scheme to increase profitable efficiency poses as the final fulfillment of individualism, ending up with a demand to "develop the individuality of the workers."[16]

The idea of compliant efficiency perfectly illustrates the structure of technological rationality. Rationality is being transformed from a critical force into one of adjustment and compliance. Autonomy of reason loses its meaning in the same measure as the thoughts, feelings and actions of men are shaped by the technical requirements of the apparatus which they have themselves created. Reason has found its resting place in the system of standardized control, production and consumption. There it reigns through the laws and mechanisms which insure the efficiency, expediency and coherence of this system.

As the laws and mechanisms of technological rationality spread over the whole society, they develop a set of truth values of their own which hold good for the functioning of the apparatus – and for that alone. Propositions concerning competitive or collusive behavior, business methods, principles of effective organization and control, fair play, the use of science and technics are true or false in terms of this value system, that is to say, in terms of instrumentalities that dictate their own ends. These truth values are tested and perpetuated by experience and must guide the thoughts and actions of all who wish to survive. Rationality here calls for unconditional compliance and coordination, and consequently, the truth values related to

---

15 Robert F. Hoxie, *Scientific Management and Labor*, New York 1916, p. 140f.
16 *Ibid.*, p. 149.

this rationality imply the subordination of thought to pregiven external standards. We may call this set of truth values the technological truth, technological in the twofold sense that it is an instrument of expediency rather than an end in itself, and that it follows the pattern of technological behavior.

By virtue of its subordination to external standards, the technological truth comes into striking contradiction with the form in which individualistic society had established its supreme values. The pursuit of self-interest now appears to be conditioned upon heteronomy, and autonomy as an obstacle rather than stimulus for rational action. The originally identical and "homogenous" truth seems to be split into two different sets of truth values and two different patterns of behavior: the one assimilated to the apparatus, the other antagonistic to it; the one making up the prevailing technological rationality and governing the behavior required by it, the other pertaining to a critical rationality whose values can be fulfilled only if it has itself shaped all personal and social relationships. The critical rationality derives from the principles of autonomy which individualistic society itself had declared to be its self-evident truths. Measuring these principles against the form in which individualistic society has actualized them, critical rationality accuses social injustice in the name of individualistic society's own ideology.[17] The relationship between technological and critical truth is a difficult problem which cannot be dealt with here, but two points must be mentioned. (1) The two sets of truth values are neither wholly contradictory nor complementary to each other; many truths of technological rationality are preserved or transformed in critical rationality. (2) The distinction between the two sets is not rigid; the content of each set changes in the social process so that what were once critical truth values become technological values. For example, the proposition that every individual is equipped with certain inalienable rights is a critical proposition but it was frequently interpreted in favor of efficiency and concentration of power."[18]

The standardization of thought under the sway of technological rationality also affects the critical truth values. The latter are torn from the context to which they originally belonged and, in their new form, are given wide, even official publicity. For example, propositions which, in Europe, were the exclusive domain of the labor movement are today adopted by the

---

17 Cf. Max Horkheimer and Herbert Marcuse, "Traditionelle und kritische Theorie," in *Zeitschrift für Sozialforschung*, VI (1937), pp. 245ff.

18 Cf. the discussion on the law Le Chapelier in the National Assembly of the French Revolution.

very forces which these propositions denounced. In the Fascist countries, they serve as ideological instruments for the attack on "Jewish capitalism" and "Western plutocracy," thereby concealing the actual front in the struggle. The materialistic analysis of present day economy is employed to justify Fascism to the German industrialists in whose interest it operates, as the regime of last resort for imperialistic expansion.[19] In other countries, the critique of political economy functions in the struggle among conflicting business groups and as a governmental weapon for unmasking monopolistic practices; it is propagated by the columnists of the big press syndicates and finds its way even into the popular magazines and the addresses to manufacturers' associations. As these propositions become part and parcel of the established culture, however, they seem to lose their edge and to merge with the old and the familiar. This familiarity with the truth illuminates the extent to which society has become indifferent and insusceptible to the impact of critical thought. For the categories of critical thought preserve their truth value only if they direct the full realization of the social potentialities which they envision, and they lose their vigor if they determine an attitude of fatalistic compliance or competitive assimilation.

Several influences have conspired to bring about the social impotence of critical thought. The foremost among them is the growth of the industrial apparatus and of its all-embracing control over all spheres of life. The technological rationality inculcated in those who attend to this apparatus has transformed numerous modes of external compulsion and authority into modes of self-discipline and self-control. Safety and order are, to a large extent, guaranteed by the fact that man has learned to adjust his behavior to the other fellow's down to the most minute detail. All men act equally rationally, that is to say, according to the standards which insure the functioning of the apparatus and thereby the maintenance of their own life. But this "introversion" of compulsion and authority has strengthened rather than attenuated the mechanisms of social control. Men, in following their own reason, follow those who put their reason to profitable use. In Europe, these mechanisms helped to prevent the individual from acting in accordance with the conspicuous truth, and they were efficiently supplemented by the physical control mechanisms of the apparatus. At this point, the otherwise diverging interests and their agencies are synchronized and adjusted in such a manner that they efficiently counteract any serious threat to their dominion.

---

19 Hitler's speech before the Industry Club in Düsseldorf, January 27, 1932, in *My New Order*, New York 1941, pp. 93ff.

The ever growing strength of the apparatus, however, is not the only influence responsible. The social impotence of critical thought has been further facilitated by the fact that important strata of the opposition have for long been incorporated into the apparatus itself – without losing the title of the opposition. The history of this process is well known and is illustrated in the development of the labour movement. Shortly after the First World War, Veblen declared that "the A.F. of L. is itself one of the Vested Interests, as ready as any other to do battle for its own margin of privilege and profit. . . . The A.F. of L. is a business organization with a vested interest of its own; for keeping up prices and keeping down the supply, quite after the usual fashion of management by the other Vested Interests."[20] The same holds true for the labor bureaucracy in leading European countries. The question here pertains not to the political expediency and the consequences of such a development, but to the changing function of the truth values which labor had represented and carried forward.

These truth values belonged, to a large extent, to the critical rationality which interpreted the social process in terms of its restrained potentialities. Such a rationality can fully develop only in social groups whose organization is not patterned on the apparatus in its prevailing forms or on its agencies and institutions. For the latter are pervaded by the technological rationality which shapes the attitude and interests of those dependent on them, so that all transcending aims and values are cut off. A harmony prevails between the "spirit" and its material embodiment such that the spirit cannot be supplanted without disrupting the functioning of the whole. The critical truth values borne by an oppositional social movement change their significance when this movement incorporates itself into the apparatus. Ideas such as liberty, productive industry, planned economy, satisfaction of needs are then fused with the interests of control and competition. Tangible organizational success thus outweighs the exigencies of critical rationality.

Its tendency to assimilate itself to the organizational and psychological pattern of the apparatus caused a change in the very structure of the social opposition in Europe. The critical rationality of its aims was subordinated to the technological rationality of its organization and thereby "purged" of the elements which transcended the established pattern of thought and action. This process was the apparently inevitable result of the growth of large scale industry and of its army of dependents. The latter could hope effectively to assert their interests only if these were effectively

20 Veblen, *The Engineers and The Price System*, New York 1940, pp. 88ff.

coordinated in large scale organizations. The oppositional groups were being transformed into mass parties, and their leadership into mass bureaucracies. This transformation, however, far from dissolving the structure of individualistic society into a new system, sustained and strengthened its basic tendencies.

It seems to be self-evident that mass and individual are contradictory concepts and incompatible facts. The crowd "is, to be sure, composed of individuals – but of individuals who cease to be isolated, who cease thinking. The isolated individual within the crowd cannot help thinking, criticizing the emotions. The others, on the other hand, cease to think: they are moved, they are carried away, they are elated; they feel united with their fellow members in the crowd, released from all inhibitions; they are changed and feel no connection with their former state of mind."[21] This analysis, although it correctly describes certain features of the masses, contains one wrong assumption, that in the crowd the individuals "cease to be isolated," are changed and "feel no connection with their former state of mind." Under authoritarianism, the function of the masses rather consists in consummating the isolation of the individual and in realizing his "former state of mind." The crowd is an association of individuals who have been stripped of all "natural" and personal distinctions and reduced to the standardized expression of their abstract individuality, namely, the pursuit of self-interest. As member of a crowd, man has become the standardized subject of brute self-preservation. In the crowd, the restraint placed by society upon the competitive pursuit of self-interest tends to become ineffective and the aggressive impulses are easily released. These impulses have been developed under the exigencies of scarcity and frustration, and their release rather accentuates the "former state of mind." True, the crowd "unites," but it unites the atomic subjects of self-preservation who are detached from everything that transcends their selfish interests and impulses. The crowd is thus the antithesis of the "community," and the perverted realization of individuality.

The weight and import of the masses grow with the growth of rationalization, but at the same time they are transformed into a conservative force which itself perpetuates the existence of the apparatus. As there is a decrease in the number of those who have the freedom of individual performance, there is an increase in the number of those whose individuality is reduced to self-preservation by standardization. They can pursue their self-interest only by developing "dependable reaction patterns" and by performing pre-arranged functions. Even the highly differentiated

21 E. Lederer, *State of the Masses*, New York 1940, p. 32f.

professional requirements of modern industry promote standardization. Vocational training is chiefly training in various kinds of skill, psychological and physiological adaptation to a "job" which has to be done. The job, a pre-given "type of work . . . requires a particular combination of abilities,"[22] and those who create the job also shape the human material to fill it. The abilities developed by such training make the "personality" a means for attaining ends which perpetuate man's existence as an instrumentality, replaceable at short notice by other instrumentalities of the same brand. The psychological and "personal" aspects of vocational training are the more emphasized the more they are subjected to regimentation and the less they are left to free and complete development. The "human side" of the employee and the concern for his personal aptitudes and habits play an important part in the total mobilization of the private sphere for mass production and mass culture. Psychology and individualization serve to consolidate stereotyped dependability, for they give the human object the feeling that he unfolds himself by discharging functions which dissolve his self into a series of required actions and responses. Within this range, individuality is not only preserved but also fostered and rewarded, but such individuality is only the special form in which a man introcepts and discharges, within a general pattern, certain duties allocated to him. Specialization fixates the prevailing scheme of standardization. Almost everyone has become a potential member of the crowd, and the masses belong to the daily implements of the social process. As such, they can easily be handled, for the thoughts, feelings and interests of their members have been assimilated to the pattern of the apparatus. To be sure, their outbursts are terrifying and violent but these are readily directed against the weaker competitors and the conspicuous "outsiders" (Jews, foreigners, national minorities). The coordinated masses do not crave a new order but a larger share in the prevailing one. Through their action, they strive to rectify, in an anarchic way, the injustice of competition. Their uniformity is in the competitive self-interest they all manifest, in the equalized expressions of self-preservation. The members of the masses are individuals.

The individual in the crowd is certainly not the one whom the individualistic principle exhorted to develop his self, nor is his self-interest the same as the rational interest urged by this principle. Where the daily social performance of the individual has become antagonistic to his "true interest," the individualist principle has changed its meaning. The protagonists of individualism were aware of the fact that "individuals can be developed only by being trusted with somewhat more than they can, at the

---

22 Albert Walton, *Fundamentals of Industrial Psychology*, p. 27.

moment, do well"; [23] today, the individual is trusted with precisely what he can, at the moment, do well. The philosophy of individualism has seen the "essential freedom" of the self to be "that it stands for a fateful moment outside of all belongings, and determines for itself alone whether its primary attachments shall be with actual earthly interests or with those of an ideal and potential 'Kingdom of God.'" [24] This ideal and potential kingdom has been defined in different ways, but it has always been characterized by contents which were opposed and transcendent to the prevailing kingdom. Today, the prevailing type of individual is no longer capable of seizing the fateful moment which constitutes his freedom. He has changed his function; from a unit of resistance and autonomy, he has passed to one of ductility and adjustment. It is this function which associates individuals in masses.

The emergence of the modern masses, far from endangering the efficiency and coherence of the apparatus, has facilitated the progressing coordination of society and the growth of authoritarian bureaucracy, thus refuting the social theory of individualism at a decisive point. The technological process seemed to tend to the conquest of scarcity and thus to the slow transformation of competition into cooperation. The philosophy of individualism viewed this process as the gradual differentiation and liberation of human potentialities, as the abolition of the "crowd." Even in the Marxian conception, the masses are not the spearhead of freedom. The Marxian proletariat is not a crowd but a class, defined by its determinate position in the productive process, the maturity of its "consciousness," and the rationality of its common interest. Critical rationality, in the most accentuated form, is the prerequisite for its liberating function. In one aspect at least, this conception is in line with the philosophy of individualism: it envisions the rational form of human association as brought about and sustained by the autonomous decision and action of free men.

This is the one point at which the technological and the critical rationality seem to converge, for the technological process implies a democratization of functions. The system of production and distribution has been rationalized to such an extent that the hierarchical distinction between executive and subordinate performances is to an ever smaller degree based upon essential distinctions in aptitude and insight, and to an ever greater degree upon inherited power and a vocational training to which everyone could be subjected. Even experts and "engineers" are no exception. To be sure, the gap between the underlying population

---

23 W. E. Hocking, *The Lasting Elements of Individualism*, New Haven 1937, p. 5.
24 *Ibid.*, p. 23.

and those who design the blueprints for rationalization, who lay out production, who make the inventions and discoveries which accelerate technological progress, becomes daily more conspicuous, particularly in a period of war economy. At the same time, however, this gap is maintained more by the division of power than by the division of work. The hierarchical distinction of the experts and engineers results from the fact that their ability and knowledge is utilized in the interest of autocratic power. The "technological leader" is also a "social leader"; his "social leadership overshadows and conditions his function as a scientist, for it gives him institutional power within the group . . . ," and the "captain of industry" acts in "perfect accordance with the traditional dependence of the expert's function."[25] Were it not for this fact, the task of the expert and engineer would not be an obstacle to the general democratization of functions. Technological rationalization has created a common framework of experience for the various professions and occupations. This experience excludes or restrains those elements that transcend the technical control over matters of fact and thus extends the scope of rationalization from the objective to the subjective world. Underneath the complicated web of stratified control is an array of more or less standardized techniques, tending to one general pattern, which insure the material reproduction of society. The "persons engaged in a practical occupation" seem to be convinced that "any situation which appears in the performance of their role can be fitted into some general pattern with which the best, if not all, of them are familiar."[26] Moreover, the instrumentalistic conception of technological rationality is spreading over almost the whole realm of thought and gives the various intellectual activities a common denominator. They too become a kind of technique,[27] a matter of training rather than individuality, requiring the expert rather than the complete human personality.

The standardization of production and consumption, the mechanization of labor, the improved facilities of transportation and communication, the extension of training, the general dissemination of knowledge – all these factors seem to facilitate the exchangeability of functions. It is as if the basis were shrinking on which the pervasive distinction between "specialized (technical)" and "common" knowledge[28] has been built, and

---

25 Znaniecki, *The Social Role of the Man of Knowledge*, pp. 40, 55.
26 Op. cit., p. 31, Znaniecki's description refers to a historical state of affairs in which "no demand for a scientist can arise," but it appears to refer to a basic tendency of the prevailing state of affairs.
27 Cf. Max Horkheimer, "The End of Reason," *Studies in Philosophy and Social Science*, IX, p. 380.
28 Znaniecki, p. 25.

as if the authoritarian control of functions would prove increasingly foreign to the technological process. The special form, however, in which the technological process is organized, counteracts this trend. The same development that created the modern masses as the standardized attendants and dependents of large scale industry also created the hierarchical organization of private bureaucracies. Max Weber has already stressed the connection between mass-democracy and bureaucracy: "In contrast to the democratic self-administration of small homogeneous units," the bureaucracy is "the universal concomitant of modern mass democracy."[29]

The bureaucracy becomes the concomitant of the modern masses by virtue of the fact that standardization proceeds along the lines of specialization. The latter by itself, provided that it is not arrested at the point where it interferes with the domain of vested control, is quite compatible with the democratization of functions. Fixated specialization, however, tends to atomize the masses and to insulate the subordinate from the executive functions. We have mentioned that specialized vocational training implies fitting a man to a particular job or a particular line of jobs, thus directing his "personality," spontaneity and experience to the special situations he may meet in filling the job. In this manner, the various professions and occupations, notwithstanding their convergence upon one general pattern, tend to become atomic units which require coordination and management from above. The technical democratization of functions is counteracted by their atomization, and the bureaucracy appears as the agency which guarantees their rational course and order.

The bureaucracy thus emerges on an apparently objective and impersonal ground, provided by the rational specialization of functions, and this rationality in turn serves to increase the rationality of submission. For, the more the individual functions are divided, fixated and synchronized according to objective and impersonal patterns, the less reasonable is it for the individual to withdraw or withstand. "The material fate of the masses becomes increasingly dependent upon the continuous and correct functioning of the increasingly bureaucratic order of private capitalistic organizations."[30] The objective and impersonal character of technological rationality bestows upon the bureaucratic groups the universal dignity of reason. The rationality embodied in the giant enterprises makes it appear as if men, in obeying them, obey the dictum of an objective rationality. The private bureaucracy fosters a delusive harmony between the special and the common interest. Private power relationships appear not only

29 Max Weber, *Wirtschaft und Gesellschaft*, Tübingen 1922, p. 666.
30 Weber, p. 669.

as relationships between objective things but also as the rule of rationality itself.

In the Fascist countries, this mechanism facilitated the merger between private, semi-private (party) and public (governmental) bureaucracies. The efficient realization of the interests of large scale enterprise was one of the strongest motives for the transformation of economic into totalitarian political control, and efficiency is one of the main reasons for the Fascist regime's hold over its regimented population. At the same time, however, it is also the force which may break this hold. Fascism can maintain its rule only by aggravating the restraint which it is compelled to impose upon society. It will ever more conspicuously manifest its inability to develop the productive forces, and it will fall before that power which proves to be more efficient than Fascism.

In the democratic countries, the growth of the private bureaucracy can be balanced by the strengthening of the public bureaucracy. The rationality inherent in the specialization of functions tends to enlarge the scope and weight of bureaucratization. In the private bureaucracy, however, such an expansion will intensify rather than alleviate the irrational elements of the social process, for it will widen the discrepancy between the technical character of the division of functions and the autocratic character of control over them. In contrast, the public bureaucracy, if democratically constituted and controlled, will overcome this discrepancy to the extent that it undertakes the "conservation of those human and material resources which technology and corporations have tended to misuse and waste."[31] In the age of mass society, the power of the public bureaucracy can be the weapon which protects the people from the encroachment of special interests upon the general welfare. As long as the will of the people can effectively assert itself, the public bureaucracy can be a lever of democratization. Large-scale industry tends to organize on a national scale, and Fascism has transformed economic expansion into the military conquest of whole continents. In this situation, the restoration of society to its own right, and the maintenance of individual freedom have become directly political questions, their solution depending upon the outcome of the international struggle.

The social character of bureaucratization is largely determined by the extent to which it allows for a democratization of functions that tends to close the gap between the governing bureaucracy and the governed population. If everyone has become a potential member of the public

---

31 Henry A. Wallace, *Technology, Corporations, and the General Welfare*, Chapel Hill 1937, p. 56.

bureaucracy (as he has become a potential member of the masses), society will have passed from the stage of hierarchical bureaucratization to the stage of technical self-administration. Insofar as technocracy implies a deepening of the gap between specialized and common knowledge, between the controlling and coordinating experts and the controlled and coordinated people, the technocratic abolition of the "price system" would stabilize rather than shatter the forces which stand in the way of progress. The same holds true for the so-called managerial revolution. According to the theory of the managerial revolution,[32] the growth of the apparatus entails the rise of a new social class, the "managers," to take over social domination and to establish a new economic and political order. Nobody will deny the increasing importance of management and the simultaneous shift in the function of control. But these facts do not make the managers a new social class or the spearhead of a revolution. Their "source of income" is the same as that of the already existing classes: they either draw salaries, or, insofar as they possess a share in the capital, are themselves capitalists. Moreover, their specific function in the prevailing division of labor does not warrant the expectation that they are predestined to inaugurate a new and more rational division of labor. This function is either determined by the requirement of profitable utilization of capital, and, in this case, the managers are simply capitalists or deputy-capitalists (comprising the "executives" and the corporation-managers);[33] or it is determined by the material process of production (engineers, technicians, production managers, plant superintendents). In the latter case, the managers would belong to the vast army of the "immediate producers" and share its "class interest," were it not for the fact that, even in this function, they work as deputy-capitalists and thus form a segregated and privileged group between capital and labor. Their power, and the awe which it inspires, are derived not from their actual "technological" performance but from their social position, and this they owe to the prevailing organization of production. "The leading managerial and directorial figures within the inner business sancta . . . are drawn from, or have been absorbed into, the upper layers of wealth and income whose stakes it is their function to defend."[34] To sum up, as a separate social group, the managers are thoroughly tied up with the vested interests, and as performers of necessary productive functions they do not constitute a separate "class" at all.

---

32 J. Burnham, *The Managerial Revolution*, New York 1941, pp. 78ff.
33 *Ibid.*, p. 83f.
34 Robert A. Brady, "Policies of National Manufacturing Spitzenverbände," in *Political Science Quarterly*, LVI, p. 537.

The spreading hierarchy of large scale enterprise and the precipitation of individuals into masses determine the trends of technological rationality today. What results is the mature form of that individualistic rationality which characterized the free economic subject of the industrial revolution. Individualistic rationality was born as a critical and oppositional attitude that derived freedom of action from the unrestricted liberty of thought and conscience and measured all social standards and relations by the individual's rational self-interest. It grew into the rationality of competition in which the rational interest was superseded by the interest of the market, and individual achievement absorbed by efficiency. It ended with standard-ized submission to the all-embracing apparatus which it had itself created. This apparatus is the embodiment and resting place of individualistic rationality, but the latter now requires that individuality must go. He is rational who most efficiently accepts and executes what is allocated to him, who entrusts his fate to the large scale enterprises and organizations which administer the apparatus.

Such was the logical outcome of a social process which measured individual performance in terms of competitive efficiency. The philoso-phers of individualism have always had an inkling of this outcome and they expressed their anxiety in many different forms, in the skeptical conformism of Hume, in the idealistic introversion of individual freedom, in the frequent attacks of the Transcendentalists against the rule of money and power. But the social forces were stronger than the philosophic pro-tests, and the philosophic justification of individualism took on more of the overtones of resignation. Toward the end of the nineteenth century, the idea of the individual became increasingly ambiguous: it combined insistence upon free social performance and competitive efficiency with glorification of smallness, privacy and self-limitation. The rights and liber-ties of the individual in society were interpreted as the rights and liberties of privacy and withdrawal from society. William James, faithful to the indi-vidualistic principle, asserted that, in the "rivalry between real organizable goods," the "world's trial is better than the closet solution," provided that the victorious keep "the vanquished somehow represented."[35] His doubt, however, as to whether this trial is really a fair one seems to motivate his hatred of "bigness and greatness in all their forms,"[36] his declaration that "the smaller and more intimate is the truer, – the man more than the home, the home more than the state or the church."[37] The counterposition

---

35 *The Thought and Character of William James*, ed. R. B. Perry, Boston 1935, II, p. 265.
36 *Ibid.*, p. 315.
37 *Ibid.*, p. 383.

of individual and society, originally meant to provide the ground for a militant reformation of society in the interest of the individual, comes to prepare and justify the individual's withdrawal from society. The free and self-reliant "soul," which originally nourished the individual's critique of external authority, now becomes a refuge from external authority. Tocqueville had already defined individualism in terms of acquiescence and peaceful resignation: "a mature and calm feeling, which disposes each member of the community to sever himself from the mass of his fellow-creatures; and to draw apart with his family and his friends; so that, after he has thus formed a little circle of his own, he willingly leaves society at large to itself."[38] Autonomy of the individual came to be regarded as a private rather than a public affair, an element of retreat rather than aggression. All these factors of resignation are comprehended in Benjamin Constant's statement that "our liberty should be composed of the peaceful enjoyment of private independence."[39]

The elements of restraint and resignation which became increasingly strong in the individualist philosophy of the nineteenth century elucidate the connection between individualism and scarcity. Individualism is the form liberty assumes in a society wherein the acquisition and utilization of wealth is dependent on competitive toil. Individuality is a distinct possession of "pioneers"; it presupposes the open and empty spaces, the freedom of "hewing out a home" as well as the need to do so. The individual's world is a "world of labor and the march," as Walt Whitman says, one in which the available intellectual and material resources must be conquered and appropriated through incessant struggle with man and nature, and in which human forces are released to distribute and administer scarcity.

In the period of large scale industry, however, the existential conditions making for individuality give way to conditions which render individuality unnecessary. In clearing the ground for the conquest of scarcity, the technological process not only levels individuality but also tends to transcend it where it is concurrent with scarcity. Mechanized mass production is filling the empty spaces in which individuality could assert itself. The cultural standardization points, paradoxically enough, to potential abundance as well as actual poverty. This standardization may indicate the extent to which individual creativeness and originality have been rendered unnecessary. With the decline of the liberalistic era, these qualities were vanishing from the domain of material production and becoming the ever more exclusive property of the highest intellectual activities. Now, they seem to

---

38 *Democracy in America*, transl. H. Reeve, New York 1904, II, p. 584.
39 Quoted in E. Mims, *The Majority of the People*, New York 1941, p. 152.

disappear from this sphere too: mass culture is dissolving the traditional forms of art, literature and philosophy together with the "personality" which unfolded itself in producing and consuming them. The striking impoverishment which characterizes the dissolution of these forms may involve a new source of enrichment. They derived their truth from the fact that they represented the potentialities of man and nature which were excluded or distorted in the reality. So far were those potentialities from their actualization in the social consciousness that much cried out for unique expression. But today, *humanitas*, wisdom, beauty, freedom and happiness can no longer be represented as the realm of the "harmonious personality" nor as the remote heaven of art nor as metaphysical systems. The "ideal" has become so concrete and so universal that it grips the life of every human being, and the whole of mankind is drawn into the struggle for its realization. Under the terror that now threatens the world the ideal constricts itself to one single and at the same time common issue. Faced with Fascist barbarism, everyone knows what freedom means, and everyone is aware of the irrationality in the prevailing rationality.

Modern mass society quantifies the qualitative features of individual labor and standardizes the individualistic elements in the activities of intellectual culture. This process may bring to the fore the tendencies which make individuality a historical form of human existence, to be surpassed by further social development. This does not mean that society is bound to enter a stage of "collectivism." The collectivistic traits which characterize the development today may still belong to the phase of individualism. Masses and mass culture are manifestations of scarcity and frustration, and the authoritarian assertion of the common interest is but another form of the rule of particular interests over the whole. The fallacy of collectivism consists in that it equips the whole (society) with the traditional properties of the individual. Collectivism abolishes the free pursuit of competing individual interests but retains the idea of the common interest as a separate entity. Historically, however, the latter is but the counterpart of the former. Men experience their society as the objective embodiment of the collectivity as long as the individual interests are antagonistic to and competing with each other for a share in the social wealth. To such individuals, society appears as an objective entity, consisting of numerous things, institutions and agencies: plants and shops, business, police and law, government, schools and churches, prisons and hospitals, theaters and organizations, etc. Society is almost everything the individual is not, every-thing that determines his habits, thoughts and behavior patterns, that affects him from "outside." Accordingly, society is noticed chiefly as a power of restraint and control, providing the framework which integrates

the goals, faculties and aspirations of men. It is this power which collectivism retains in its picture of society, thus perpetuating the rule of things
and men over men.

The technological process itself furnishes no justification for such a
collectivism. Technics hampers individual development only insofar as they
are tied to a social apparatus which perpetuates scarcity, and this same
apparatus has released forces which may shatter the special historical form
in which technics is utilized. For this reason, all programs of an anti-
technological character, all propaganda for an anti-industrial revolution[40]
serve only those who regard human needs as a by-product of the utilization
of technics. The enemies of technics readily join forces with a terroristic
technocracy.[41] The philosophy of the simple life, the struggle against big
cities and their culture frequently serves to teach men distrust of the potential instruments that could liberate them. We have pointed to the possible
democratization of functions which technics may promote and which
may facilitate complete human development in all branches of work and
administration. Moreover, mechanization and standardization may one
day help to shift the center of gravity from the necessities of material
production to the arena of free human realization. The less individuality is
required to assert itself in standardized social performances, the more it
could retreat to a free "natural" ground. These tendencies, far from
engendering collectivism, may lead to new forms of individualization.
The machine individualizes men by following the physiological lines of
individuality: it allocates the work to finger, hand, arm, foot, classifying
and occupying men according to the dexterity of these organs.[42] The
external mechanisms which govern standardization here meet a "natural"
individuality; they lay bare the ground on which a hitherto suppressed
individualization might develop. On this ground, man is an individual
by virtue of the uniqueness of his body and its unique position in the space–
time continuum. He is an individual insofar as this natural uniqueness
molds his thoughts, instincts, emotions, passions and desires. This is the
"natural" *principium individuationis*. Under the system of scarcity, men

---

40 See for example Oswald Spengler, *Man and Technics*, New York 1932, p. 96f.,
    and Roy Helton, "The Anti-Industrial Revolution," in *Harpers*, December 1941,
    pp. 65ff.
41 In National Socialist Germany, the ideology of blood and soil and the glorifica-
    tion of the peasant is an integral part of the imperialistic mobilization of industry
    and labor.
42 For examples of the degree to which this physiological individualization has been
    utilized see *Changes in Machinery and Job Requirements in Minnesota
    Manufacturing 1931–36*, Works Projects Administration, National Research
    Project, Report No. 1–6, Philadelphia, p. 19.

developed their senses and organs chiefly as implements of labor and competitive orientation: skill, taste, proficiency, tact, refinement and endurance
were qualities molded and perpetuated by the hard struggle for life,
business and power. Consequently, man's thoughts, appetites and the
ways of their fulfillment were not "his," they showed the oppressive and
inhibitive features which this struggle imposed upon him. His senses,
organs and appetites became acquisitive, exclusive and antagonistic. The
technological process has reduced the variety of individual qualities down
to this natural basis of individualization, but this same basis may become
the foundation for a new form of human development.

The philosophy of individualism established an intrinsic connection
between individuality and property.[43] According to this philosophy, man
could not develop a self without conquering and cultivating a domain of
his own, to be shaped exclusively by his free will and reason. The domain
thus conquered and cultivated had become part and parcel of his own
"nature." Man removed the objects in this domain from the state in which
he found them, and made them the tangible manifestation of his individual
labor and interest. They were his property because they were fused with the
very essence of his personality. This construction did not correspond to
the facts and lost its meaning in the era of mechanized commodity production, but it contained the truth that individual development, far from
being an inner value only, required an external sphere of manifestation and
an autonomous concern for men and things. The process of production
has long dissolved the link between individual labor and property and now
tends to dissolve the link between the traditional form of property and
social control, but the tightening of this control counteracts a tendency
which may give the individualistic theory a new content. Technological
progress would make it possible to decrease the time and energy spent in
the production of the necessities of life, and a gradual reduction of scarcity
and abolition of competitive pursuits could permit the self to develop from
its natural roots. The less time and energy man has to expend in maintaining his life and that of society, the greater the possibility that he can
"individualize" the sphere of his human realization. Beyond the realm of
necessity, the essential differences between men could unfold themselves:
everyone could think and act by himself, speak his own language, have
his own emotions and follow his own passions. No longer chained to
competitive efficiency, the self could grow in the realm of satisfaction. Man
could come into his own in his passions. The objects of his desires would be
the less exchangeable the more they were seized and shaped by his free self.

---

43 See Max Horkheimer, "The End of Reason," p. 377, *op. cit.*

They would "belong" to him more than ever before, and such ownership would not be injurious, for it would not have to defend its own against a hostile society.

Such a Utopia would not be a state of perennial happiness. The "natural" individuality of man is also the source of his natural sorrow. If the human relations are nothing but human, if they are freed from all foreign standards, they will be permeated with the sadness of their singular content. They are transitory and irreplaceable, and their transitory character will be accentuated when concern for the human being is no longer mingled with fear for his material existence and overshadowed by the threat of poverty, hunger, and social ostracism.

The conflicts, however, which may arise from the natural individuality of men may not bear the violent and aggressive features which were so frequently attributed to the "state of nature." These features may be the marks of coercion and privation. "Appetite is never excessive, never furious, save when it has been starved. The frantic hunger we see it so often exhibiting under every variety of criminal form, marks only the hideous starvation to which society subjects it. It is not a normal but a morbid state of the appetite, growing exclusively out of the unnatural compression which is imposed upon it by the exigencies of our immature society. Every appetite and passion of man's nature is good and beautiful, and destined to be fully enjoyed. . . . Remove, then, the existing bondage of humanity, remove those factitious restraints which keep appetite and passion on the perpetual lookout for escape, like steam from an overcharged boiler, and their force would instantly become conservative instead of destructive."[44]

---

44 Henry James, "Democracy and Its Issues," in *Lectures and Miscellanies*, New York 1852, p. 47f.

II

STATE AND INDIVIDUAL UNDER NATIONALSOCIALISM

Herbert Marcuse
218 – 18 St.
SANTA MONICA, CALIF.

Today, we no longer need refute the opinion that National-socialism signifies a revolution. This movement, we now see, has not changed the basic relationships of the productive process that is still administered by special social groups which control the instruments of labor regardless of the needs and interests of society as a whole. [1] The economic organization of the Third Reich

[1] The material for the verification of this interpretation is found in F. Neumann, Behemoth. The Origin and Structure of Nationalsocialism. New York 1942.

is built around the great industrial combines which, to a large extent with governmental help, had steadily increased their hold before Hitler's ascent to power. They maintained their key position in the production for war and expansion. Since 1933, they have been amalgamated with a new "elite", recruited from the top ranks of the Nationalsocialist party, but they have not lost their decisive social and economic functions. [2]

[2] For the "division of power" between the political machine and big business see Gurland, "Technological Trends under National-socialism", in Studies in Philosophy and Social Science, 1941, no. 2, p.245 ff., and Kirchheimer, "Changes in the Structure of Political Compromise", op. cit., p.275 ff. - Cf. below p.11 f.

On the other hand, Nationalsocialism is not a social and political restoration, although the Nationalsocialist regime to

† In the Marcuse archives, there are both a lecture on National Socialism without a
   title (numbered 118.01) and what appears to be a prepared article on "State and
   Individual Under National Socialism" (#118). There is no date on either
   manuscript, but the address under Marcuse's name on the latter (218 – 18 St.,
   Santa Monica, California) suggests that it was prepared shortly after Marcuse's
   lecture in New York, while he was in California and before he moved to
   Washington, D.C. in late 1942. Wiggershaus indicates in *The Frankfurt School*
   that Marcuse's text was to be published in book form along with Gurland's study
   of "Private Property under National Socialism" Neumann's text on "The New
   Rulers in Germany," Kirchheimer on "Law and Justice under National Socialism,"
   and Pollock's study "Is National Socialism a New Social and Economic System?"
   The proposed book never appeared, and we publish the manuscript as prepared
   for publication, although as a supplement we include the final pages from the
   lecture manuscript which deals with National Socialism and art, a theme not
   developed in the manuscript prepared for publication.

STATE AND INDIVIDUAL
UNDER NATIONAL
SOCIALISM†

Today, we no longer need refute the opinion that National Socialism signifies a revolution. This movement, we now see, has not changed the basic relationships of the productive process that is still administered by special social groups which control the instruments of labor regardless of the needs and interest of society as a whole.[1] The economic organization of the Third Reich is built around the great industrial combines which, to a large extent with governmental help, had steadily increased their hold before Hitler's ascent to power. They maintained their key position in the production for war and expansion. Since 1933, they have been amalgamated with a new "elite", recruited from the top ranks of the National Socialist party, but they have not lost their decisive social and economic functions.[2]

On the other hand, National Socialism is not a social and political *restoration*, although the National Socialist regime to a large extent restored to power those forces and interests which had been threatened or even frustrated by the Weimar republic: the army has again become a state within the state, the authority of the entrepreneur within the enterprise has been freed from numerous limitations, and the working class has been brought under totalitarian control. But this process did not bring back the old forms of domination and stratification. The National Socialist state as it exists has little in common with the political structure of the old Reich. The army, once the breeding ground for Prussian drill and feudalism, has

---

1 The material for the verification of this interpretation is found in F. Neumann, *Behemoth. The Origin and Structure of National Socialism*. New York 1942.
2 For the "division of power" between the political machine and big business see Gurland, "Technological Trends under National Socialism", in *Studies in Philosophy and Social Science*, 1941, no. 2, p. 245ff., and Kirchheimer, "Changes in the Structure of Political Compromise", p. 275ff. Cf. below p. 74f.

been reorganized according to more democratic principles of selection, while outside the army a network of pseudo-democratic measures has been spread over social relationships. Entrepreneur and worker are brought together in the German Labor Front, are made to participate shoulder on shoulder in the same demonstrations and parades, and are held to be committed to the same rules of behavior. Numerous privileges and distinctions, vestiges of the feudal order, have been abolished. Moreover, and most important, the old state bureaucracy and the top ranks in industry and finance have recognized a new master and new methods of government.

If National Socialism is neither a revolution nor a restoration, what is it?

The usual approach to National Socialism is influenced by two most conspicuous facets of it: (1) the totalitarian character of the *state*, and (2) the authoritarian character of the *society*. These phenomena induce us to see in National Socialism the absolute rule of the state over all private and social relationships, and the absolute repression of the individual with all his rights and abilities. We shall try to show that this interpretation is at best highly questionable.

The proposition which we are going to develop is that National Socialism has done away with the essential features which characterized the modern state. It tends to abolish any separation between state and society by transferring the political functions to the social groups actually in power. In other words, National Socialism tends toward direct and immediate selfgovernment by the prevailing social groups over the rest of the population. And it manipulates the masses by unleashing the most brutal and selfish instincts of the individual.

The modern state – and we deal only with this form of the state – was instituted and organized outside a realm of human relationships which was regarded as *non*-political and subject to its own laws and standards. The private life of the individual, the family, the church, large sectors of economic and cultural life belonged to this realm. This does not mean that the state was to refrain from interfering with the social relationships; not only the absolutist but also the democratic states claimed and exercised the right of interference. In doing so, however, the state recognized that certain inherent social rights anteceded its own power, and its interference was justified and accepted only insofar as it safeguarded, promoted or restored these rights. The rights of men as social beings, as members of society, have been defined in different ways – (the liberty to buy and to sell, to enter into contracts, to choose one's own abode and profession, to earn a living) – in any case, the state found in them the limit or the end of its dominion. The state constituted a realm of calculable administration which remained distinguished from the realm of society proper. This holds true for the absolutistic state, which even in the form discussed in the *Leviathan*, was meant to promote and sustain the fundamental liberties of competitive society. The progressive function of the absolute state, namely that of balancing the competing social activities into a steady and calculable order, came to fruition in the liberalistic form of the state. The rule of law, the monopoly of coercive power, and national sovereignty were the three features of the modern state which most clearly expressed the rational division of functions between the state and society. National Socialism has abolished this division.

During the modern era, the *rule of law* has, to an ever increasing extent, become the medium through which the state operated as a system of rational administration. The law treated men, if not as equal, at least without regard for the most obvious social contingencies; it was, so to speak, the court of appeal that mitigated the hazards and injustice which men suffered in their social relationships. The universal character of the law offered universal protection to all citizens, not only from the disastrous play of conflicting self-interests, but also from governmental caprice.

The National Socialist regime has done away with these properties of the law which had raised it above the hazards of the social struggle. The very concept of the law as universally valid and equally applicable has been abandoned and replaced by a diversity of particular rights: one for the party, another for the army, a third for the ordinary *Volksgenossen*.[3] The residue of universality which still remained in these group rights has been further limited by the practice of enhancing the authority of the judge and freeing him from the fetters of written law. Law made subordinate to such standards as the feeling of the racial community (*Rechtsempfinden*)[4] in reality to political expediency, serves to heighten existing social and political privileges. The promulgation of retroactive laws destroys the calculability and rationality of the administration of justice. Law is no longer an established and generally known reality which balances the social and political interests, it is rather the direct expression of these interests themselves, constantly changing as social and political requirements change.

True, the rule of law characterized the state only during the liberalist era.

---

3 Carl Schmitt has furnished the ideological justification for the abolition of the universality of law: "In a people stratified according to estates, there always prevails a plurality of orders each of which has to form its own estate law (*Standesgerichtsbarkeit*) – 'as many estates, as many benches'" (*Über die drei Arten des rechtswissenschaftlichen Denkens*, Hamburg 1934, p. 63ff.).

4 Hermann Göring, *Die Rechtssicherheit als Grundlage der Volksgemeinschaft*, Hamburg 1935, p. 13.

In the absolutist state, law was reduced to the command of the sovereign. Even so, however, this state was an institution separate from society. It assumed this independent and autonomous form because no single social group was powerful enough to dictate to the whole of society; the state thus could obtain and make secure an operational field of its own, against the nobility as well as the clergy and the middle classes. In contrast, the National Socialist state has been casting away the last remnants of independence from the predominant social groups – it is becoming the executive organ of the imperialist economic interests.

If there is anything totalitarian in National Socialism, it is certainly not the state. The "abstract State" was "an idea of the liberalist era". The State, as a "technical instrument of power, was set apart from economy and culture". The Third Reich does not bring about "the so-called totality of the State, but of the National Socialist movement".[5] Hitler himself has protested against the totalitarian state and proclaimed that National Socialism is typified by the fact that it denies the independence and superiority of the state: "the basic realization is that the State represents not an end, but a means. It is indeed the presumption for the formation of a higher human culture, but not its cause. On the contrary, the latter lies exclusively in the existence of a race capable of culture".[6] Hitler and his official spokesmen have frequently expressed the view that they consider the state merely as a part of a much more comprehensive scheme. Wherever they have refrained from ideological glorification, they have stated that this scheme is set and determined by the expanding needs of German capitalism.

In Europe, autonomy, the power monopoly and the rule by law characterized the state as long as industrial capacity could produce for internal and external markets that were still open. For Germany this period came to an end with the First World War. Germany rebuilt and modernized her industrial apparatus at an incredible rate, but the shrinking of the internal market, the loss of external outlets, and, above all, the social legislation of the Weimar republic prevented the profitable utilization of this apparatus. Under these circumstances, return to a direct imperialist policy offered itself as the most plausible solution. It was violently opposed by the majority of the social groups which had organized the democratic state. Industrial expansion and, with it, the social order based on this expansion could be maintained only through the transformation of the democratic state into an authoritarian political system.

---

5 Alfred Rosenberg, *Gestaltung der Idee*, München 1936, p. 20f.
6 *Mein Kampf*, Reynal and Hitchcock, New York 1939, p. 592.

This may sound like an extremely one-sided interpretation, but it is the explanation of National Socialism which *Hitler himself* has given. He has elaborated this point of view in a speech free from the usual ideological trappings and for that reason particularly revealing. The speech was delivered before the *Industry Club* in Düsseldorf in January 1932, one year before his ascent to power. Hitler starts from the fact that, in the modern world, private as well as social and political life is based upon the "principle of efficiency". According to this principle individuals as well as social groups and nations receive a share in the social product measured by their performance in the competitive struggle – regardless of the means through which this performance has been achieved, and regardless of its ends, provided that they keep within the established social pattern. To Hitler, modern society is perpetuated by *ruthless competition* among unequal groups and individuals: only the most ruthless and most efficient competitor can get along in this world. The first task of National Socialism is, therefore, to restore Germany's position as a powerful competitor on the international market. He says:

"The world situation today can be briefly stated: Germany, England, France, and further – but not by reason of compulsion – the American Union, together with a whole series of small states, are industrial nations dependent on export. After the close of the war all these peoples were faced with a world market comparatively emptied of commodities. Methods in industry and in factories had been improved . . . with vast ingenuity on account of the War, and armed with these new methods men rushed into this great void, began to remodel their works, to invest capital and under the compulsion of this invested capital sought to raise production to the highest possible level. This process could continue with success for two, three, four or five years. It could be continued successfully for a further period if new possibilities for export could be created which should correspond to the rapid increase and improvements in production and in methods. This was of primary importance, for the rationalization of business . . . leads to a reduction in the number of men engaged in work, a reduction which is useful only if the men thus turned out of employment can be easily in their turn transferred into new branches of economic activity . . . But we see that since the World War there was no further important extension of export markets; on the contrary, we see that relatively those export markets contracted, that the number of exporting nations gradually increased, and that a great many former export markets became themselves industrialized . . .

"The essential thing is to realize that, at the present moment, we find ourselves in a condition which has occurred several times before in the history of the world: already there have been times when the volume of certain products in the world exceeded the demand . . . there has arisen such an increase in productive capacity that the present possible consumption market stands in no relation to this increased capacity. But if Bolshevism . . . tears the Asiatic continent out of the human economic community, then the conditions

for the employment of these industries which have developed on so gigantic a
scale will be no longer even approximately realized . . . "

In such a situation, the functioning of the economic apparatus can no
longer be secured by "voluntary economic resolutions but only by political
decisions . . . In my view it is to put the cart before the horse when today
people believe that by business methods they can . . . recover Germany's
power-position instead of realizing that the power-position is also the
condition for the improvements of the economic situation."[7]

What consequences does Hitler draw from this picture? Under the
prevailing external and internal conditions, the German economy is no
longer capable of functioning by means of its own inherent forces and
mechanisms. The *economic relations* must therefore be *transformed into
political relations*, economic expansion and domination must not only be
supplemented, but superseded by political expansion and domination.
Hitler promises that the new state shall become the executive agent of
the economy, that it shall organize and coordinate the entire nation for
unhampered economic expansion, that it shall make German industry the
winner in the international competition. And he furthermore promises
that he will furnish the weapon which alone will enable German industry
to run down its competitor and to open up the required markets,
namely, the most formidable army in the world. And 8 years after Hitler's
promise, Robert Ley, the leader of the German Labor Front, happily
declares that Hitler has fulfilled his promise: "Capitalist economy had
reached a barrier which it could not overcome by its own means. The risk
of conquering new economic territory was so great that it could not be
taken by private capital; capital had retreated and merely defended its
previous position. It thus happened that, on the one side, gigantic productive capacities and even more gigantic supplies of commodities remained
unused, while, on the other side, millions of men were barely able to avoid
starvation. Then, National Socialism ventured on the successful attempt
to open up new ways for an economy which was frustrated and had
reached the limits of its own power".[8] The National Socialist state itself
assumed the risk which the private entrepreneur no longer dared to
assume, or, in Ley's words, the state undertook to provide new space
for the initiative of the entrepreneur.

This, however, could not be accomplished within the framework of the
established state. In the speech we quoted, Hitler frightens the industrialists

---

7 Hitler, *My New Order*, ed. by R. De Roussy de Sales, Reynal and Hitchcock, New
   York 1941, pp. 105–106, 110–111.
8 *Neue Internationale Rundschau der Arbeit*, April 1941, p. 137.

with the statement that 50% of the German population have become bolshevist. He means that 50% of the German population were not willing to sacrifice their wants and perhaps their lives for imperialist expansion, and that the democratic state gave them the means of effectively expressing their unwillingness. To secure industrial capacity and its full utilization all the barriers between politics and economy, between state and society had to be removed, the intermediate institutions which mitigated the oppressive social and economic forces had to be abandoned, the state had to identify itself directly with the predominant economic interests and order all social relationships according to their requirements.

In the same measure, however, as the economic forces became direct political forces, they lost their independent character. They could rid themselves of their inherent limitations and disturbances only by surrendering their freedom. The restoration of their full efficiency was conditioned upon a strong regulation of the market, a coordination of production, control of investment and consumption, and, above all, a curbing and compensating of all those groups which had to be sacrificed to the necessities of rationalization. The principle of efficiency favored the great monopolies and combines, the plants with the most powerful technical equipment, and demanded the exclusion from the productive process of all those who could not keep pace with the giants. The increase of industrial capacity on an imperialist scale meant the exclusion of all inefficient enterprises from the productive process, the transformation of the remaining independent middle classes into vassals of the monopolies, and the enslavement of the atomized working class. Never before have the interests of the predominant social groups been so strikingly at odds with the interests of the majority of the population – a population which had just experienced fourteen years of democratic liberty. The terrible failure of the Weimar Republic drove the masses into the camp of the new rulers, but their social and political consciousness was sharp enough to make them recognize their old masters even in a new streamlined form and setting. German society could not be reorganized and coordinated directly by the imperialist forces. The latter were divided against the other social groups and also among themselves. They could maintain and expand their dominion only by accepting a new *division of power*. The National Socialist *party* and its leader offered the indispensable terroristic apparatus which welded together the antagonistic whole. It supervises the education and training of the youth, monopolizes the power of the secret and open police, corrects the process of law whenever expedient, and creates and perpetuates the official ideology. The task of the party, however, is by no means exhausted by its terroristic and ideological functions. Its vast bureaucracy offers numerous opportunities for new jobs and creates a new elite which rises into the highest ranks of the ruling class and amalgamates with the old captains of industry and finance.

Beside the dominion of the party, and frequently overlapping it, stands the powerful dominion of the *army*. It has succeeded in retaining a considerable degree of independence, and the party has acquiesced in its practices, thus recognizing not a real social or political conflict but a division of labor which served to strengthen the army's efficiency and freedom of action. In sanctioning the independence of the army, National Socialism did not accept an equally powerful opponent, but the most vital and formidable protagonist of its own imperialist interests. The National Socialist state thus emerges as the threefold sovereignty of industry, party and army which have divided up among themselves the former monopoly of coercive power.

The whole system is by no means a homogeneous one. The three ruling hierarchies frequently clash with each other and each is divided within itself. Terror might sufficiently explain the silence of the masses. But no rational plan exists which unites and organizes the various resources, instruments and interests for a pre-established common goal. Despite the diverging claims and tendencies, however, the conflicts do not break out in the open because of the deeper pre-existing harmony between the interests of industry, the party and the army.

This harmony is symbolized in the *Leader*. Ideologically, he is the embodiment of the German race, its infallible will and knowledge, and the seat of supreme sovereignty. In reality, however, he is the agency through which the diverging interests of the three ruling hierarchies are coordinated and asserted as national interests. He mediates between the competing forces; he is the locus of final compromise rather than sovereignty. His decision might be autonomous, particularly in minor matters, but it is still not free, not his own, but that of others. For it originates from and is bound to the philosophy and policy of the governing imperialist groups which he has served from the very beginning. If they accept him as their common master and put up with all the restrictions which the regime places on their liberty, they do so because they know that he, in turn, will master the people, and the the restrictions will ultimately be to their own benefit.

This harmony will prevail just as long as the system continues to expand; it is welded together only by success. In the event of failure, fear alone will remain to tie the centrifugal forces to each other. For fear of the masses and fear of each other are decisive elements in this harmony. Moreover, the ruling groups realize clearly that they can survive only by showing themselves efficient to the utmost. They know that they can keep their efficiency only through aggressive expansion, and that they have to carry on the war and win the war, regardless of costs. They will do everything to that end, and they do not need a plan to unite their efforts. The investment is risky, but it is the only possible investment, and the eventual profit is worth the risk. Hitler has promised them continents as their exclusive markets and the whole populations of conquered territories as compulsory customers and suppliers. The Germany army is on the march to make good these promises. The present rulers of Germany do not believe in ideologies and in the mysterious power of the race, but they will follow their leader as long as he remains what he has hitherto been, the living symbol of efficiency.

A dreadful efficiency, to be sure, one that has nothing left in it of the progressive character of efficiency in advancing liberal society. In such a society efficiency may conform with the development of truly productive forces, intellectual as well as material, and may be a lever for expanding and enriching the range of human satisfaction. National Socialist efficiency is of a different brand. It is in the total service of imperialist expansion. And it implies the very opposite of what efficiency originally meant, for it can operate only through impoverishment and oppression on an international scale. The New Order tends to transfer the internal social antagonisms to an international plane. The German Reich proper, as the core of this order, is to be surrounded by concentric circles of satellite states, feeding and working for the "master race".

The structure of the National Socialist state is not adequately described, however, by the threefold sovereignty of industry, party and army, with the Leader as the seat of the ultimate compromise. The competing forces execute their decisions through a *bureaucracy* which is one of the most highly rationalized and efficient administrations of the modern era. It is, at the same time, the least novel element of the Third Reich, to a considerable extent identical with the vested bureaucracy of the Weimar Republic, purged of its "unreliable" members. The terror which holds the National Socialist society together is not only that of the concentration camps, prisons and pogroms; it is not only the terror of lawlessness, but also the less conspicuous though no less efficient legalized terror of bureaucratization.

In the administration of the state, National Socialism has developed and employed a peculiar type of rationality as an instrument of mass domination. We may call it technical rationality because it is derived from the technological process and therefrom applied to the ordering of all human relationships. This rationality functions according to the standards of efficiency and precision. At the same time, however, it is severed from everything that links it with the humane needs and wants of individuals; it is entirely adapted to the requirements of an all-embracing apparatus of domination. The human subjects and their bureaucratically organized work are but the means for an objective end, which is nothing other than the maintenance of the apparatus on an increasingly efficient scale. National Socialism has transformed all personal and social relationships into the minutely supervised and controlled functions of such an apparatus. The irrational slogans of the National Socialist philosophy conceal a most brutal rationality in which everything is subordinated to the values of speed, precision and efficiency. Hans Frank, Governor General of Poland and president of the Academy for Germany Law, has revealed that the strength of the Third Reich depends, to a large extent, upon a bureaucratic administration which functions with the precision and consistency of a machine. "The state machine, consisting of the wheels of the administrative activities which are connected and timed through command and obedience" provides the "clearly structurized, simply organized and precisely functioning" foundation for the "state will" of National Socialism.[9]

The state – a machine: this materialistic conception reflects the National Socialist reality much better than do the theories of the racial community and the leader state. This machine, which embraces the life of men everywhere, is the more terrifying since, with all its efficiency and precision, it is totally incalculable and unpredictable. Nobody, except perhaps the few "insiders", knows when and where it will strike. It seems to move by virtue of its own necessity and is still flexible and obedient to the slightest change in the set-up of the ruling groups. All human relations are absorbed by the objective wheelwork of control and expansion. National Socialism presents its state as the personal rule of certain powerful figures; in reality, however, the persons succumb to the mechanisms of the apparatus. What actually strikes and commands is not Himmler, Göring, Ley, but the Gestapo, the "air arm," the labor front. The various administrative machines are coordinated in a bureaucratic apparatus which integrates the interests of industry, army and party. Here again, the supreme power is not vested in the individual captains of industry, generals and bosses, but in the big industrial combines, in the military machinery, in the political position. The National Socialist state is the government of hypostatized economic, social and political forces.

These competing elements converge on one definite goal: imperialist expansion on an inter-continental scale. To achieve this, the regime calls

---

9 "Technik des Staates", in *Zeitschrift der Akademie für Deutsches Recht*, 1941, no. 1, p. 2.

for an utmost exertion of labor power, a vast reservoir of man power, and an intellectual and physical training for the exploitation of all conquered natural and human resources. Here, where the functioning of the apparatus depends upon essentially subjective factors, it also finds the limits of terroristic oppression. An expanding social system, based upon full technological and industrial efficiency, cannot but release those human faculties and impulses which render such efficiency possible. The most valuable source of energy and power is the human individual, and, in this function, he becomes the pet child of the National Socialist regime. Its social policy endeavours "to develop all the slumbering faculties in man, to increase his capacity, to enrich the essence of his personality".[10] The National Socialists blame the capitalist economy for its "depersonalization" of man. "Where everyone thinks in terms of capital, factors of production, interest and profitability, the living human being is easily degraded to a lifeless factor".[11] No wonder the workers rose against such an economy. In contrast, the National Socialist economy wants to reinstate man and to emancipate his full individual performance. The enterprise as well as the nation as a whole must be a "community in which his achievement alone gives to every individual his place, a community, however, in which every contribution (*Einsatz*) is assured of its full equivalent. In this community, each individual must have the opportunity to rise through his own abilities – regardless of status or birth".[12]

All this sounds like the individualistic philosophy of the heyday of liberalism. And indeed, in focusing its attention on the human individual as the primary source of labor, National Socialism consummates certain fundamental tendencies of individualist society. This society's principle it was that everyone be given according to his free performance in the social division of labor, and that the pursuit of self-interest should be the guiding motive in all performances, but the every increasing inequality of wealth resulting from this process has led to the demand that government regiment the free play of economic forces. It must be noted, however, that the National Socialist regimentation of social and economic life is essentially different from that advocated and practiced in democratic countries. Whereas governmental regimentation in these countries is supposed to mitigate the detrimental effects of concentration of economic power, National Socialist control tends to abolish or correct the mechanisms which

---

10 *Neue Internationale, Rundschau der Arbeit*, p. 156f.
11 *Soziale Praxis*, 1939, no. 10, p. 589.
12 *Deutsche Sozialpolitik*. Bericht der Deutschen Arbeitsfront, Zentralbureau, Sozialamt. Berlin 1937, p. 20.

might hamper such concentration.[13] The National Socialist regimentations are, to a large extent, restrictions on those vestiges of the liberalist past which themselves restricted the ruthless exertion of economic power. They revolve around the institution through which, blindly and anarchically, the *whole* of society had asserted itself against *particular* interests; they revolve around the institution of the market. They remove the waste and backwardness caused by uncontrolled competition and the inefficient performance of plants and shops not adapted to the highest standards of technology. They subordinate the profitability of the individual enterprise to the full utilization of the entire industrial apparatus which is bound to yield even greater profits to those who control it. Owing to the harmony of interests that converge upon imperialist expansion, such subordination might appear as the triumph of common welfare over private advantage, but the community whose welfare is thus at stake is one based upon perpetual scarcity and oppression. It may be compared with a gigantic monopolistic combine which has succeeded in controlling competition within and subduing the masses of the workers, and which has set out to conquer the world market. The emergence of the Third Reich is the emergence of the most efficient and ruthless competitor.

The National Socialist state is not the reversal but the consummation of competitive individualism. The regime releases all those forces of brutal self-interest which the democratic countries have tried to curb and combine with the interest of freedom.

Like any other form of individualist society, National Socialism operates on the basis of private ownership in the means of production. Accordingly, it is made up by two polar strata, the small number of those who control the productive process and the bulk of the population which, directly or indirectly, is dependent upon the former. Under National Socialism it is the status of the individual in this latter stratum that has most drastically changed. Here, too, however, the changes bring to fruition rather than contradict certain tendencies of individualist society.

At the broad base of the social pyramid, the most conspicuous change is that the individual has sunk to the position of a number of the "*crowd*". The Third Reich is, indeed, a "state of the masses" in which all individual interests and forces are submerged into an emotional human mass, skilfully manipulated by the regime.[14] These masses, however, are not united by a common interest and common "consciousness". They are rather made up of individuals each of whom follows only his most primitive self-interest, and their unification is brought about by the fact that this self-interest

---

13 See Gurland, "Technological Trends under National Socialism", p. 247f.
14 E. Lederer, *State of the Masses*, New York 1940, particularly p. 30f.

is reduced to the bare instinct of self-preservation which is identical in all of them. The coordination of individuals into a crowd has intensified rather than abolished their atomization and isolation from each other, and their equalization only follows the pattern on which their individuality has been previously molded.

Under capitalism, the free individual performance of the majority of the population had become the expenditure of labor power. The industrial process had made all the various modes of individual qualitative labor commensurable; work had become a quantitative unit. The social division of labor and the technological process had equalized individuals, and their liberation seemed to call for a union of men acting in the solidarity of a common interest which superseded the interest of individual self-preservation. Such a union is the very opposite of the National Socialist mass.

From the beginning, the social policy of the Third Reich was directed to prevent the crystallization and expression of a common interest. The emphasis on the individual which permeates its ideological proclamations finds its counterpart in the National Socialist organization of the masses, guided by the principle of atomization and isolation. In the organization of labor, the individual plant is isolated from all other plants, and the various divisions within the plant are isolated from each other. Wages and working conditions are military secrets; their betrayal even to a fellow worker of another plant or division is treason. The individuals know little of each other; they are suspicious and shrewd, and have learned to be silent. They are susceptible to manipulation and unification from above because they are stripped of everything that might transcend their self-interest and establish a real community. They are led to entertainment, they rest and holiday in masses. The very mass of the participants in Strength Through Joy intensifies their isolation: the unknown neighbor might be "unreliable" or a henchman of the Gestapo. Reduced to that brute and abstract instinct of self-preservation which is equal in all of them, they are easily forced into masses which, by their mere weight, prevent any articulation of a common interest.

This atomization and isolation provides the safe ground on which the individual's forces and faculties can issue into the service of the regime. The Labor Front "has to see that in the economic life of the nation every individual holds his position in that mental and physical condition which enables him to highest efficiency and thus guarantees the greatest advantage for the racial community."[15] The same principle of efficiency that, in

---

15 Edict of October 24, 1934, in *Deutsche Sozialpolitik*, p. 4.

the organization of business, led to the regimentation of industry, benefit-
ting the most powerful combines, leads, in the organization of labor, to the
total mobilization of labor power. For the expenditure of labor power is
the only free performance left to the man at the base of the social pyramid.
The most valuable possession of the people is its "labour power, and the
greatness and power of the nation is founded on this. To maintain and
increase it is the foremost duty of the National Socialist movement, and the
most urgent task of the German enterprises, the existence and efficiency
of which is determined by the quantum of labor power and the degree of
labor capacity."[16] National Socialism has introduced an elaborate system
of physical, moral and intellectual education which aims to increase the
efficiency of labor by means of highly refined scientific methods and
techniques. Wages are differentiated according to the efficiency of the
individual worker.[17] Psychological and technological institutions are set up
to study appropriate methods for the individualization of labor and to
counteract the detrimental effects of mechanization. The factories, schools,
training camps, sport arenas, the cultural institutions and the organization
of leisure are true laboratories of the "scientific management" of work.

The integral mobilization of the individual's labor power tears down the
last protective wall which shielded him from society and the state: it does
away with the privacy of his leisure time. During the liberalist era the
individual was distinguished from the society by virtue of a recognized
distinction between his work and his leisure. Under National Socialism this
distinction, like that between society and state, is abolished altogether.

The German Labor Front, which directs this process, wages a violent
war against the dualism of work and leisure, which it regards as a mark of
the old liberalist capitalist order. In contrast, it bases itself on the principle
that the gulf between work and leisure must be bridged, and the organization of leisure must be assimilated to the organization of work.[18]

The National Socialist regime has realized that although leisure under
the old system meant chiefly a re-creation of energy expended in work, the
traditional way of recreation threatened to exhaust the source of all profitable energy, namely, man as the bearer of labor power. Physiological and
psychological tests have shown that the individual's performance could be
made more efficient if his leisure time was extended and made attractive,[19]

---

16 R. Ley, "Anordnung über den Leistungskampf der deutschen Betriebe", in
    Deutsche Sozialpolitik, p. 14.
17 Ibid., p. 21.
18 H. Dressler-Andress, "Die kulturelle Mission der Freizeitgestaltung", in
    Weltkongress für Freizeit und Erholung, Hamburg 1937, p. 69f.
19 *Deutsche Sozialpolitik*, p. 208.

and since National Socialism subordinates all purely economic profitability to political expansion, it spared no expense to fulfill this goal.

The extension of leisure (which has, of course, been abolished by the war) is a health requirement, serving to supplement the National Socialist breeding policy and helping to create a vast and fitting reservoir of man power for the dominion of the German master race. Accordingly, one of the features of Strength through Joy is compulsory enjoyment of open-air. We need not dwell upon the numerous activities of the Strength through Joy organizations, they have frequently been described. We must discuss, however, one aspect of the organization of leisure which elucidates the fundamental antagonisms of National Socialism, namely, its treatment of the traditional taboos on privacy.

In mobilizing leisure, National Socialism encountered one of the last bulwarks behind which the progressive elements of individualism were still alive. The mere fact that during the pre-fascist era the individual could be "with himself" (in his leisure time) and thus abstain from all competitive performances, left him at least the possibility of escaping the repressive framework of his professional life. It was good, here and there, to "draw apart" from society at large, especially when society did not care very much about those desires and abilities which did not fit into the scheme of efficiency. For the very reason that man's private life could be a thing apart from his social life, he could still obtain a measure of true satisfaction.

This privacy and the taboos imposed on it tended, however, to aggravate the antagonism between individual satisfaction and social frustration; the former was kept apart from society and, by this very fact, retained elements of a freedom and happiness which were alien to the social reality. One of the most daring enterprises of National Socialism is the struggle against these taboos on privacy.

The integral mobilization of labor power could not be carried through without compensating the individual for the loss of his independence. National Socialism has offered two compensations: a new economic *security* and a new *license*. The fact that the imperialist economy of the Third Reich has created full employment and thus assured basic economic security for its citizens is of utmost importance. The liberty enjoyed by the individual in the pre-Fascist era was, for the majority of the German population, equivalent to perpetual insecurity. Ever since 1923 militant efforts to establish a truly democratic society had ceased and there came in its stead the pervasive spirit of resignation and despair. No wonder, then, that the liberty was not a high price in exchange for a system offering full security to every member of every German family. National Socialism transformed the free into the safe economic subject; it obscured the dangerous ideal of freedom with the protective reality of security.

This security, however, binds the individual to the most oppressive apparatus modern society has ever seen. The open terror, to be sure, strikes only against "the enemies", the aliens and those who do not or cannot cooperate. But the hidden terror, the terror behind the total supervision and regimentation, war and scarcity, reaches everyone. The regime cannot enhance economic security so far that it may become the foundation of freedom; that is to say, it cannot increase the standard of living so that the individual has the possibility to find proper uses for his abilities and satisfaction for his desires. For such a liberation would be incompatible with social domination based upon imperialistic economy. The National Socialist emphasis on the duty of sacrifice has more than ideological significance; it is not only a propagandistic but also an economic principle. National Socialist security is essentially bound up with scarcity and oppression. Economic security, if it is any compensation at all, must be supplemented by some form of liberty and National Socialism has granted this liberty by abolishing certain fundamental social taboos.

The *abolition of highly sanctioned taboos* is one of the most daring enterprises of National Socialism in the field of mass domination. For, paradoxical as it may seem, the liberty or license implied in this abolition serves to intensify the "Gleichschaltung" of individuals into the National Socialist system.

The facts are well known[20] and need only be mentioned. The Third Reich has done away with discrimination against illegitimate mothers and children, it has encouraged extra-marital relations between the sexes, introduced a new cult of nudity in art and entertainment, and dissolved the protective and educational functions of the family. These changes have frequently been interpreted as tending to a destruction of the socio-psychological foundations of Western civilization. True, this civilization has been based, to a considerable extent, on the Christian taboos of chastity, monogamy and the sanctity of the family. The abolition of these taboos designates a turning point in the history of civilization, but the question is whether the turn is towards greater individual liberty or towards greater repression of liberty. In other words, the question is whether the manner in which the drives and desires of the individual are now released does not deepen rather than abate his allegiance to a system based upon restraining his actual potentialities.

---

20 Cf. C. Kirkpatrick, *Nazi Germany: Its Women and Family Life*. New York 1938, and G. Ziemer, *Education for Death*, New York 1941.

Three factors efficiently counteract the liberty granted by the National Socialist abolition of taboos:

1 The emancipation of sexual life is definitely connected with the population policy of the Third Reich.[21] The sexual relations are perverted into rewarded performances: controlled mating and breeding. They are means for achieving a political end, posited and propagated by the government. The drives and impulse thus released are fastened to an external end and are thus muzzled and deprived of their dangerous force. For their threat to society derived from the fact that they offered a satisfaction and happiness with which the social agencies and standards could least interfere, and that they thus constituted a realm of individual freedom segregated from and alien to the realm of social conformity and frustration. And this satisfaction and freedom was conditioned upon the fact that these essentially "private" relations were not aiming at a "social need", but were an end in themselves. The traditional taboos served to substitute another end for them by connecting sexual satisfaction with (marital) love. The National Socialist regime, in dissolving this connection, replaces it with a perhaps stronger tie to a political end.

2 The relations between the sexes belonged to that realm of protected privacy which granted the individual a considerable degree of freedom from a society and a state incapable of fulfilling his innermost potentialities and desires. This privacy naturally became a haven for protest, opposition and the image of possible happiness. The National Socialist regime has set out to conquer this haven for the state. Together with the entire sphere of physical and intellectual education, beginning not only with the new-born child but with the "young mother",[22] sexual life has become a matter of political training and manipulation. Consequently, even the most independent and presocial relations among men are being transformed into competitive public services. The reward is a spiritual as well as a material one, varying from honor and prestige bestowed upon illegitimate mothers to financial benefits such as marriage loans and premiums for child bearing. Official encouragement is expressed in the deliberate herding of boys and girls in and near the labor camps, and in the stimulating distinctness with which National Socialist artists expose the erogenous zones of the human body. Hitler established the combination of "expediency and beauty" as the highest principle of

---

21 D. V. Glass, *Population*. Oxford 1940, p. 282, where most of the material has been collected and discussed.
22 Hitler, *Mein Kampf*, p. 615.

art, and supplemented it with the demand for "absolute correctness in the presentation of the female and male body."[23] This new National Socialist realism fulfills its political function as an instrument for sexual education and inducement. The political utilization of sex has transformed it from a sphere of protective privacy in which a recalcitrant freedom could endure to a sphere of acquiescent license. The individuals whose most intimate enjoyment is urged and sanctioned by the state are apt to become its obedient followers.

3 The factor which contributed most to diverting the new license into channels desired by the regime is the connection of it with drives and impulses directed against the chosen enemies of the Third Reich. The new individual liberties are by their very nature exclusive liberties, the privilege of the healthy and approved members of the German race. The satisfaction is granted to manipulated masses which are distinguished from certain conspicuous groups of aliens and outsiders: Jews, foreigners, feeble-bodied and feeble-minded, "traitors" and the insane. The member of the "master race" is imbued with a feeling of superiority which makes the outsider the natural object of contempt and oppression – in accordance with Hitler's command that "his entire education and development has to be directed at giving him the conviction that he is absolutely superior to the others".[24] This is more than megalomania; it is a shrewdly handled means for mass domination. As a matter of fact, the National Socialist abolition of taboos is conditioned upon the simultaneous creation of new objects of humiliation and enslavement. The individuals can be released only insofar as they are at the same time elevated above social groups which are infinitely more fettered, helpless and unhappy than they are. Their liberators appeal to impulses which have tied the released individuals to social frustration and submissiveness: they appeal to resentment, envy, cruelty, hatred of the weaker fellow man. These impulses thrive only in an antagonistic social system, and by fostering them the regime perpetuates the prevailing system in the character structure of the individuals and turns their claims and protests from the executioners to their victims.

The working of these socio-psychological mechanisms cannot be verified by official or semi-official documents; it must be elucidated by a careful interpretation of the behavior and utterances of National Socialist groups

---

23 Speech of September 5, 1934, in *Der Kongress zu Nürnberg vom 5. bis 10. September 1934*, München 1934, p. 99.
24 Hitler, *Mein Kampf*, p. 618.

in certain characteristic situations. We can here venture only two minor contributions to such an interpretation.

Reliable neutral eye-witnesses were stunned by the evident enjoyment of suffering and sacrifice among the National Socialist youth. There is a hidden truth in the proud declarations of these girls that they love to bear children because they may suffer in doing so, or of these boys that they love to be beaten and killed for the Leader.[25] It is as if this youth has readily responded to Hitler's dictum that "sufferings and adversities have to be borne in silence".[26] The point is that the demanded sufferings and sacrifices are conspicuously irrational and unnecessary; they are of a provocative character. The natural attitude of youth in the face of such suffering and sacrifice would be protest and rebellion. National Socialist education has broken this protest and rebellion, and has done so by playing on the mechanisms of identification. Through the elevation of the German "master race" above the persecuted aliens and outsiders, the National Socialist youth has been identified with those who *inflict* suffering and sacrifices. The concentration camps explain the joy of suffering which animates the strong and healthy youth of the Third Reich.

The National Socialist regime has given its followers the good conscience of their frustration. They have been maltreated, restrained and distorted in their desires and faculties, but now they are the masters and may do what their old masters rarely dared to do. E.R. Pope quotes an illuminating passage from the official program of the famous orgiastic Night of the Amazons: "That which was formerly guarded carefully and offered to a select few behind high walls, today comes to life for all of us – in the nocturnal magic of Nymphenburg Park . . . in the scanty clothing of the Muses, in the undressed freedom of beautiful figures . . . Those who shout exultantly, filled with the joyful enthusiasm of action and gazing, are the German youth of 1939 . . . "[27] This is the entertainment of men who are allowed to revel in their prison, to release themselves in the park of their former kings, to act and to "gaze" at previously forbidden wonders. The glamour, beauty and license of the National Socialist pageants retain the features of submissiveness and domination. The beautiful nude girls and colorful landscapes in the paintings of National Socialist artists fit in perfectly with the classical assembly halls and the beautified factories, machines and uniforms. They transform stimuli for protest and rebellion into stimuli for coordination. They merge into the image of

---

25 Georg Ziemer's book, quoted above, is full of such reports.
26 Hitler, *Mein Kampf*, p. 623.
27 *Munich Playground*, New York 1941, p. 40.

an order which has succeded in coordinating even the most hidden danger-zones of individualist society, and they induce the individual to like and perpetuate a world which uses him only as a means for oppression.

SUPPLEMENT[†]

The extension of leisure (which has, of course, been abolished by the war) is a health-requirement, serving to supplement the National Socialist breeding-policy and helping to create a vast and fitting reservoir of man power for the dominion of the German master race. Accordingly, one of the features of Strength through Joy is compulsory enjoyment of open-air. We need not dwell upon the numerous activities of the Strength through Joy Organizations: they have frequently been described. We must discuss, however, one aspect of the organization of leisure which elucidates the fundamental antagonisms of National Socialism, namely, its treatment of intellectual culture.

In mobilizing leisure, National Socialism encountered one of the last bulwarks behind which the progressive elements of individualism were still alive. We have sketched the development which adapted the free time to the working time and standardized the individuals at leisure. Nevertheless, the mere fact that, in the pre-fascist era, the individual could, in his leisure time, stay "with himself" and refrain from all competitive performances left him at least the possibility to go beyond the repressive framework of his professional life. It might be good, here and then, to "draw apart" from society at large, when this society did not care very much about those desires and capacities of man which did not fit into the scheme of efficiency. In the solitude of peaceful enjoyment, the individual may come to *think*, his impulses, feelings and thoughts may be driven into regions which are foreign and inimical to the prevailing order. We mention here only two stimuli of this tendency: *sex* and *art*.

---

† The concluding pages of Marcuse's lecture "State and Individual Under National Socialism" (#118.01) contain some comments on sex and art under National Socialism left out of the article prepared for publication which we include above.

Individualist society, while guarding and restricting these spheres by strong taboos, had made them a domain of private satisfaction and realization. This very privacy and the taboos imposed on it rather aggravated the antagonism between individual satisfaction and social frustration; the former was kept apart from society and, by this very fact, retained elements of a freedom and happiness which was alien to the social reality. One of the most daring enterprises of National Socialism is the struggle against these taboos on privacy. With regard to sexual taboos, we need only point to the deliberate herding of boys and girls in the training camps, to the license granted to the racial elite, to the facilitation of marriage and divorce, to the sanctioning of illegitimate children, to the anti-semitic pornography. All this is, of course, in line with the population policy of the Reich, which calls for an ever greater supply of man power. But the policy has still another aspect, which is far more hidden and touches the roots of National Socialist society.

The abolition of sexual taboos tends to make this realm of satisfaction an official political domain. Just as National Socialism denies the distinction between state and society, so it denies the distinction between society and the individual. The individual is "socialized" in the distorted sense that society itself takes over his oppressed and deteriorated instincts and interests and asserts them on an international scale. National Socialism makes them the interests of the *nation* and pursues them through conquest and war. The abolition of cultural taboos is the last stone in this edifice. The individual recognizes his private satisfaction as a patriotic service to the regime, and he receives his reward for performing it. By this very fact individual satisfaction loses the character which made it such. In "nationalizing" the sacred privacy of individual satisfaction National Socialism conquered the last position which man still held against a repressive public order, the last domain in which he could live up to his potentialities and desires. It is an old story that boys and girls, when they are compelled to enjoy each other, don't do it. The story is more than a truism. It says that individual happiness and fulfillment might have something to do with factors which lie beyond the reaches of society as it is, which even may be essentially foreign to it. The distinction between the individual and society was closer to the goal of human fulfillment than its National Socialist abrogation. The National Socialist abolition of taboo has a definitely repressive function.

This becomes particularly clear in the National Socialist attitude towards *art*. During the liberalist era, the fine arts fulfilled, to a considerable extent, the function of enchanting and edifying the independent individual. Removed from the sphere of daily life in society and politics, they developed standards and ideals of their own which transcended those prevalent in the social reality. The standards of beauty, truth, harmony, reason, as they were preserved in the fine arts, were, in their innermost meaning, alien and antagonistic to the current social standards. They envisioned a world in which man's true potentialities were at stake and thus kept alive promises which reality has not made true. National Socialism has done away with this function of art by amalgamating and adjusting art to the pattern of daily life. From the top of the party hierarchy came the command that culture was no longer to be a possession of the privileged few, but a factor of daily life. But in popularizing culture, National Socialism was careful enough to purge from itself all those elements which destroyed the illusion that man's true potentialities were preserved in the existing forms of life. National Socialist art tends to exclude everything that is ugly and shocking, everything that responds to the human situation by presenting a distorted and deteriorated world. Hitler has declared that the artist is to be guided only by the ideal of the sublime and beautiful,[1] and the National Socialist artists, in following his command, have fused the sublime and the beautiful into a real orgy of beauty.

This might at first seem to be a rejuvenation of traditional aesthetic norms. However, the beauty of National Socialist art is of a peculiar brand, which conforms perfectly to the streamlined apparatus of control and oppression. The smoothness and glamor of this beauty absorbs all discord and disharmony, and its conspicuous character stimulates those instincts which the regime wants to be stimulated. The nude human body looms large in the National Socialist paintings and is pictured with pornographic distinctness. According to Stendhal, beauty contains a "promise of happiness." But the happiness which the National Socialist beauties promise is no other than that which the S.A. and S.S. men are allowed to enjoy: it appeals to the same instincts that are in another form satisfied in the torturing of the helpless and weak. This art stimulates and gratifies the impulses of individuals who have educated to inhibit all desires which might transcend the prevailing system of force, toil and efficiency.

Hitler has one defined the essence of art as "expediency." The expediency of National Socialist art is to reconcile men with the world as it is. Art has forsaken all elements of protest and estrangement and become an integral part of the daily life of manipulated masses: it adorns the factories in which men work 10 and more hours for war supplies, the assembly

---

1 Speech of September 11, 1935: *Die Reden Hitlers am Parteitag der Freiheit*, München 1935, p. 36.

halls in which the leaders map the strategy of terror, the ministries which plan for conquest and destruction. National Socialist art bestows upon this world the grandeur of a natural harmony.

The domestication of art follows the same pattern as the domestication of sex. Art, adjusted to a world hostile to its original promises, changes its content and functions: it becomes itself a lever for adjusting man to the forces which rule his social and political life. The beautiful nude girls and colorful landscapes in the paintings of National Socialist artists fit in perfectly with the classical assembly halls and the beautified factories, machines and uniforms. They transform stimuli for protest and rebellion into stimuli for coordination. They merge into the image of an order which has succeeded in coordinating even the most hidden danger-zones of individualist society, and they induce the individual to like and perpetuate a world which uses him only as a means for oppression.

We have come to the end of our introductory survey. We have attempted to show that National Socialist society tends to become the direct government of the most powerful social groups which have conquered or abolished all the intermediary legal and political institutions that stood between their particular interests and the commonwealth. Their regime, far from suppressing him, has emancipated the human individual in his most sinister instincts and aspects. National Socialism is neither an absolutist nor a socialist nor a nihilist revolution. The New Order has a very affirmative content: to organize the most aggressive and destructive form of imperialism which the modern age has ever seen.

III

Herbert Marcuse, Peter Marcuse, Franz Neumann, Sophie Marcuse, Inge Neumann (c. 1937)

A HISTORY OF THE DOCTRINE OF SOCIAL CHANGE

by

Herbert Marcuse and Franz Neumann

International Institute of Social Research

(Columbia University)

429 West 117th Street.

Since sociology as an independent science was not established before the 19th century, the theory of society up to that time was an integral part of philosophy or of those sciences (such as the economic or juristic), the conceptual structure of which was to a large extent based upon specific philosophical doctrines. This intrinsic connection between philosophy and the theory of society (a connection which will be explained in the text) formulates the pattern of all particular theories of social change occuring in the ancient world, in the middle ages, and on the commencement of modern times. One decisive result is the emphasis on the fact that social change cannot be interpreted within a particular social science, but must be understood within the social and natural totality of human life. This conception uses, to a large extent, psychological factors in the theories of social change. However, the derivation of social and political concepts from the "psyche" of man is not a psychological method in the modern sense but rather involves the negation of psychology as a special science. For the Greeks, psychological concepts were essentially ethical, social and political ones, to be integrated into the ultimate science of philosophy.

I

In ancient philosophy the theories of social change were basically determined by a search for the most fruitful existence, for adequate intercourse between individuals, for the fulfillment of the highest

---

† A 17-page manuscript in the Marcuse archives is titled "A History of the Doctrine of Social Change," by Herbert Marcuse and Franz Neumann, with the Institute (Columbia University) address following (#118.00); it is accompanied by a longer 47-page manuscript with a "Contents" page, but no title, that provides a substantive overview of the project (#118.04), and which we reproduce on page 105. There is also a short precis of the "Theory of Social Change" project (#118.01), which appears to be a proposal for a lecture course, with some handwritten additions by Marcuse (#118.01). Since there is no date on the manuscripts, or external references to the project in other documents, it is unclear when the texts were written, though the Institute address on one of the texts suggests that it was a pre-war product, as the move to Washington of Marcuse, Neumann and other Institute members in 1942 effectively ended their affiliation with the Institute. Consequently, the project was probably undertaken in the late 1930s or early 1940s when Marcuse and Neumann were most active in the Institute and were working closely together in New York. The existence of a proposed lecture course on "Theories of Social Change" would suggest that the project was underway in 1941–2 when the Institute was proposing lectures to Columbia University.

A HISTORY OF THE DOCTRINE OF SOCIAL CHANGE[†]

Herbert Marcuse and Franz Neumann

Since sociology as an independent science was not established before the 19th century, the theory of society up to that time was an integral part of philosophy or of those sciences (such as the economic or juristic), the conceptual structure of which was to a large extent based upon specific philosophical doctrines. This intrinsic connection between philosophy and the theory of society (a connection which will be explained in the text) formulates the pattern of all particular theories of social change occurring in the ancient world, in the middle ages, and on the commencement of modern times. One decisive result is the emphasis on the fact that social change cannot be interpreted within a particular social science, but must be understood within the social and natural totality of human life. This conception uses, to a large extent, psychological factors in the theories of social change. However, the derivation of social and political concepts from the "psyche" of man is not a psychological method in the modern sense but rather involves the negation of psychology as a special science. For the Greeks, psychological concepts were essentially ethical, social and political ones, to be integrated into the ultimate science of philosophy.

I

In ancient philosophy the theories of social change were basically determined by a search for the most fruitful existence, for adequate intercourse between individuals, for the fulfillment of the highest potentialities of man,

for conditions resulting in well-being and happiness. The ancient philoso-
phers considered social change as a process which could for the most part
be identified with the progress of human life, and was to be measured
according to the given possibilities of human life.

This humanization of the theory of society assumes its first radical
form in the doctrine of the **Sophists**. Social institutions are subject to the
wants of the individuals for whose sake they have been established. If there
are universal obligations and a universal order of society, they must be
interpreted as originating in a contract between the individuals. Since the
Sophists protested against those traditional forms of the city state which
were no longer in conformity with the progressive material and intellectual
forces, they opposed the institutionalized standards of the Polis to a law
of nature. The latter, however, merely contained the recognition of the
natural inequality of man and the demand that the unequal individuals
should have the unrestricted right to realize their natural strength. Thus
their theory, in contrast to those preceding, merely implied the possibility
of social change by the conscious act of man. But it did not contain any
statement regarding the laws to which social change is subject. The doctrine of the Sophists is the prototype of all theories by which ancient
philosophy in the name of the interest of the individual protested against
the hypostization of the existing social institutions and conventions. The
development of these oppositional theories will be treated *in extenso*, since
they embody elements of the theory of social change which are constitutive
factors of the modern doctrines of social change. (Sophists: Protagoras,
Gorgias, Thrasymachus, Callicles; Cyrenaics: Antisthenes, Aristippus.)

Plato's theory of social change will not be discussed in the traditional
terms of his utopian idealism and reactionary totalitarianism. Plato's ideal
state is neither an utopia nor the violent perpetuation of the existing
city state. Rather he elaborates that form of social order which can best
guarantee the development of human potentialities under the prevailing
conditions. Plato definitely links social change with the psychological
structure of man, and the latter with the economic structure. The order of
private property ruins the psyche of man to such an extent that he becomes
incapable of discovering unaided the correct form of social and political
relations. Thus the individual can no longer himself decide upon the order
of state and society. Its construction becomes the task of the philosopher
who, by virtue of his knowledge, possesses the truth according to which
the order of life must be established. The radical change of the traditional
city state into the Platonic state of estates implies a reconstruction of
the economy in such a manner that the economy no longer determines
the faculties and powers of man, but is rather determined by them. The

diversity of work and the division of labor is arranged to conform with the most adequate development of the diversity of human faculties. State and society are primarily a work of psychological reconstruction. Since the latter, however, depends upon a total change of the existing material order of society, the true state is first the product of political reconstruction. The subordination of political to psychological theory is bound up with a complete change of the meaning of psychology. With Plato, psychology becomes a kind of universal science and as such identical with philosophy. Not only the social, but also the natural objective order is exclusively considered in its import to the truth and righteousness of the human psyche.

Aristotle is the first philosopher who attempted to elaborate a general theory of social and political development. His theory is based upon the first philosophical analysis of movement as presented in his metaphysics. Aristotle conceived Being in terms of movement and movement as the realization of the substantial potentialities of Being. In his description of the various modes of movement, Aristotle established a basic distinction between the types of movement in the human and in the natural world. Historical movement is a conscious development in the course of which something actually new is produced, whereas change in the world of nature merely means a cycle in which identical things keep recurring. There is a definite purposive direction in the development of social relations from the family to the state. Only the state is capable of realizing all the potentialities which man as a rational being possesses. Like Plato, Aristotle measures the order of the state according to its ability to fulfill these potentialities. His politics constitute the direct continuation of his Nicomachean Ethics. In expounding his political theory, Aristotle systematically investigates the concrete causes of the corruption of the existing forms of the state and of their degeneration. This theory is not merely a political one, but is also a theory of social development, since the divorce of state from society runs counter to the whole Greek philosophy. At the same time his theory of social and political change is a criticism of the platonic doctrine of the inevitable degeneration of all forms of political life. According to him, such a degeneration can be avoided only if the principle of proportionate justice in state and society is maintained. Since the influence of the Aristotelian ethics and politics has received enormous political and social significance, particularly from the 13th century on, his concept of proportionate justice, in connection with the social stratification and the social institutions of Greece, will be discussed in detail.

With the dissolution of the Greek city states, political theory incorporated the concept of the equality and universality of human nature as the highest standard of social and political organization. The theory of social change is viewed under the aspect of a universal law which equally rules man and external nature. It will be shown how the then prevailing historical conditions led to a fatalistic view of historical development. The problem of how the **Stoic** doctrine of a cycle of death and re-incarnation of the world is connected with a particular theory of society will be discussed. The Stoic contribution to the theory of society, which outlived all other contributions of this philosophy, was their theory of natural Law. This deeply influenced the teaching of the Church Fathers, Roman legal thought, and the oppositional attitudes of the later middle ages and of modern times. Their teachings were based on Heraclitus' ontology and on the political doctrines of the Sophists. Due to the identification of man with external nature, man was subject to eternal and immutable laws standing above the political institutions and unifying mankind into a society of equals. (Greek Stoics: Zeno, Chrysippus, Cleanthes; Roman Stoics: Cicero, Seneca, Marcus Aurelius.)

The individualistic reaction to the disintegration of the traditional forms of Greek life is to be found in the teachings of the **Epicurean** school. Since the prevailing forms of Greek society no longer guaranteed the realization of the individuals's happiness, Epicurus renounced any theory of political and social development. He was content with the existence of any state which left the individual free to pursue his own happiness. (Greek: Epicurus; Roman: Lucretius.)

Retrospectively, the theories of social change in early and classical Greek philosophy appear to be neither sociological, political, nor psychological in the modern sense. They cannot conceive of separating man, society and nature. The true order of human life embraces all three realms of reality, and the laws ruling that order are at the same time psychological, sociological and natural laws. We shall attempt to show that this theory of integration reappears in the latest stage of the development of modern thought.

II

With respect to **early Christianism**, we propose to lay emphasis on the radical social opposition inherent in the theology of the Church Fathers. Furthermore, we suggest a rather extensive study of the heretic religious doctrines, which gain increasing significance as medieval society develops.

Medieval theory views the problem of social change within the totality of the static hierarchic order of the creative world in its relation to the *Civitas Dei*. Accordingly, every social change is, in the last analysis, an ontological change standing beneath the eternal law of the *Mundus Creatus*. The direction of this change as well as its value is predetermined.

The most significant document prior to the reception of the Aristotelian philosophy is **John of Salisbury**'s Polycraticus, which without introducing startling innovations, summarizes medieval social and political philosophy. He is one of the first to expound an organic theory of society after the pattern of man's body, thus confining social changes to the narrow limits given by the organic structure of state and society.

In the section dealing with the height and decline of the middle ages, this contribution will advance the thesis that the birth of modern society from the very structure of medievalism must be traced not so much to the orthodox doctrines of Thomism, but rather to the critical and heretic teachings of Latin Averroism. This heretic philosophy received practical, political and social significance in three spheres: i.e. in the struggle between the church and the secular powers, in the disputes within the church; and, finally, in the discussion within the secular society caused by the disputed realm of temporal and secular powers. The extraordinary significance of this heretic social philosophy can best be understood by contrasting it with the orthodox Thomist Doctrine.

The **Thomistic social philosophy** is the attempt to reconcile the natural law doctrine of the Stoics with the existing feudal, hierarchically organised estate. The Stoic natural law had certain revolutionary implications. In the Thomistic philosophy, it becomes the justification of a hierarchical society based on a clear distinction between the three estates. Besides the *Summa Theologia* there exist innumerable pamphlets, the sole intention of which is to equip the existing society with the dignity of moral law. In the Thomistic philosophy, this reconciliation is made possible by the reception of the Aristotelian philosophy. Thomistic philosophy is thus necessarily hostile to social changes seeping into the ordained division of society.

In contrast to this levelling of social change within the eternally valid order of given society, the main concepts of **Latin Averroism** envisage a dynamic process which leads eventually to the construction of an entirely new order of life. The idea of the unity and equality of reason, in addition to the demand that man himself as the bearer of this reason be held responsible for the organization of his life, is definitely connected with the requirements of early capitalistic society. Accordingly, the problem of social change is already viewed in the light of a materialistic critique of feudalism. These theories were advanced in the struggle of the rising temporal state with the well established church. One can find innumerable contributions to a new materialistic conception of social change in the discussions of the partisans of the independent secular state with the defenders of the supremacy of the church (particularly during the struggle of Philipp the Fair with Boniface VIII and of Lewis of Bavaria with Pope John XXII, John of Paris, Pierre Dubois; Marsilius of Padua, John of Jandum and William of Occam). Similar ideas, even if more moderate, can be seen in the conciliar movement aiming at the democratization of the church, or at least at the supercession of the papal sovereignty by the aristocracy of the church dignitaries. In the philosophical field, Latin Averroism, in the 13th and 14th centuries, produced a whole set of materialistic social psychologies and ethics, intended as a critique of the traditional modes of life and aiming at the freeing of the productive forces of society from the fetters of feudal and clerical domination.

III

The process leading to the ideological divorce of the secular society from the church is completed in the work of **Machiavelli**. Here, the problem of social change is openly and without any philosophical or theological glorification put forth as a problem of the stability and integrity of the rising national state. Social change evolves into the pragmatic problem of the technique of dominating the masses in the interest of the absolute sovereign power. Machiavelli's theory of social change, however, is incorporated into a more comprehensive psychological and sociological theory. The outstanding feature of Machiavelli's social psychology is the radical subordination of psychology to the requirements of modern government. If he assumes a uniform nature of man from which the basic laws of social change and progress are derived, he uses this assumption in the service of supplying the sovereign with certain distinct rules for the government of the state. There are no longer any eternally valid forms of political life; any of these will degenerate and be replaced by another form. Machiavelli not only secularizes state and civil society, but also implicitly rejects the view that the development of humanity follows a pattern of a pre-established harmony realizing some idea of progress. With the establishment of modern society, the whole conceptual structure of theory changes. Rationalism becomes predominant. The progress of science and technique, the opening of the world markets and the progressive subjection of every country to an all embracing uniform system of production and the foundations of society upon the principle of free labor were reflected in a theory which claimed to comprehend the whole universe under rational unified concepts. That is, nature and society, earth and heaven, are governed by the same inevitable objective laws which can be discovered by the power of human reason and used for the rational domination of the world. Social change thus becomes merely a particular phenomenon of universal change. The problem is, according to the different patterns of rationalistic theory, discussed either in terms of mechanistic (Hobbes), mathematical (Spinoza), or dynamic (Leibniz) philosophy. This entire trend involves a very **positivistic element**, insosfar as the prevailing structure of society provides the final framework for the analysis of social change. This positivistic side becomes predominant in the **empiricist doctrines**, where the existence of immutable objective laws and of innate ideas is rejected, and where nature and the development of human society are entirely understood in terms of reduction to sensual perceptions and their corollaries (Condillac, Locke, Hume, John Stuart Mill).

The rational and empirical theories will also be evaluated according to their different psychological and sociological foundations. Three different trends may be discerned. The first two theories begin with a certain hypothesis on the character structure of man and the predictable attitudes derived from them. **Optimistic philosophies** assume that man is essentially good. Consequently, they express or imply a theory of social evolution embodying the idea of progress and asserting that man's potentialities can be fully developed in an orderly progress of society without revolution and retrogression (Grotius, Locke, Christian Wolff, Thomasius, Shaftesbury, Hutcheson, Benjamin Franklin and Thomas Jefferson). **Pessimistic theories** reject the possibility of peaceful and continuous progress. They find their most vigorous expression in Lutheranism and Calvinism, culminating in the repudiation of any kind of social change which might endanger the existing social order (also the later counterrevolutionary theories: de Maistre, Bonald, also Mandeville and Burke).

From the commencement of modern society, there exists a strong non-conformist critical and predominantly **materialist trend** opposing the above rationalistic and empiricist doctrines. These doctrines base their criticism of society on the material needs of man. To these, social change is equivalent to the complete transformation of society, particularly to a complete change of the system of private property. This materialistic criticism is the link unifying the philosophy of French enlightenment (Holbach, Helvetius, Morelly, Mably, Meslier, and Linguet) and is still operative in Rousseau's critique of the traditional society.

In periods of social disintegration, the critique assumes an openly revolutionary character demanding the reconstruction of a new order of freedom and reason (Thomas Münzer, the Anabaptist movement, the

Taborties, the chiliastic trends in the Puritan Revolution like the Diggers and the Fifth Monarchy Men, and Roger Williams in Rhode Island).

In the period when the middle classes gained political and social recognition, the **Physiocrats** and the **Classical Economists** attempted to converge the optimistic and pessimistic trends into a theory of society governed by a preestablished harmony. Possible disturbances and unequal developments were acknowledged. Yet these could be overcome by the free play of economic forces. These theories led to a completely optimistic doctrine of evolution and progress. To them social change is merely the adjustments of avoidable disturbances.

The antagonistic tendencies of modern rationalism culminate in the theory of **German idealism**. On the one hand, the principle of individual freedom and of the sovereignty of critical reason is maintained as the standard of social and political organization. Social change is viewed in the light of the realization of reason. On the other, freedom and reason are brought into conformity with the material structure of the given society, and are thus changed into ideals which the individual must unaided realize within his isolated personality (Kant, Fichte). **Hegel**'s philosophy marks the culmination of the philosophical treatment of the theory of society. Society is, in its entirety, subordinated to the standards of reason and freedom. At the same time, the realization of reason is conceived as a historical process producing during varying stages different forms of state and society. Modern civil European society and its adequate political organization, the constitutional monarchy, is considered as that stage of the process in which the two antitheses of modern society, freedom of the individual and reason of the whole, are reconciled. The unconditional consequence with which Hegel treats the basic ideas of modern society however, changes his social and political theory into a definitely critical doctrine. He expounded the belief that civil society is based on the inevitable antagonisms of private property, and can therefore never attain that form of universality in which the interest of the individual is united with the interest of the whole. This recognition leads to the fundamental distinction between state and society, as realms based on two different principles of existence, a distinction inaugurating modern sociology. The problem of social change assumes an entirely new form within the general structure of Hegel's dialectics. The dialectical method will be discussed as an adequate theoretical structure capable of coping with the dynamic character of modern society. Social change is no longer a particular event within a rather static reality, but the primary reality itself from which all static [conditions] must be explained. The interpretation of social change becomes identical with the theory of society.

IV

This conceptual transformation corresponds to that stage of the historical development where the antagonisms inherent in modern society have attained their full force. In the face of these antagonisms, the problem no longer is one of the adjustment of the lasting structure of society to social changes, but one of clarifying the realization that, regardless of social changes, there still exists a lasting society in permanent process of reproduction. This new problem necessitated a critique of the existing society as such. It was first prepared by **Sismondi** and **Saint-Simon** in France, and **Lorenz von Stein** in Germany, who either restricted their critique to certain important phenomena or attacked existing society in a rather utopian way.

In contrast to these doctrines, **Marx** retains Hegel's demand that the theory of society must, in every concept, aim at the totality of a rational society. The dialectical method had led to the understanding of the labor process as the process which decides upon all forms and spheres of human life. The ways in which the labor process of society is organized (economic relationships, legal, political and social institutions), which are termed by Marx "relationships of production", come, under capitalistic forms of production, into an inevitable conflict with the productive forces in such a manner that the latter are fettered and restricted by the maintenance of this organization. Consequently, the problem of social change is not a problem within the prevailing form of society, but of the substitution of this society for a socialist one. This theory also claims to furnish a method by which changes within the existing societies can be uniformly explained.

In the later part of the 19th century the discussion of the problem of social change is largely determined by the impact of the Marxian theory. Only from that angle can the syndicalist theories of **Proudhon-Sorel** and the anarchist theory of **Bakunin** be fully understood.

Modern sociology has severed the intrinsic connection between the theory of society and philosophy which is still operative in Marxism and has treated the problem of social change as a particular sociological question. This separation results in the increasing import of the more or less independent special sciences in the analysis of social change. Anthropology, biology, physics and psychology are supposed to furnish the conceptual basis for the analysis of the problem. The various sociological theories of social change will be examined; we *do not* think it necessary to mention them in this outline. Special emphasis will be placed on the growing predominance of positivism in the theory of society. The positivistic tendency produces a new kind of adjustment of social theory to the prevailing social order. The dynamic character of the positivistic doctrines of social change is a mere shell, only slightly concealing a fundamentally static conception. This pattern will be shown in the discussion of **Pareto**'s sociology. To Pareto, social change is essentially a movement of particular social groups attempting to organize society according to their particular interest. The structure of these groups, however, is conceived in terms of an individualistic psychology working with rather abstract concepts of individual drives and instincts. In the last analysis, Pareto's idea of the elites involves an *a priori* acceptance of the rule of those groups which have the actual power in a given society. His concept provides no standards by which the elites themselves can be measured.

Our conclusion will discuss the new setting of the problem of social change during the preparation of Fascist and National Socialist philosophy (Germany: **Moeller van den Broek, O. Spann, E. Juenger;** Italy: **G. Gentile,** Corradini, Rocco).

Finis

IV
$$$$

Contents

I. Introduction

II. The Pragmatistic Pattern
(XVI. and XVII. century)

III. The Cultural Integration
(Vico - Montesquieu)

IV. The Rationalistic Pattern
(Helvetius, French and British
Enlightenment)
The Idea of Progress: Condorcet
Rousseau

V. Counter - Revolution
Burke - Bonald - De Maistre

VI. The Idealistic Pattern
Kant - Hegel

VII. The Administrative Pattern
Saint-Simon, Comte
Spencer
The Socialist Critique

VIII. The Dialectical Conception
Hegel, Marx, L.v.Stein
Reformist and Radical Marxism

IX. The End of the Philosophical Integration
Lester Ward

† Untitled manuscript, no authors, no date, on theories of social change. This text, close in content to the previous titled manuscript, and thus presumably by Marcuse and Neumann (#118.04), is a more detailed explication of the project and the "Contents" page seems to suggest a prospectus being prepared for a publisher.

THEORIES OF SOCIAL CHANGE†

Herbert Marcuse and Franz Neumann

If we attempt to give a historical review of some major issues in the theory of social change, we find ourselves in a rather awkward position. The scientific concept of social change is one of the achievements of present day sociology; in a strict sense, it does not appear prior to our century and has thus not yet a historical tradition. The earlier forms of sociology and social philosophy were occupied with the idea of universal social laws, with the conception of social progress and evolution, but they did not arrive at a philosophically and ethically neutral notion of social change. On the other hand, we cannot hope to understand this notion and its far-reaching implications without taking into account the preceding theoretical conceptions from which it was derived and which continue to operate in the doctrines that have replaced them. Our historical survey must therefore trace the problems of social change in theories the conceptual structure of which is quite different from that of modern sociology, and only slowly and step by step can we arrive at the properly sociological formulations.

The first fact that has to be taken into consideration is that, up to the XVIIIth century, the theory of social change was essentially a *philosophical* theory. Men did not look upon society as a relatively independent entity or process, they did not separate the social facts and relations from the comprehensive context in which nature and society was merged into an organic whole. The obvious changes which stimulated theoretical reflection (growth and decline of cities, ruling houses and empires, the overthrowing of governments, population movements, the consequences of war, plague and poverty) were related to more universal changes and derived from certain general laws governing history as well as nature. To be sure, there were thorough analyses of social phenomena, particularly the causes of unrest and revolution, the conditions of wealth and power, the stability and adequacy of various forms of government, the mechanisms of social control and public opinion. All these phenomena, however, were studied under definitely pragmatic aims, in connection with definite social and political interests, and wherever the investigation went beyond this framework, it was directed by philosophical or even theological ideas.

In the modern era, the philosophical setting of the doctrine of social change was chiefly determined by one basic question: how can a stable social order be established and perpetuated? Since the German Reformation, the Religious Wars and the ever aggravating struggles between the rising middle class and the secular and ecclesiastical nobility, this question obtained a new and threatening significance. The feudal system had been undermined, in all its ramifications, by a new mode of production and division of labor which cut across the fixed distinctions of the hierarchy of Estates. Expanding commodity production abolished the prevailing order of "natural" and personal dependence which had hitherto secured the functioning of society. This order was now being replaced by a violently dynamic system, relating men to each other as free and equal economic subjects. The very form of society became the result of the emancipated individualistic interests and of the ever changing constellation of economic forces.

It must be noted that it was precisely the dynamic character of the new order which induced its theorists to subordinate the problem of social change to the problem of social stability. The almost incessant series of inventions and discoveries, the opening up of new natural resources and the constant transformation of all social relations was simply a fact to be accepted; it seemed to be founded in the very nature of man that the productive forces were utilized by the dangerous dynamic of conflicting self-interests. Society itself was change and nothing but change, and the only question was whether and how change could be controlled so as to secure an at least provisional order of the whole. The various answers to this question were all given along the following line: the functioning of society can be guaranteed only by the establishment of a strong and undisputed government to whose authority the individuals transfer the task of integrating their diverging interests and of asserting them within and without. Whether the government was to be constituted in a democratic or absolutistic form was a minor matter, depending upon the particular situation of the country and the relation of the competing groups; the only thing that mattered was the government's ability to control the social dynamic and to secure prosperity and order.

Ever since Machiavelli, social change has been interpreted in terms of order and disorder. Maintenance of order was the one vital aim of social theory and practice, and all other problems had to be subordinated to this goal. This accounts for the strikingly cynical character which distinguishes the political doctrines of the XVIth and XVIIth centuries. Today, we look upon the problem of social change primarily under the aspect of adjusting our material culture to the developing faculties and wants of men. We do not separate the efforts for controlling and directing the social dynamic from the efforts to preserve and expand human rights, liberties and satisfaction. We evaluate the tendencies and ideas which propagate the perpetuation or the transformation of our culture and measure them according to the standards of freedom and reason. In the social teachings of Luther and Calvin, Machiavelli, Bodin and Hobbes, even Spinoza, such considerations do not determine the question and its solution. The rights of the free individual and their constitutional guarantee appear only insofar as they are already vested in an orderly functioning political system, and they are in any case subject to the requirements of the established order. Or, if they are advanced by a party which fights the established order, they are pragmatic means for discrediting the opposed order and recede before the interests of that party as soon as it has attained its goal.

Even the search for the general laws of change which had animated social philosophy since Aristotle was, in the XVIth and XVIIth century, undertaken in the pragmatic interests of the "cause of order." The revival of the ancient doctrine of the cyclical course of constitutions and of cultural growth and decline certainly retained its deterministic tinge, but in its concrete setting, in the work of Machiavelli, for example, it sounded a different tone: the cycle was essentially one of order and disorder, prosperity and impoverishment, and its threatening inevitability was meant to exhort the people to forget their petty interests and to unite in collaboration for the power of the whole.

We can exactly define the point at which new historical issues shatter this conceptual framework and transform the doctrine of social change into a sociological doctrine. This takes place in the period in which the French middle class overthrows the rule of feudal absolutism and sets out to adapt the social and political institutions to the actual stage of the material culture. In England, the feudal nobility had been amalgamated with the middle class since the XVIth and XVIIth centuries and no new political revolution was necessary in order to consummate this tendency. In Central Europe, absolutism remained still unchallenged; only in France, the conflicting social forces were driven towards a revolutionary situation. The same movement that gave birth to American independence, made, in

France, the changing of the adaptive culture the cause of a revolution. Here, the tension between the progressing material culture and the obsolete social and political institutions was so strong that it put the problem of change in the center of social and political thought. It was no longer a problem of maintaining order but one of destroying it. Society, as the organic unity of material and non-material culture, was something that had only to be created, and this task was no more a primarily political one but affected all human relations and institutions, private as well as public. Society appeared as the totality of the relations and institutions which determine the content and direction of human life and particularly the range of human freedom. For the creation of an adequate social order was tantamount to the abolition of an oppressive system of domination and to providing the means for greater human satisfaction.

In this situation, thought assumed an essentially critical function. New impulses, ideas and values came into conflict with the prevailing patterns of life which were, in their totality, patterns of maladjustment. All inquiry into the given potentialities of man and nature hit upon the fact that they were fettered by the existing social and political relations, and this antagonism stimulated the analysis of the inherent laws which governed the social process, the part of human reason and freedom, the position of the various social groups in the division of labor, the distribution and utilization of wealth. The doctrine of social change was stirred by new issues, and these were the very same ones that rejuvenate it again in our days.

Before we proceed to a brief survey of these issues, we must take account of a singular phenomenon in the history of our problem, the work of Giambattista Vico. He was the first who treated change as a primarily sociological problem; his conception emancipated the analysis of the social process from an alien metaphysical and theological framework as well as from a narrow pragmatic aspect. His work, the *Scienza Nuova*,[1] appeared first in 1725; it had hardly any bearing upon the development of French thought in the XVIIIth century, although Montesquieu might have incorporated some of Vico's ideas in his *Esprit des Loix*.

The subject matter of Vico's work is the totality of the material and non-material culture in their historical development and interrelation. He views this totality – and this is his decisive achievement – as "the work of men",[2] thus terminating the vain search for universal cosmic laws under which the social process appeared as the result of more or less suprasocial

---

1 We quote from Michelet's edition of Vico's works, 2 vols., Paris 1855.
2 I, pp. 396, 412.

forces. The social world emerged as the realm of human wants, desires and interests, as the ever renewed contest between man and nature and history, and when Vico set out to establish the general tendencies of this contest, he tried to do this on a definitely empirical basis. To be sure, there is constant emphasis on the course of Providence, but this is only a thin veil before the essentially secularized historical conception. On the other hand, Vico does not limit the scope of his work to the pragmatic interests of a particular state or power. He views the individual persons, groups, nations and epochs only as definite stages of the comprehensive process in which culture unfolds itself.

Vico finds the empirical basis for his new science in the "common sense" which men apply to the "necessities and utilities" of their life.[3] This common sense is the context of ideas, values and standards that the associated individuals, prior to all "reflection" and abstraction, develop in the daily maintenance of their life; it is, according to Vico, a common and universal possession, shared not only by a particular group or nation but, in the last analysis, by mankind as a whole.[4] This fund of ideas, values and standards constitutes, in various historical forms, the organic unity of a culture or age, and it is the sole foundation on which the general laws governing the course of history are to be established. Vico comprises these laws in a cycle which leads from a pre-civilizatory Heroic Age over the different stages of an increasingly refined civilization to another state of "reflected barbarism"[5] out of which the whole cycle begins anew. The important point is that Vico transforms the traditional cycle of political orders into one of social orders: the relations that mark the transition from one stage to another are the social relations in which men have organized the material culture. The development of all forms of society commences with the organization of mere necessities, is then determined by utilities and commodities, and ends with the rule of pleasure, luxury and wealth.[6] These relations give shape to the moral, political, artistic and religious forms which characterize the individual historical cultures.

This rough outline of Vico's conception might suffice to indicate the pattern of social change in his work. According to Vico, no isolated factor can be singled out and made responsible for the occurrence of social change. In an established culture, all factors and spheres are so interrelated that it is always the whole itself which changes; in the measure in which

---

3 I, pp. 342, 410.
4 I, p. 342.
5 II, p. 379.
6 I, p. 366.

material culture proceeds, new forms of settlement and collaboration are found, new tools invented, new resources opened up, "common sense" itself changes and proceeds to new forms in the non-material culture. The material culture, however, does not unilaterally determine the other spheres, it is itself shaped by the imaginative and speculative forces of man, and Vico places great emphasis on their part in the evolution of humanity. Nevertheless, when he pictures the concrete history of the Romans (to Vico the prototype of every national history), he orients his analysis to the constant struggle between Patricians and Plebeians so that the whole seems to be structurized after the foundational social relations.

In Vico's conception of culture as an organic totality, the question for the stimuli of social change is overshadowed by the question for its direction. It is here where his philosophy is most distinctly connected with the subsequent theories of the French enlighteners. For Vico, the passage from one to another historical stage is a passage from a lower to a higher form of reason; as civilization develops, man liberates himself from the sway of dark and unconscious forces that ruled his primitive life and expands the domain of conscious and rational action. It is the trained reflection on himself and his world, the progress of consciousness which, itself stimulated by the progress of material culture, gives man mastership over nature as well as society, produces increasing wealth and luxury, but, at the same time, promotes the decline of the entire culture in a new age of barbarism.

The idea of progress by reason, so dear to the enlighteners, is thus, in Vico's work, counteracted by the conception that cultural progress necessarily unfolds the inherent contradictions by virtue of which mankind again plunges into barbarism. The evolution of accumulative culture does not signify a straightforward development of human faculties and satisfaction; progress in reason is not progress in happiness, and the increasing rational control over nature and society cannot invalidate the eternal laws that govern the growth and decline of nations. This is the conservative element in Vico's philosophy of history, an element which was even strengthened in Montesquieu's notion of the *"esprit d'un peuple."* Vico and Montesquieu were the first to grasp culture as a structurized totality of historical and natural relations, but in doing so they conceived this totality as an organic whole, evolving according to inevitable laws with which man cannot tamper without endangering the order of his entire life. The historical method which Vico and Montesquieu opposed to the doctrine of abstract rights and to the metaphysical construction of state and society contained tendencies that surrendered the present and future to the past and came close to a justification of all that had become and sustained itself in the course of history.[7] It has correctly been emphasized that Montesquieu's influence on American political thought was with the conservative authors of the *Federalist Papers* rather than with the radical representatives of Jeffersonian democracy, and Vico's idea came to fruition in the doctrine of the counter-revolution, in Burke and De Maistre, and in the conservative Romanticist and Historical School of Germany.

The French enlighteners were well aware of the conservative implications in Montesquieu's work and they did not hesitate to reject it notwithstanding its great contribution to the cause of freedom and the struggle against despotism. Their criticism is in line with the new impulses that guided their approach to the problem of social change and made them place their analysis into a revolutionary framework. Space forbids dealing with the various social doctrines of the enlightenment; we shall limit ourselves to illustrate the new issues by the work of that philosopher who, although he cannot stand for the whole movement, represents most clearly its basic tendencies, that is, Helvétius.

The comment with which Helvétius returned the manuscript of Montesquieu's *Esprit des Lois* elucidates his whole position. He said: "I have never understood the incessantly repeated subtle distinctions between the different forms of government. I know only of two forms: the good ones, which are still to be created, and the bad ones, whose entire art consists in making pass, by different means, the money of the governed part into the pockets of the governing part."[8] Against Montesquieu's historical method which derives the forms of government from their origin and the particular physical and cultural climate in which they move, Helvétius holds a critical method, evaluating these forms according to definite universal standards. At a first glance, these standards seem to be purely arbitrary moral norms with a dogmatic orientation to economic status. In the context of Helvétius' philosophy however, his standards reveal their concrete empirical foundations.

Helvétius starts from the obvious fact that, in his days, man's physical and intellectual faculties were totally restricted and distorted by oppressive forms of political and spiritual domination. To him, the abolition of absolutism and the fight against the Church was not only a matter of expediency, required by the interest of a particular group or nation, but a matter deciding upon the fate of mankind itself. He raised the question whether the given forms of government and society were not subject to

---

7 See for example Vaughan, *Studies in the History of Political Philosophy Before and After Rousseau*, Manchester 1939, vol. I, p. 291f.
8 *Correspondance de Montesquieu*, Paris 1914, vol. II, p. 21.

standards which could not be derived from their particular historical structure and function but had to be obtained by measuring them against the nature of man and his task as a social being. For Helvétius, this was not a metaphysical question but one which destroyed the very basis of metaphysics and paved the way for the social and political emancipation of man. Helvétius started from the assumption of sensualistic philosophy, particularly Locke and Condillac, that our ideas and values derive, in the last analysis, from the senses, and he drew from this the conclusion that, the senses being the real organon of the truth, their development and satisfaction was the primary task of human life, private as well as social. Time and again, he proclaimed that to seek pleasure and to avoid pain was the driving motive of all action.[9]

From here, Helvétius' philosophical materialism evolved at once into a radical social and political theory. The promotion of happiness, the greatest possible satisfaction of human needs and desires being the ultimate aim of private and public life, it followed that the social and political institutions must be adapted and, in their functioning, directed to this aim. Again, there could be no doubt that the institutions of absolutism patently contradicted such principles. Men lived in a state of misery, wickedness and oppression, and a change of this state was impossible without changing the "legislation" that caused and perpetuated it. "If one wishes to destroy the vices attached to the legislation of a people without changing this legislation, one pretends the impossible and rejects the right consequences of the principles which one admits."[10] Change is not the slow and organic evolution of an established culture nor the source of eternal historical laws, but the conscious and free adaptation of all forms of life to the principle of happiness, the creation, may it even be a revolutionary one, of a society promoting the satisfaction of an ever greater part of the population. As against Montesquieu's respect for what has grown and sustained itself in history, Helvétius holds that precisely "the weakening of the peoples' stupid veneration for ancient laws and usages enables the sovereign to purge the earth from most of the evils which devastate the earth."[11]

Happiness, however, the satisfaction of material needs and desires, is an individualistic principle, and social change thus seemed to be surrendered to divergent personal interests. Indeed, Helvétius repeatedly stressed that the "personal interest" of individuals is the driving motive power behind all

---

9 See *De L'Esprit*, *Oeuvres Complètes*, London 1777, vol. II, pp. 187, 295; *De L'Homme*, London 1773, vol. I, pp. 102, 106, 119f., 124.
10 *De L'Esprit*, p. 225.
11 *Ibid*. p. 136.

private and social actions and institutions.[12] To be sure, state and society are integrated by and to be organized according to the common interest, but the latter is nothing other than the sum-total of personal interests,[13] or, the interest of the greatest number.[14] The question then arises: how can the multitude of individual interests ever yield a common good? How can conformity be achieved between the private and the public interest?

The answer, we know, implied, according to Helvétius, the abolition of the then prevailing political system and some sweeping social reforms as regarded the distribution of wealth and labor.[15] But this did not dispose of the problem itself. The individualistic principle, which vested the power of social change in the development of personal interests and at the same time justified such power as the proper basis of all social progress, this principle – particularly in the materialistic form Helvétius gave it – obviously threatened the very foundations of state and society. Faced with this difficulty, Helvétius set out to show that it was precisely the *unrestricted* realization of the individualistic principle that alone could create a true community of interests.

In the hitherto known societies, individual interests not only conflicted with each other but individuals were unequal to such an extent that a unified culture, based upon the happiness of men, could hardly be imagined. The "spirit" of a people was indeed in every case a very particular one, and their particular customs, mores and institutions were far from converging upon the general happiness of mankind. This fact, however, did not express an eternal law but the rule of unmastered natural and oppressive political conditions over the life of men. That inequality and diversity which stood in the way of a true community was, in the last analysis, the result of an inadequate form of government and education.[16] These causes once removed, man will develop his faculties and wants in such a way that, pursuing his individual interest, he will simultaneously promote the common wealth. If happiness has really become the legitimate aim, if its pursuit has been liberated from the interest of domination and oppression, then it will become manifest that the most individualistic principle is also the most universalistic one. For happiness is incompatible with misery; he who is happy has no longer any motive for making or keeping others unhappy. "The

---

12 *Ibid.* p. 40f.; *De L'Homme*, vol. I, pp. 261, 268.
13 *De L'Esprit*, p. 75.
14 *Ibid.* p. 180.
15 *De L'Homme*, II, pp. 164–69.
16 *De L'Esprit*, pp. 207, 349, 379; *De L'Homme*, II, pp. 119 (Section VII, ch. I), 370 (Section X, ch. 10).

happy man is the humane man."[17] Helvétius thus formulated the essence of his philosophy in the equation between self-interest, happiness, virtue, justice and common interest.[18]

The emancipation of man to the knowledge of his true interest, however, can only be the result of a long process of education, or, happiness itself is the "work of education."[19] As soon as absolutism is overthrown and the basic social reforms are introduced, change becomes the steady evolution of all human faculties, guided and controlled solely by reason. Reason, the totality of those human activities and ideas which are directed to the promotion of happiness, will at first be vested in the individuals who, owing to the preceding conditions of inequality, have most freely developed their humane potentialities. But the privilege of reason will soon become a common property and alone guide the constant adjustment of all relations and institutions to the progress of the material culture.

In this doctrine of social change, all the elements are already assembled which determined the approach to the problem for at least a century. This approach is perhaps best characterized by the fact that the pattern of social change is conceived as a *pattern of Reason*. We may roughly define this pattern as follows:

If social change is governed by perpetual historical laws, such laws are at least in a more or less perfect harmony with the increasing domination of nature by man's conscious activity and with the development of all his faculties, physical as well as intellectual. We could even say that the historical process was identified with progress, that is with the achievement of ever higher and more rational forms of association, were it not for the fact that even the most optimistic enlighteners expected periods of grave retrogression and had their doubts whether the growth of technique and industry was *eo ipso* a growth of freedom and happiness. Moreover, we need only mention the names of Rousseau, Burke, Bonald and De Maistre in order to see that the rationalistic idea of progress was from the beginning opposed by a philosophy which was fully aware of the dangers involved in the developing individualistic society. Nevertheless, the enlighteners were convinced that mankind had reached the stage at which, after the necessary political and social reforms, the natural, technological and cultural order were in an essential equilibrium and that its recurring disturbances could be overcome by the increased rational control which the associated individuals exercised over these orders. As regards the relationship among the

---

17 *De L'Homme*, II, p. 16 (Section V, ch. 3).
18 For example *ibid.*, I, p. 151f (Section II, ch. 16).
19 *Ibid.*, II, p. 17 (Section V, ch. 3).

three orders, emphasis was to an ever greater extent laid upon the cultural order, since industry and technique, once freed from external regulations and left to their own inherent power, seemed to guarantee an ever greater exploitation of nature and satisfaction of material wants. Philosophic rationalism thus joined forces with economic liberalism, and the issues which occupied the doctrine of social change in the subsequent period were closely connected with the issues of liberalistic society.

Before turning to this period, we have still to consider some important aspects of the rationalistic pattern of social change. We have indicated the rapprochement between the ideas of change and progress that took place after the French Revolution. To be sure, the perfect equilibrium between the three orders was still laid in the future, but it was a future growing out of the present without revolutionary leaps. This conviction is most strikingly expressed in the famous passage from Condorcet's *Esquisse d'un Tableau Historique de Progrès de l'Esprit Humain*:[20] "that there is no limit to the perfection of human faculties, that man's perfectibility is actually indefinite, that the progress of this perfectibility, having become independent of all the powers that wished to stop it, now has no other limit than the duration of the glove upon which nature has thrown us. No doubt, this progress might follow a more or less rapid course but it will never be retrograde, provided that the earth stays in her place in the system of the universe, and the general laws governing this system don't produce a general revolution nor a change which no longer permits mankind to maintain itself, to unfold the same faculties and to find the same resources." This doctrine implied that not only human faculties and natural resources remained fundamentally the same but also their social organization and utilization. Apart from the radical wing of the enlightenment above all represented by Meslier, Mably, Morelly and Linguet, nobody advocated a new social organization of production and labor. The form of society which consolidated itself in and after the French Revolution was increasingly interpreted as the "natural" form, meaning lasting as well as adequate, in accordance with nature as well as reason. The pattern of reason, originally opposed to and transcending the prevailing order, was slowly adjusted to it. While Helvétius had linked the principle of self-interest with a principle of happiness calling for the equal satisfaction of all human desires with the utility the individual could expect from the satisfaction of his pleasure, and such satisfaction was subordinated to personal advantage in the competition of daily life, the notion of self-interest came soon to be tied up. The emancipation of the individual was

---

20 Second edition, Paris 1796, p. 4f.

shaped after the emancipation of the economic subject, a process the results of which were already contained in the liberal utilitarianism of Hume and Adam Smith.

The social dynamic was divided in two spheres: the industrial and technical order and the intellectual culture. In the former, social change appeared as the "natural" progress to ever greater prosperity, stimulated by accumulating inventions, more efficient modes of labor, more rational administration. This process could be left to the free play of its inherent forces precisely because it was a "natural" one, an organic or even auto-matic evolution. The problem of human control over change here came down to the problem of finding the most inconspicuous form of adminis-tration, with as little interference and domination as possible. The sphere of intellectual culture, on the other hand, was the realm of conscious freedom, especially of liberalistic freedom of thought, speech and religion. Change here was the result of the unhampered development of human reason in the variety of its manifestations, and it was expected to be a rich reservoir of the ideas and norms which guided the organization of material progress.

The rationalistic conception, by leaving the development of the material culture to the inherent mechanisms of progress, tended to dissolve the problem of control over social change into that of educational guidance. Some form of guidance, of leadership towards progress, was necessary since the harmony between the different spheres of culture was a task still to be accomplished, and since men were still far from knowing their true interest. To be sure, the Declaration of the Rights of Man marked the point at which humanity had reached the threshold of a free and rational society,[21] but obsolete ideas, customs, values and morals still held sway over a population misled by centuries of oppression and ignorance. It followed from the rationalistic conception that the emancipating leadership was conceived as a primarily intellectual one, based upon reason and setting free the powers of reason in every individual. Educational control should take its justification and its standards solely from reason, that is to say, it should act as every individual would act if he would use his liberated and developed faculties, disregarding any external authority. Control thus became an intellectual factor, and the intellectuals seemed to be those best equipped to discharge this task. The large part played by the intellectuals in the preparation of the French Revolution and in its execution has frequently been stressed.

It must be noted, however, that the idea of educational control was not the exclusive characteristic of the rationalistic conception but found

---

21 Condorcet, *Tableau*, p. 240f.

likewise expression in the work of its most ardent enemy, Rousseau. His doctrine, which treated the notion of progress with contempt and refused to make the establishment of a free society dependent upon the evolution and the mechanisms of the material culture, is much more dynamic than that of the rationalists. To him, the leap into a free society can only be the result of a free decision of the individuals, and the constitution of an absolute democracy is its sole lever. It implies a retrogression rather than a progress of the economic and technological order, above all the prevalence and equal distribution of small property. Once the absolute democracy has been established, all change will be introduced and executed by the free decision of the sovereign people. However, Rousseau's contempt for the historical method, for the veneration of the past, did not blind him against the factual rule of the past over the present. The problem of how a hitherto unfree people can suddenly know and utilize freedom looms largely in his work and is concentrated in his striking formula that "men must be forced to be free".[22] This brings the question of social control to the fore and makes it the vital point of the most radical theory of democracy: what is the legitimation of him who forces men to be free? Rousseau did not elaborate the social stages which precede the consolidation and functioning of the general will. His answer might be indicated by the strange figure of the original legislator who is the vessel of charismatic forces and acting with an unconditional, almost divine authority.[23] However closely this leadership might resemble recent national socialist ideas, Rousseau remained faithful to his revolutionary impulses in that he envisioned the compulsion to freedom as a purely educational dictatorship that tended to its own abolition in the measure in which men became conscious of their true interest.

One fundamental aspect unites Rousseau with his rationalist opponents. He as well as the rationalists derived the adequate form of state and society from the needs and the will of emancipated individuals. This is to say, they viewed social and political transformations under the aspect of adapting state and society to the developing wants and faculties of man. They subjected the given social institutions and relations to the standards of freedom and they were convinced that its realization would result from the conscious activity of the combined individuals. This conception implied a definite program of change: (1) the mastering of the pregiven natural conditions, (2) their utilization in accordance with the greatest possible freedom of all associated individuals, (3) the establishment of the autono-

---

22 Rousseau, *The Social Contract* (Everyman's Library), pp. 36–8.
23 *Ibid.*

mous control of these individuals, united in a sovereign body politic, over all social and political relations. It was this conception which caused the most violent opposition and brought to the fore the first consistent theory of the counterrevolution. This theory set the conceptual framework for the subsequent struggle against European liberalism on all fronts and furnished a reservoir of ideas which fed the antiliberalist trends until our days.

Historically, the opposition fought against the revolution of 1789 and its immediate aim was the restoration of the hereditary monarchy with the predominance of the Church and nobility in the shaping of public life. We shall here disregard the often essential differences between the British (Burke) and the French (Bonald, De Maistre) doctrine and limit ourselves to show the new pattern of social change with its antiliberalist features.

Its first outstanding characteristic is that the part played by human will and action in producing, directing and controlling social change is, if not entirely rejected, greatly reduced. This becomes manifest in the attack on the notion of social contract, particularly violent in the work of Bonald and De Maistre. They thought it the original sin of political philosophy to derive state and society from voluntary consent and action of individuals. To them, state and society were the result of divine ordinance, and social and political obligations inherent natural obligations, prior to all expediency and conditioning all contracts and agreements.[24] Consequently, the real constitution of the state is not the written one, not that which was the work of human deliberation, but the unwritten natural and divine order around which all written constitutions center. Burke held that the more elaborate a constitution is, the worse it is, and De Maistre proclaimed that "no constitution originates from mere deliberation" and that "no human assembly whatsoever can give to a people a constitution."[25] "Society is not the work of man, but is the immediate result of the will of the Creator who has willed that man be what he has always and everywhere been".[26] If this is the case, any change in the constitution produced by the free will and conscious action of men is not only inexpedient and a change to the worse but a crime and a sin, for the constitution is part and parcel of the order of the universe, "linking the lower with the higher natures, connecting the visible and invisible world" and keeping all moral natures "in their appointed place".[27]

---

24 Burke, *Reflections on the Revolution in France*, second ed., London 1790, p. 144.
25 De Maistre, *Essai sur le principe générateur des constitutions politiques*, Preface.
26 De Maistre, *Considérations sur la France*, Oeuvres complètes, Lyon 1891–2, vol. I, p. 317.
27 Burke, *Reflections on the Revolution in France*.

From here, the doctrine of the counterrevolution proceeds to a wholesale defamation of human reason which, in adapting the established constitutions to its standards, "would only pervert and destroy them".[28] Left to the development of his rational forces, emancipated from the divine force of absolute government, man becomes a wild beast that has to be tamed by all means.[29] "In general, as an individual, he is too wicked to be free".[30] This is the counterthrust against the very principle of liberalism.

The pattern of social change thus emerging is essentially antirationalistic and deterministic. The only genuine change that conforms to the universal order is the slow natural growth of the social and political body in its history. State and society develop from their original constitution by virtue of their inherent nature, through the preestablished concord of all its spheres, and any interference from without is nothing but destruction. The natural and the existing, the true and the prevailing order are fused together. Moral obligation becomes respect for the given, and positive right tends to assume the form of natural right. This conception guided the development of antiliberalist philosophy throughout the xixth century, particularly in the Historical School of Right in Germany. It was one of the theoretical pillars of authoritarianism as long as the latter fought the liberal and democratic forces which prevented its establishment as a social and political system.

We shall now indicate some of the consequences of the doctrine of the counterrevolution which had most bearing upon the subsequent theory of antiliberalism.

Undoubtedly, a criterion was needed to distinguish the order of natural growth from destructive changes. This criterion was found in the charismatic character of established authority. The monarchs and princes were regarded as the immediate delegates of God, and obedience to them as an unconditional obligation. The vested authorities alone could decide whether and what changes should be introduced and how they should be directed. The divine character of their rule had to be protected from all questioning. There was no rational justification for the sanctioned institutions and relations, and it was not in the power of the governed to alter them in accordance with their wants. Burke and De Maistre outlined a theory of mass domination that foreshadowed recent fascist and national socialist practices. The people must be constantly handled and manipulated. The cynical frankness with which these writers proclaimed

---

28 De Maistre, *Considérations sur la France*, vol. I, p. 367.
29 *Ibid.*, vol. I, p. 357.
30 *Ibid.*, vol. II, p. 399.

the principles of mass domination again resembles the methods of present-day authoritarianism. Prejudices and superstition must be fostered, patriotism must be utilized as an expedient dogma. Every government ought to have its dogmas, mysteries and priests, removed from the profane ways of the people. "Man's primary need is that his nascent mind be best under a double yoke, that it humble and lose itself in the national spirit".[31] Nothing is more important for man than his prejudices, they are "the real elements of his happiness and the palladium of the empires." And for all spiritual and secular government, De Maistre gives the following advice: "Man does not need problems but beliefs for his conduct. His cradle must be surrounded by dogmas, and when his reason awakes, he must find all his opinions ready-made, at least those which bear upon his conduct".[32]

The doctrine of the counterrevolution had rejected the rationalistic and harmonistic pattern of social change mainly on the ground that the very principles of individualistic society from which this pattern was derived contained the germ of inevitable destruction. The organization and reform of the social order could not be left to the will and deliberation of the combined individuals nor oriented to their freedom and happiness because the corrupted nature of man made him incapable of discharging such a task. The social order was rather to be based on super-human authority; it was to be an order of control, punishment and compulsion in which the intellectual was the eternal enemy and the executioner "the corner stone of society".[33] The defenders of the counterrevolution justified their verdict by a dogmatic philosophy of man, implying the corruption of his nature and reason. It must be noted, however, that this philosophy was buttressed by a far-reaching analysis of the French Revolution and the turmoil of devastating conflicts which followed the period of the Terror. No wonder that Burke, Bonald and De Maistre identified deliberate change with revolution and revolution with annihilation. De Maistre did not hesitate to extend its verdict to the American Revolution and to predict that the city of Washington would never be built and that Congress would never assemble there.[34]

The events in France seemed to bear out the indictment pronounced by the theorists of the counterrevolution, and their philosophy was, to a considerable extent, connected with a critique of rising middle class society,

---

31 *Ibid.*, vol. I, p. 376.
32 *Ibid.*, p. 375; compare Burke's hymn on prejudice as the source of wisdom and virtue, in *Reflections*, p. 130.
33 De Maistre, *Les Soirées de Saint-Pétersbourg.*
34 See W. Montgomery McGovern, *From Luther to Hitler*, Houghton Mifflin Company 1941, p. 103.

particularly with the new distribution of property and the dangers involved in it.[35] The attack on rational control over social change and the justification of authoritarianism came thus to be linked with a critique of the actual foundations of individualistic society. At about the same time, this tendency was pursued and strengthened by a quite different philosophy, that of German Idealism.

It might, at a first glance, appear as strikingly inconsistent that Kant, who based his theoretical and practical philosophy on the autonomous reason and will of the free subject, arrived, in his social doctrine, at the refutation of the right to resistance and the demand for unconditional obedience to the established authorities. It seems likewise inconsistent that Hegel, whose system elevated reason to the rank of the sole reality and identified it with the realization of freedom, regarded the monarchic state of the Restoration as the final period of history and equipped this state with divine powers. To be sure, Kant retained the rationalistic optimisms of the enlightenment in his conception of a progress towards a world community united in perpetual peace, and he as well as Hegel defended the French Revolution as one of the greatest events in the emancipation of mankind.[36] Nevertheless, Kant envisioned such progress only as one "from above" and his acceptance of the fact of revolution was tantamount to a recognition of a successfully established and consolidated government.[37] Hegel's doctrine of social change will be dealt with in connection with the dialectical theory; here, we shall limit ourselves to interpret the apparent inconsistency in the social philosophy of German Idealism.

The idealists repudiated interference with the social order by the free decision of the emancipated people because they were convinced that civil society, as the association of free individuals, could function only if it was integrated and dominated by a strong state. The famous distinction between state and society, which was the conceptual precondition for the development of modern sociology, is guided by this conviction. According to Kant, and particularly to Hegel, a social system built upon the diverging self-interests of independent proprietors must necessarily engender increasing inequality and injustice.[38] The idealists identified society with

---

35 See Burke's remarks on the social and political function of landed property in *Reflections*, pp. 62ff., 75ff.
36 Kant, *Werke*, ed. Cassirer, vol. VII, p. 398f.; Hegel, *Philosophy of History*, transl. J. Sibbree, New York 1899, p. 447.
37 Kant, *ibid.*, p. 129f.
38 Kant, *ibid.* p. 66f. derives the civil order from the "accidental character" of acquisition. Hegel's exposition of the inherent contradictions of civil society [is] in his *Philosophy of Right* §§ 246–248.

the relations of civil society, that is to say, with the integration of men by means of the free play of private interests. All change in this sphere was, in the last analysis, stimulated and directed by private interests, chiefly the interests of private property, and their dynamic, if left to its free course, seemed to tend to destruction since it was not guided by a conscious and united community. Such a community must therefore be established from without or rather from above civil society, and this was the task of the state. The state, the "system of government" must be removed from the destructive antagonisms of society; it is the realm of static order to be erected above the realm of destructive change which is society. Social change is thus controlled and directed by a power which itself is not drawn into the turmoil of change.

It is obvious that this statism called for a system of government which was as little as possible amenable to diverging social interests. This conception did not only favor the hereditary monarchy as that form of government which corresponded mostly to such demand but also laid increasing emphasis on the role of the *bureaucracy* in the social process. An "estate" of government officials responsible solely to the sovereign and occupied exclusively with the business of government seemed to be the principal means for achieving independence of the state from the pressures of social interests.[39]

In the idealist conception, the distinction between state and society led to an interpretation of social change in terms of social motives and effects as contrasted with political forms and institutions. This distinction, however, was placed in a conceptual framework in which the state dominated society and exercised supreme control over the range and direction of social change. Notwithstanding its individualistic foundation, the idealistic doctrine arrived at a strongly authoritarian pattern of social change. The idealists did not develop the strictly sociological interpretation of social change. This was rather accomplished in the work of that man who can rightly be called the founder of social science, namely, Saint-Simon.

Saint-Simon was the first to derive his doctrine entirely from the empirical analysis of the prevailing social process, to exclude all transcendental standards and to elaborate a pattern of change according to the tendencies of progressing industrial society. He took the decisive step from political to social science in his programmatic declaration that "the law which constitutes the power and form of government is not as important and does not influence the welfare of nations as much as the law that

---

39 Hegel, *Philosophy of Right*, §§ 289f.

constitutes property,"[40] meaning the social distribution and function of property in a given social order. We remember that the rationalistic conception of the XVIIIth century regarded the form of government as the essential factor of social progress, subordinating the latter to the task of finding that political form which was most adequate to the unhampered development of the social forces. According to Saint-Simon, this task had been accomplished by the French Revolution; society had liberated itself from the fetters of governmental absolutism and was now to proceed to the stage of free self-organization. Such self-organization was to follow the "law of property", that is to say, the mechanisms and interests which factually determined the production of national wealth. At the attained stage of social development, all national wealth was, in the last analysis, the result of industrial production. "Society as a whole is based on industry. Industry is the only guarantor of its existence, and the unique source of all wealth and prosperity. The state of affairs which is most favorable to industry is, therefore, most favorable to society."[41] Industry (which, according to Saint-Simon, includes agriculture, insofar as it is not idle feudal property) is not only the "sole useful class"[42] but also the sole class whose activity and interests are in harmony with the whole and whose growth means growing prosperity of the whole.[43]

Saint-Simon derives from this conception the entire pattern of social and political change. Industry is a dynamic process in which every step leads to increasing social wealth, every change is progress in productivity and power, provided that it is caused by the free development of industrial activity and dictated by the free interests of industry itself. Industry is the sole true factor of social change and all conscious direction and control of the social dynamic is to be guided by industrial interests: all laws and administrative measures are to be judged according to their utility for industry.[44] This implies a complete subordination of the political to the social or rather economic relations and institutions; the state is absorbed by society, and government is restricted to technical administration.

Saint-Simon draws these conclusions with unerring consequence. All governmental functions as well as the decisive political and legislative initiative is to be transferred to the industrialists.[45] The industrialist class

---

40 Saint-Simon, *L'Industrie*, vol. II, in *Œuvres*, ed. Enfantin, Paris 1868 ff., vol. III, p. 82.
41 *L'Industrie, Prospectus*, vol. II, p. 13.
42 Ibid., vol. III, p. 74.
43 Ibid., p. 47f., 168f.
44 Ibid., p. 74.
45 Ibid., p. 83.

comprises the "theoretical industrialists" (scientists and technicians) and the "immediate producers", the "applied" theory and science.[46] For Saint-Simon, government by industry signifies the final adequate organization of society, the organization of indefinite progress. Industrial government is distinguished from the preceding inadequate forms of government by the following features: the people is united with its "chiefs" instead of being dominated and regulated by them; it is directed instead of being commanded; disorder is replaced by order;[47] the governing are merely the "administrators" of society,[48] occupied with "subaltern functions and police duty",[49] in brief, all action against men is replaced by action against things, that is to say, by the collective domination and exploitation of nature for the welfare of society as a whole.[50]

We have dealt with Saint-Simon's conception rather extensively because it set a new framework for the doctrine of social change as it developed not only in XIXth century sociology but also in socialist theories and in more recent ideas of a planned society. We may characterize the new conception as the organizational or administrative pattern of social change (Saint-Simon himself called his doctrine a *"philosophie organisatoire"*.)[51] The social process is interpreted in terms of the industrial process of technique, and the problem of directing and controlling it becomes a problem of organization and administration, to be treated as a technical task. The administrative pattern of social change grows out of the conviction that, in the material culture, everything is in order, that production has reached its adequate form, and that all further changes would be but changes within this form, its inherent development, and not changes affecting the form itself. The idea of progress and of a purposive direction of the social process is being combined with a technological determinism according to which progress in all spheres of culture is conditioned by the free and full unfolding of industrial technique. Society is again conceived as governed by necessary natural laws, although these laws are no longer those of the geographical or biological but of the technological order. They are natural insofar as they operate with an automatic necessity and that their utilization implies obedience to their dictum and the abolition of all metaphysical standards. The philosophers of the enlightenment had measured the progress of material culture against the still unfulfilled potentialities of

---

46 Ibid., p. 60.
47 *L'Organisateur*, vol. IV, p. 150f.
48 Ibid., p. 187.
49 Ibid., p. 202.
50 Ibid., pp. 192, 161f.
51 Ibid., vol. I, p. 138.

men and against the goal of the universal satisfaction of their needs. Such critical aspects are now disappearing; the conception becomes essentially harmonistic. The gap between factual and potential productivity, between the new impulses and forces and the existing relationships of labor no longer stands in the center of the doctrine of social change; the latter is narrowed down to the question of the most rapid and secure adaptation of the intellectual to the material culture, and the question is answered by the call for efficient technical organization.

We have mentioned the ideological justification of the political bureaucracy in Hegel's system; we now find, in the philosophy of Saint-Simon, an even more striking justification of the industrial and technical bureaucracy. Social and political control is transferred to the latter, which emerges as the sole guarantor of progress and order. It must be noted that this conception was accompanied by a decisive shift in the emphasis on social values: the interest of the consumer was subordinated to that of the producer,[52] happiness and freedom to technical reason, efficiency and order. These tendencies are consummated in Comte's sociology. In his principles, Comte does not go beyond Saint-Simon and we may therefore refrain from their discussion.[53] Comte gave Saint-Simon's ideas a larger philosophical and scientific foundation and filled his conceptual framework with a greater empirical material. With respect to the doctrine of social change, however, Comte only strengthened and elaborated the trends already visible in Saint-Simon's work. His Law of the Three Stages placed increased emphasis on the "natural" and almost automatic character of progress based upon the development of industry and science. He viewed social dynamics chiefly under the aspect of the accumulative growth of intellectual culture, particularly of "intelligence and *sociabilité*".[54] The laws governing social dynamics were derived from the conception that each state of society was "the necessary result of the preceding one of the indispensable motor of the succeeding one".[55] Social change was thus conceived as a leapless sequel of transformations, starting from the material culture and assuming, in the age of positivism, the form of a harmonious evolution of industrial and intellectual productivity. Political domination will be replaced by the self-government of the "productive classes" and by technical and scientific administration. Revolution and anarchy will be abolished, for these disturbances resulted only from the immaturity of the

---

52 See the characteristic passage in Saint-Simon, ibid., vol. III, p. 83.
53 For this discussion see Herbert Marcuse, *Reason and Revolution*, New York 1941, pp. 340–360.
54 *Discours sur l'esprit positif*, Paris 1844, p. 56.
55 *Cours de philosophie positive*, 4th ed., Paris 1877, vol. IV, p. 263.

productive process and its subjection to external and obsolete forms of government. Progress will be based on order and finally become identical with order: order is the "fundamental condition of progress," and "all progress ultimately tends to consolidate order".[56]

Notwithstanding its harmonistic and liberalistic implications, the administrative pattern of social change exhibited the features of *authoritarianism*. They were almost negligible in Saint-Simon's doctrine, but became very definite in Comte's sociology. We have seen that Comte as well as Saint-Simon supplemented industrial government by a government of scientists. They regarded science as the adequate embodiment of that technical reason which was supposed to give man perfect mastery over nature and society. Organization and administration should proceed according to scientific principles which were not only in conformity with the requirements of industrial progress but also guaranteed the emancipation of mankind from all prejudices and dogmas. Naturally, these principles were taken from physical science, founded on observation and guided by empirical verification. The conviction, however, that men would voluntarily bow to the verdicts of scientific reason implied a too high opinion of the inner rationality and goodness of human nature which was not at all borne out by the facts. It is thus easily understandable that Comte consolidated his scientific government by a system of totalitarian control, vested in an elaborate hierarchy of authorities and exalted by numerous symbols and dogmas.

The authoritarian trend was furthermore strengthened by the fact that the plea for industrial and scientific self-government was inevitably linked with the plea for an efficient regulation of all social relationships. Government by technical administration called for scientific control over the social process, and such control seemed to be impossible without a conscious manipulation of all decisive rapports [i.e. relations] among men in society. At this point, Comte's conception became distinctively opposed to the ideals of liberalism. He envisioned a state in which the fundamental social relations, particularly that between worker and entrepreneur, would no longer be "sufficiently guaranteed in the free natural antagonism between them" but would require to be regulated "toward an indispensable harmony".[57]

The authoritarian elements hidden in the administrative pattern of social change were soon to recede before the sway of liberalism in the second half of the XIXth century. The pattern was developed along its foundational

---

56 *Discours*, p. 56; *Cours de philosophie positive*, vol. IV, p. 17.
57 *Cours de philosophie positive*, vol. IV, p. 485.

harmonistic lines. Social science, strengthened in its claim for independence by John Stuart Mill's *Logic*, focussed its interest upon the immutable general laws which were supposed to transform all development into progress. In the theoretical justification of the idea of progress, the biological and psychological factors gained momentum. Spencer's sociology viewed social change not as much under the aspect of physical laws as of organic evolution. Society appeared as a living organism, constantly adapting itself, by virtue of its inherent power, to the changing environment. Adaptation was, to a large extent, a psychical process: the younger generation inheriting and developing those faculties and impulses which the older had acquired in their struggle with nature. Since this struggle tended to an ever greater domination of nature and satisfaction of happiness, the psychical process quite naturally tended to mental and cultural growth. Owing to the strong emphasis placed upon the psychical factors, education assumed an important role in controlling and directing social change: the liberal educator replaced Comte's authoritative scientist. The economic sphere, which played such a large part in Saint-Simon's and Comte's work, no longer stood in the center of the social orbit. Spencer was convinced that the economy was on the level of historical progress and he took it for granted that all disturbances and deficiencies could be removed without establishing new social and political forms.

This conviction gave Spencer's utilitarianism the harmless and renunciatory tinge which already characterized Bentham's and Mill's philosophy and so clearly distinguished it from the conception of the enlightenment. The enlighteners demanded, as much as Bentham, Mill and Spencer did, that the pursuit of self-interest be in accord with the interest of the others and that happiness should and could not be achieved at the expense of the fellow-man's unhappiness. The enlighteners held, however, that such union between the personal and common interest could only be achieved in a state to come, and that under the prevailing conditions the self-interest of the one was incompatible with the self-interest of the other. In contrast, Spencer's brand of utilitarianism did not imply such a gap and leap between the present and the future. Consequently, the demand for the union of personal and common interest subordinated the pursuit of happiness to the prevailing social constellation of interests which appeared as the pre-given barrier for happiness as well as utility. The motives for social change derived from utility and self-interest became as many motives for maintaining and complying with the existent order and relations. Notwithstanding its claims for happiness and progress, Spencer's utilitarian conception struck the note of resignation rather than liberation.

It is a peculiar fact that the same impulses and events that gave birth to the harmonistic and administrative pattern of social change led to the opposite conception, namely, to the revolutionary doctrine of social change. Saint-Simon had based his philosophy on the development of industrial society, implying that the economic structure of society decided upon the progress in all spheres of culture. Some of his most ardent disciples, while maintaining the master's conception, drew the conclusion that the factual organization of industrial society did not guarantee the full development of its capacities, that the industrial interests were not at all in harmony with the interest of the whole, and that the economic relations themselves called for a revolutionary change. The recurrent crises which shook France in the post-Napoleonic period seemed to buttress this opinion. Already before the revolution of 1830, Saint-Simonism had become a radical doctrine. Together with Sismondi's economic critique of capitalist commodity production and with the writings of the early British socialists, it constituted a body of socialist ideas which grew constantly throughout the XIXth century until it was overshadowed by the Marxian theory.

In the lectures which Saint-Simon's pupil Bazard published as the *Doctrine Saint-Simonienne*, the harmonistic picture is already destroyed. Industry is interpreted as the "exploitation of man by man", as the ever aggravating struggle between the "whole mass of workers" and those "whose property it utilizes", and the existing social order is viewed as general disorder, resulting from "the principle of unlimited competition".[58] Since these conditions are, according to Bazard, bound up with private property and command of the instruments of labor,[59] the transition to a state of rational administration can only be achieved through a new revolution "that will finally do away with the exploitation of man by man in all its insiduous forms" and with the institution of property which perpetuated this exploitation.[60]

The social contradictions, and the revolution which is to dissolve them, appear in the radical version of Saint-Simonism as rather unique events. In the dialectical conception, which we shall now briefly discuss, they determine the general pattern of social change throughout history.

The dialectical conception of change was first elaborated in Hegel's philosophy. It reversed the traditional logical setting of the problem by taking change as the very form of existence, and by taking existence as a totality of objective contradictions. Every particular form of existence contradicts its content, which can develop only through breaking this form

---

58 Bazard, *Doctrine Saint-Simonienne – Exposition*, Paris 1854, pp. 123f., 145.
59 Ibid., p. 124.
60 Ibid., p. 127.

and creating a new one in which the content appears in a liberated and more adequate form. Full liberation and adequacy is only reached in the totality of all forms, when this totality is comprehended and made the realization of reason. Such realization is, according to Hegel, the result and good of the historical process, and is identical with the achievement of free and rational forms of state and society. This process is motivated by the material wants and interests of men and advances through their thoughts and actions, but these are only the instruments of objective reason which asserts itself in the history of mankind.[61]

What were the consequences of this conception for the problem of social change? (1) Social change was no longer an event occurring in or to a more or less static system, but the very *modus existentiae* of the system, and the question was not how and why changes took place but how and why an at least provisional stability and order was accomplished. (2) Any harmonistic interpretation of a historical system was repudiated since such a system was only the integration of inherent contradictions which could be resolved only through the destruction of the system. (3) All particular stimuli and causes of change were to be derived from the very structure of the whole system which was in itself an antagonistic and destructive structure. (4) The direction of change was an objective one, determined by the given content of the system and by the necessarily antagonistic and restrictive relations in which this content was organized. (5) Such objective determination pointed in the direction of increasing freedom and rationality because the historical process itself made available, to an ever greater extent, the means for fulfilling human freedom and satisfaction. The transition from the progressing "consciousness of freedom" to its realization was not an automatic one but required the conscious action of men. Hegel himself used the dialectical conception in the field of social philosophy by analyzing Civil Society as developing through the antagonism between self- and common interest, accumulating wealth and increasing poverty, growing productivity and expansionist war.[62] He thought that these antagonisms could be coped with by a strong state, and he saw in the monarchic state of the Restoration the appropriate master of destructive social mechanisms. Lorenz von Stein detached the dialectical conception from the philosophical systematic and applied it to a concrete sociological analysis, namely, the analysis of the social struggles in France from the revolution of 1789 to that of 1848. He saw the motor of the social dynamic in the inevitable struggle between

---

61 For a more detailed account of Hegel's philosophy see Herbert Marcuse, *Reason and Revolution.*
62 *Philosophy of Right*, §§ 185, 243ff., 248, 333ff.

capital and labor for the possession of state power, a struggle that must necessarily lead to a revolution. The revolution, however, contains a new dialectic: the victorious class will exclude other groups from the government and organize the state according to its particular interests. Lorenz von Stein held that the ruinous dialectic could be brought to a standstill by a comprehensive social reform for which the warring classes would eventually unite themselves.[63]

The dialectical conception unfolded its full impact, however, only in the Marxian theory. We shall consider here only those of its aspects which have a direct bearing upon the problem of social change.

Marx derived every kind of social change from the antagonism between the productive forces operating in a given form of society and the relationships in which the same society organized the utilization of these forces. According to Marx, every society develops to a point at which these relationships hinder and eventually prevent the full utilization of the productive forces in the interest of the whole. This, he holds, is caused by the fact that society is a class society, that one social group possesses the means of production as its exclusive property and uses them in its particular interest. The ruling class at first fulfills a progressive social function because its own interest and position compels it to abolish obsolescent forms of production and domination, to unfold the economic potentialities, to create new wants and new means for their satisfaction. This process integrates an ever larger part of the population in the social division of labor, but can only do so by extending and intensifying exploitation. Marx set out to demonstrate this dynamic in his analysis of capitalism. In capitalist society, commodity production has embraced the earth, the productive forces have grown to an hitherto unknown extent, man has brought nature under his dominion, and the means for the satisfaction of all human needs, for the establishment of a free and rational society are at hand. However, these forces are developed through the utilization of capital, and the latter requires the continuous appropriation of surplus value, which, in turn, can be achieved only by continuous exploitation of free labor power. Competition among the independent entrepreneurs leads to the ever increased use of machinery in the productive process, thereby, on the one hand, reducing the share of "living labor", employment and the rate of profit, and, on the other hand, accelerating the concentration and centralization of capital in the hands of a few. These tendencies, according to Marx, plunge the capitalist system into ever aggravating crises which

---

63 *Geschichte der sozialen Bewegung in Frankreich von 1789 bis auf unsere Tage*, ed. G. Salomon, München 1921, vol. I, Introduction.

can be overcome only by a revolution, transferring the means of production to the proletariat. The revolutionary dictatorship of the proletariat will abolish the classes, and society will then become a "union of free men" who collectively decide upon the organization of their life.

It was necessary to sketch the well known basic conception of Marxian theory in order to gain a starting point for indicating the new pattern of social change. We may say that this pattern combines and at the same time transforms the decisive features of the preceding doctrines. We may recognize the rationalistic pattern, the idea of progress, the cultural integration, the search for the "natural laws" of the social process. In the new conceptual framework, however, all these notions assume an entirely different significance. We shall illustrate this by two examples which might elucidate two of the most widely discussed issues involved in the doctrine of social change: (1) the problem of determinism, and (2) the part played by ideological factors in social change.

1   Marx was convinced that the laws governing capitalist society operated with the necessity of natural laws,[64] that tendencies asserted themselves in the actions and thoughts of men which overruled their particular intentions, motives and interests. The "law of value" comprises all these tendencies: it determines the mechanisms of exchange, of supply and demand, centralization and concentration, crisis and breakdown of the system. Here, however, the rule of physical laws comes to an end. The act of the revolution, and the construction of a free and rational society is not determined by such laws but can, although dependent upon "objective conditions," be only the result of the free decision of the associated workers. For Marx, society is governed by natural laws precisely insofar as it is not yet a free and rational association. The natural character of the social system, which, to Comte, was the token of progress and reason, is, to Marx, the mark of its irrationality and bondage, and the equilibrium constituted by the natural laws of society is the integration of anarchy, waste and oppression. Consequently, Marx denied the entire development of class society the title of human history and contrasted it as pre-history or *Entstehungsgeschichte* with the real history of mankind which, according to him, would begin only with the functioning of classless society.[65] The idea of progress is thus transposed to a new realm: the economic and technological growth that culminated in capitalism, the entire process of

---

64   *Capital*, transl. S. Moore, E. Aveling and E. Untermann, Chicago 1906–09, Preface to the first edition, and vol. I, p. 837.

65   *Ökonomisch-philosophische Manuskripte*, in *Marx–Engels Gesamtausgabe*, 1927, vol. III, p. 153.

accumulative culture in class society is progress only in an ironical sense; it is, with all its positive features, also a negative phenomenon – emancipation and, at the same time, restriction and distortion of all human and natural potentialities. Marx retained the conception that a rational society implied men's autonomous control over their social life, and that such control was to replace domination by administration, but he held that this could only be the case when freely associated individuals had constituted themselves as the conscious subjects of the social process. This event, however, was separated from the prevailing form of society by a gap which excluded all evolutionary and harmonistic interpretation of progress.

Determinism of social change thus became a historical characteristic, valid only for a particular historical form of society. The automatism of social laws was seen to be correlative to a society in which the reproduction of the whole was but the result of blind mechanisms, operating "behind the back" of the free individuals.

In the subsequent development of Marxian theory, the problem of determinism and autonomous control became one of the main points of conflict between the reformist and radical school. The former extended the automatism of social laws to the very period which, according to Marx, should abolish this automatism, namely, the revolution. It was considered to be an event which followed with natural necessity from the capitalist dynamic, and the pre-history and history of mankind were linked together in one evolutionary pattern.[66] Whereas Marx had strikingly contrasted the realm of freedom with the blind necessity governing all "pre-historical" forms of society, his theory was now praised for "weaving the realm of history into the realm of necessity".[67] All change that was taking place in society since the turn of the century was supposed to tend from liberal constitutionalism to the parliamentary and from there to the socialist democracy. At the same time, "the class interest recedes, the common interest grows in power," and legislation regulates to an ever increasing extent the economic forces "which were previously left to the blind war of particular interest".[68]

At the opposite pole of Marxism, in the radical school, all social determinism was violently rejected, and the "subjective factor" was emphasized as against the widespread fetishism of the objective conditions. This went so far that all economic determinism of social change was

66 See particularly Eduard Bernstein, *Zur Theorie und Geschichte des Sozialismus*, Berlin 1904, part III, p. 69f.
67 Karl Kautsky, in *Die Neue Zeit*, 1898–9, vol. II, p. 7.
68 Bernstein, *Zur Theorie und Geschichte des Sozialismus*, p. 69.

repudiated and "political spontaneity" made the foremost factor in revolutionary action. "Politics cannot but have precedence over economics. To argue differently, means forgetting the ABC of Marxism."[69]

2 We have mentioned that, in the dialectical conception, the various causes and impulses of social change are integrated into a whole, structurized by the tension between the productive forces and their organization. The productive forces are not identical with the prevailing industrial and technological capacity. Marx once defined them as the historical "results of applied human energy" and included among them objective as well as subjective forces. The latter comprise the developed intellectual and physical faculties of men insofar as they contradict and transcend the cultural forms in which society utilizes and satisfies them. In other words, the term productive forces is a critical concept which measures the given cultural productivity against its own content. This means that the social dynamic is again viewed under the aspect of the gap between factual and potential productivity, and is by no means identical with the full development of industrial and technological capacity. The decisive issue is the direction in which this development takes place, namely, whether it is oriented to the liberation of all material and intellectual capacities in the interest of the whole of society.

This conception yields the clue for the question of the role of the ideological factor in social change. The ideologies prevailing in a society, far from being nothing but an "illusion", provide an important standard for the objective character of the social contradictions and for the direction in which their solution can be sought. Marx himself used in this way the ideology of middle class society. This ideology claimed to organize society according to the principles of freedom, equality, just exchange, and self-interest; it thus envisioned the true principles of a free and rational society. Owing to the relationships, however, in which middle class society had ordered the productive process, these principles inevitably turned into their opposite and created bondage, inequality, injustice and exploitation. The ideological content itself, if taken seriously, points to a new order in which it would find its adequate form, and the ideology is an "illusionary" consciousness only insofar as it is the illusion of the truth.

The dialectical conception attempted to elaborate an integrative pattern of social change within a comprehensive theory of society, subjecting the particular empirical forms, causes and tendencies of social change to critical and rational standards which transcended the prevailing social

---

69 Lenin, *Selected Works*, New York 1934ff., vol. IX, p. 54.

context. In the subsequent period, the philosophical and integrative elements were increasingly removed, and the doctrine of social change took the form of a strictly empirical and specialized theorem, focussing its intention on the factual stimuli and effects of change in the existing social order. This transformation can best be seen in the sociology of Durkheim and his school and is consummated in the idea of a *wertfreie* sociology, the ideal type of which is the work of Pareto. To be sure, the impulses which animated the rationalistic and integrative conceptions do not disappear, but their influence becomes increasingly weaker, and it is only under the impact of the post-war crises and of rising European authoritarianism that sociology returns to the earlier critical patterns.

The last remnants of an integrative conception of social change can be studied in the sociology of Lester Ward. He retains the basic ideas which determined the development of the problem since the XVIIIth century. To him, happiness is the aim of private and social life, and the main issue is whether the changes occurring in society can be controlled and directed to an ever greater satisfaction of human desires, to an ever more complete abolition of pain and creation of pleasure. Moreover, Ward is convinced that society can attain this goal through the application of "scientific principles strictly analogous to those by which the rude conditions of nature have been improved upon in the process which we call civilization".[70] He holds that man is still "under the control of external nature and not under the control of his own mind",[71] and he thinks as high of the role of education in this process of improvement as did the French enlighteners. At the same time, however, he repudiates any kind of technological fetichism and harmonistic interpretation of progress. Technological progress, the accumulation of material culture, has taken place with all the blind and destructive features that characterize the natural development of a species or individual. "The same wars and wasteful methods prevail in society as in the animal and vegetable kingdom. . . . All functions of society are performed in a sort of chance way wholly analogous to the natural processes of a lower organic world."[72] The steady growth of the accumulative culture is not yet progress, for the latter can only be measured in terms of increasing human happiness and satisfaction. The very fact that moral progress lies far behind material progress is an index that society has not yet reached the level of free and consciously controlled self-development in all spheres of culture.

---

70 Lester F. Ward, *Dynamic Sociology*, 1903, vol. II, p. 2. See Samuel Chryerman, *Lester F. Ward*, Duke University Press, 1939, pp. 444–48.
71 *Dynamic Sociology*, vol. I, p. 14.
72 Ibid., vol. II, pp. 88–9.

If the social dynamic is progress at all, it is so only insofar as it develops in a way quite different from the natural processes. Ward contrasts the "genetic progress" of nature with the "telic progress" of society:[73] the latter is a planned process, rational as well as moral, and dependent upon the liberation of man's emotional and intellectual faculties. It calls not only for technological and administrative control but, even more important, for the conscious ordering of all social relationships towards the final goal of happiness. With this conception, Ward's doctrine is definitely linked to the great critical and rationalistic tradition of social philosophy.

---

73 Chryerman, p. 445.

V

THE NEW GERMAN MENTALITY

Memorandum on a Study in the Psychological
Foundations of National Socialism and the
Chances for their Destruction

By

Herbert Marcuse

c/o F. NEUMANN
403 WEST 115
NEW YORK CITY

~~110 19th St.~~
~~Santa Monica, Calif.~~   June 1942.

Table of Contents

---

† In the Marcuse archives, there is a long study of the "The New German Mentality," (#119.00) accompanied by three manuscripts which mention and build on the study (#129.00, #129.01 and #119.02). "The New German Mentality" is dated June 1942, so it was probably written in California at the time Marcuse was working on the study of "State and Individual Under National Socialism." Following Marcuse's name on the title page, his Santa Monica address is crossed out and Neumann's New York City address is written in. Marcuse apparently submitted and circulated this text for official discussion in his government work with the Office of War Information in late 1942 and early 1943, as shown by the reports which refer to "The New German Mentality," which we are also including in this volume as supplements (see pages 174–90).

THE NEW GERMAN
MENTALITY†

1 THE TWO LAYERS OF THE NEW GERMAN MENTALITY

National Socialism has changed the thought and behavior pattern of the German people in such a way that it is no longer susceptible to the traditional methods of counter-propaganda and education. The German people today is oriented to essentially different values and standards; it talks and understands a language that is different not only from that of Western civilization but also from that of the former German *Kultur*. A thorough knowledge of the new mentality and the new language is a prerequisite for the effective psychological and ideological offensive against National Socialism.

We may distinguish between two layers of the new mentality:

1 **the pragmatic layer** (matter-of-factness, the philosophy of efficiency and success, of mechanization and rationalization)
2 **the mythological layer** (paganism, racism, social naturalism)

The two layers are two sides of one and the same phenomenon.

A critical analysis of the new mentality is necessary in order to find the instruments that are most apt to destroy it.

We have two principal sources for such an analysis:

1 The actual organization of National Socialist society. We may infer the new psychological status of the people from the pattern of the social and political institutions which have been set up to govern this people.
2 The National Socialist ideology, that is to say, the philosophy by which the National Socialists explain and justify the new institutions and

relations. The ideology can only be understood, however, by analyzing it in the context of the actual organization of National Socialist society.

2 THE FEATURES OF THE NEW GERMAN MENTALITY

We may summarize the new German mentality under the following headings:

1 Integral politicalization The facts are well known, but an adequate interpretation of their scope and consequences is still lacking. In present day Germany, all motives, problems and interests pertaining to the life of individuals are more or less directly political ones, and their realization is likewise a directly political action. Social as well as private existence, work as well as leisure, are political activities. The traditional barrier between the individual and society, and between society and the state has disappeared. But it would be utterly wrong to regard this politicalization as the culmination of German etatism, authoritarianism or anti-individualism. The National Socialist politicalization rather revitalizes certain forms of terroristic politicalization which were characteristics of the middle class revolution in the Western European countries: the "bourgeois" emerges as the "citoyen" whose life is business, and whose business is a political affair.

2 Integral debunking National Socialism has trained the German people to consider everything that is not borne out by the facts as an ideological manoeuvre designed to conceal and confuse the real fronts and forces in the struggle within and without. This process did not stop short at National Socialism's own philosophy: the cynicism which pervades this philosophy has also seized those who are supposed to believe what their leaders tell them. The German people believe in the National Socialist philosophy insofar as this philosophy proves to be an efficient weapon for defense and aggression – but not farther. With the exception of the very young and the very old objects of National Socialist organization, everyone who believes in the National Socialist ideology is conscious of the fact that he believes in an ideology.[1]

3 Cynical matter-of-factness In organizing German society for total war

---

1 Paul Hagen, *Will Germany Crack?* New York 1942, p. 219. See the paper on "Private Morale in Germany," submitted to the Office of the Coordinator of Information (April 1942) by the Institute of Social Research.

expansion, National Socialism has imbued the thus mobilized population with a rationality that measures all issues in terms of efficiency, success and expediency. The German "dreamer" and "idealist" has become the world's most brutal "pragmatist." He views the totalitarian regime solely under the aspect of his immediate material advantages. He has adjusted his thoughts, feelings and behavior to the technological rationalization which National Socialism has transformed into the most formidable weapon of conquest. He thinks in quantities: in terms of speed, skill, energy, organization, mass. The terror which threatens him at any moment promotes this mentality: he has learned to be suspicious and shrewd, to weigh any step at an instance's notice, to hide his thoughts and his aims, to mechanize his actions and reactions and to adapt them to the rhythm of universal regimentation. This matter-of-factness is the very center of the National Socialist mentality and the psychological ferment of the National Socialist system.[2]

4 Neo-Paganism The pragmatic cynicism which pervades the National Socialist matter-of-factness has been pushed forward into a revolt against the basic principles of Christian civilization. To the German people, these principles were last materialized in the Weimar Republic and in the Labor movement. National Socialism has from the beginning associated the latter with the basic ideas of Christian civilization: Christian humanism, the Rights of Man, democracy and socialism have been made elements of one and the same compound.[3] This strange amalgam was rendered possible by the fact that, since the First World War, the German labor movement had become part and parcel of the system of democratic culture. The labor movement thus came to share the fate of this culture, and the failure of the Weimar Republic to fulfill its promises was used by the National Socialists to nourish distrust and hatred of the supreme ideas of Christian civilization as such, a distrust and hatred which were deeply rooted among large strata of the German population. In fostering these feelings, National Socialism appealed to the German people's experience of its most recent frustration: the revolt against Christian civilization belongs to the new spirit of matter-of-factness rather than to the spirit of "German metaphysics."

---

2 The destruction of "German metaphysics" (the people of poets and thinkers) by the new spirit of matter-of-factness began already prior to National Socialism. Oswald Spengler was perhaps the first to interpret the disillusioned, cynical, pragmatic attitude as the characteristic feature of the New Cesarism; see *Preussentum und Sozialismus*, München 1920, pp. 4, 30, and *Jahre der Entscheidung*, München 1933, pp. 9, 14. Cf. note 12 below.

3 This is one of the central propositions of Moeller van den Bruck's *Das Dritte Reich*, and Alfred Rosenberg's *Der Mythus des 20ten Jahrhundertes*. Ernst Krieck has expounded it in all his books.

The revolt against Christian civilization appears in various forms: anti-semitism, terrorism, social Darwinism, anti-intellectualism, naturalism. Common to all of them is the rebellion against the restraining and trans-cendental principles of Christian morality (the liberty and equality of man *qua* man, the subordination of might to right, the idea of universal ethics). This rebellion is an age-old German heritage which was operative in all typically German movements: in Luther's protestantism, in the "Faustic" elements of German literature, philosophy and music, in the popular upheavals during the Wars of Liberation, in Nietzsche, in the Youth Move-ment. But National Socialism has destroyed the metaphysical implications of this rebellion and transformed it into an instrument of totalitarian efficiency.

5 Shift of traditional taboos In order to actualize this rebellion, National Socialism was compelled to attack some of the taboos that Christian civilization had placed upon private and social life. The most conspicuous side of this process is the attack on certain taboos on sexuality, the family, the moral code.[4] We shall see, however, that the taboos have only been shifted, and not abolished. The result is an illusionary license and eman-cipation, accompanied by a strengthening of the taboos on other and better protected relations and institutions.

6 As the war goes on, the German population is increasingly possessed by a **catastrophic fatalism** which strengthens rather than weakens the hold of the National Socialist regime. The German masses seem to identify the annihilation of Hitlerism with annihilation as such, that is to say, with the final destruction of Germany as a nation and state, with the final loss of security, with the lowering of the standard of living below the inflation level. This catastrophic fear is one of the strongest bonds between the masses and the regime.[5]

We shall now attempt to interpret the elements of the new German mentality in the context of the National Socialist organization of society, but we shall interpret them only under the aspect of the destruction of this mentality.[6]

---

4 The material is collected in Clifford Kirkpatrick, *Nazi Germany: Its Women and Family Life*, Indianapolis 1938, and Georg Ziemer, *Education for Death*, New York 1942.

5 *Inside Germany Reports*, no. 12, 1940, p. 8; no. 20, 1941, p.3.

6 The interpretation is based on Franz Neumann, *Behemoth: The Origin and Practice of National Socialism*, New York 1942.

3 THE SOCIAL FUNCTION OF THE NEW
GERMAN MENTALITY

National Socialism may be characterized as the specifically German adaptation of society to the requirements of large scale industry, as the typically German form of "technocracy". We might even venture to say that National Socialism is the first and only "middle class revolution" in Germany, occurring at the stage of large scale industry and therefore skipping or condensing the preceding stages of the development. National Socialism has abolished the remnants of feudalism, notwithstanding the concentration of large real estate which the system promotes with all means (this concentration is a capitalistic rather than feudal process). National Socialism has furthermore abolished the relatively independent position of those groups which lagged behind the capacity of large scale enterprise, namely, the groups of small and middle business, of commerce and finance. The free market, which corresponded to the economic constellation prior to the predominance of large scale enterprise, has been regimented. National Socialism has incorporated labor into the dominion of industry and removed the barriers of social legislation which stood in the way of such incorporation. Directly political forms of control have been established (abolition of the rule of law, of free contract, representation, etc.). National Socialism has merged the industrial, governmental (ministerial) and semi-governmental (party) bureaucracy, thereby adjusting the state to the needs of the industrial apparatus. Finally, National Socialism has released the full capacity of this apparatus by embarking upon a policy of imperialist expansion on a continental scale. This sweeping adjustment in the social institutions and relations implied a not less sweeping adjustment in private as well as collective morale and psychology. The new mentality is, even in its most irrational aspects, the result of a process of totalitarian "rationalization" which removes the moral inhibition, waste and inefficiency that stand in the way of ruthless economic and political conquest.

The analysis of the new mentality will make it clear that:

1 the new mentality is the expression, not of some abtruse philosophy, but of a highly rationalized pattern of social organization;
2 there is no warranted conclusion that the new mentality will disappear with the disappearance of the National Socialist regime. For the new mentality is bound up with a pattern of social organization that is not identical with National Socialism, although National Socialism has given it its most aggressive form.

Moreover, in view of the social function of the new mentality, it is highly improbable that it can simply be retransformed into the mentality of the status quo. Since the new mentality is skilfully adapted to the latest stage of large scale industry and organization, to utmost technological capacity, any retrogression behind this stage would contradict the general trend of the international development and constitute a source of recurrent crises and conflicts. Integral politicalization is the National Socialist concomitant of the transition to a planned economy within the established social framework; integral debunking, cynical matter-of-factness and the shifting of traditional taboos are the German features of technological rationality, and neo-paganism serves to crush the psychological and emotional resistance to ruthless imperialist conquest. The whole mentality is that of the "late-comer" who tries to break into the entrenched system of powers with terroristic means.

There are other reasons against retrogression to the status quo, reasons that are founded in the new mentality itself. The matter-of-factness which, in present day Germany, provides the ground for all evaluation still gives the Hitler regime preference over the era of the democratic Republic. The German masses of today regard liberty, equality and the rights of man as a mere ideology unless these ideas are realized in material security and an adequate standard of living. The Weimar Republic was not able to achieve this realization, and the German masses care but little what happens in the other democracies as long as they themselves do not enjoy these benefits.[7] In Germany, full employment prevails, and the population does not yet starve. To be sure, the increasing hardships of war and the terrible losses will shift the balance in disfavor of the regime – but not in favor of the status quo. Here again, the evaluation is entirely pragmatic: the war has been pictured to the German population as a business proposition; the investment is high and frightfully risky, but it is the only possible investment, and the initial success is promising.[8] Entire nations have been subjected to German exploitation, and even the little man gets a small share of the booty. Moreover, it seems as if the technical character of modern warfare diminishes the weight of the moral factor and allows to continue operations even if the "spirit" is surprisingly low.

The National Socialist regime's hold over the German people is based on its efficiency and success in the international struggle, and military defeat is therefore the prerequisite for breaking this hold. But there is not the slightest guarantee that the downfall of the regime will eradicate the

---

7 Hagen, *Will Germany Crack?*, p. 165.
8 Georg Axelson's report, quoted in Thurman Arnold, *Democracy and Free Enterprise*, 1942, p. 22 f.

roots of the National Socialist mentality which made the regime possible. This mentality will disappear only when the dominion of those groups is dissolved which are for life and death tied up with the regime and, beyond the regime, with its motives and aims. It will disappear only when a social order has been established in which the achievements of the regime (full employment and material security) are preserved in a truly democratic form. To prepare the ground for such action, an attempt can be made to influence the new mentality by utilizing those of its elements which tend beyond the National Socialist form of their realization. These elements are above all the pragmatic matter-of-factness, and the integral politicalization. This, of course, does not mean that the National Socialist philosophy and propaganda are to be copied or adapted to different contents. Any concession in this direction would immediately appear as a sign of weakness and strengthen the belief in the superiority of National Socialism. It must rather be shown that National Socialism inevitably frustrates the motives and impulses which animate the new mentality, that National Socialism is the embodiment of the oppressive forces which it pretends to have conquered, and that liberation lies beyond the New Order as well as the status quo. The content and language of an effective counter-propaganda can neither be that of the New Order nor of the status quo but must develop a content and language of its own. They must respond, but not correspond, to the new mentality.

We have so far treated this mentality as a unit; we have talked of "the German people" and disregarded its differentiation in the various social strata. This is a gross over-simplification, and the adaptation of propaganda to the different social strata and interests is indispensable. We shall try such a differentiation later on. There is, however, some justification for neglecting it in a preliminary general outline. In Germany, the regimented rationalization of society is totalitarian also in the respect that it standardizes the thought and behavior pattern in all social strata. With the exception of the active opposition, they all converge on the same interests. National Socialism has furthermore "unified" the social antagonisms to such an extent that the vast majority of the population faces the small group of the industrial and governmental leadership.[9] Outside the ranks of this leadership, they are all objects of one and the same authoritarian organization, and their life depends at any moment on this organization, in the factory as well as in the shop, in the office and on the land, at home as well as in the assembly halls, clubs, theaters, hospitals and concentration

---

9 Hagen, p. 253.

camps. The dichotomy between the small ruling group and the rest of the population does not mean that the latter constitutes one oppositional mass. Unfortunately, the picture is not that simple. There is hardly any social group which, in its material interest, is not in some way or the other bound up with the functioning of the system, and wherever these ties are loosening, they are replaced by brute terror. The dichotomy rather designates the two poles on which the distribution of power centers: the policy is laid down by the ruling clique within which the conflicts of interests are fought out and the basic compromises reached, all other groups are fused together into an all-embracing organization which insures the execution of this policy. Within this regimented mass, the active opposition (that is to say, the opposition which fights the system, and not merely the more or less contingent composition of its leadership) is scattered among the factories and shipyards, road squads and labor camps, work schools and prisons. This opposition does not need "propaganda", but if the latter is addressed to the coordinated mass of the population, it will reach the opposition anyway.

4 THE NOVELTY OF NATIONAL SOCIALIST LOGIC AND LANGUAGE

The self-evident proposition that propaganda must be understandable to those whom it is addressed to is, in the case of present day Germany, no longer a truism. The change in the German mentality has been so fundamental that the German people is almost impregnable to the traditional logic and language of presentation and argumentation. It has frequently been stated that the new German language and logic are essentially irrational and illogical, and that for this reason they defy all rational discussion. To be sure, if we insulate the National Socialist philosophy from its social context and take the thus insulated philosophy as the expression of the new mentality, we are faced with nothing but illogical abstrusities. If, however, we place this philosophy and its language in the context of National Socialist policy and organization, we shall discover the perfectly rational and logical pattern behind the apparent abstrusities. Many critics of National Socialism are baffled by the fact that in present day Germany apparently two different mentalities, logics and languages coexist: the one, pertaining to the National Socialist philosophy, ideology and propaganda, utterly irrational; the other, pertaining to the realm of administration, organization and daily communication, utterly rational and technical. In reality, however, there is only one mentality, logic and language, and its two forms of manifestation are determined, pervaded and unified by one and the same rationality. This structure must be taken into account if an effective counterlanguage is to be developed.

The starting point for the understanding of a specific language is its usage.[10] The National Socialist language is used for propagating, indoctrinating and justifying large-scale imperialist expansion. In the situation of German society at the end of the Weimar Republic, this implied the subordination of all private and social relationships to the standards of mechanized and rationalized war production, and the planful elimination of all concepts and values which transcended or impaired this effort. The National Socialist language is therefore strictly *technical*: its concepts aim at a definite pragmatic goal, and fixate all things, relations and institutions in their operational function within the National Socialist system. They lose their traditional significance, their "universality" which has made them the common property of civilization – instead, they take up a new singular content, determined exclusively by their National Socialist utilization. This structure pervades the language of the totalitarian administration and bureaucracy, of the decrees, statutes, law courts, and to a great extent, of everyday life. But we shall see that the "mythological" language of National Socialist propaganda and philosophy also derives its rationality from this technical structure.

Every technical language, however, presupposes a "supra-technical" language community from which it draws its force and appeal, otherwise it could not serve as an all-embracing medium of intersubjective understanding.[11] This language community is chiefly one of sentiments, emotions, subjective desires and impulses. The National Socialist language possesses its supra-technical language community in the mythological layer of the German mentality, and particularly in that complex of ideas, impulses and instincts which constitutes the reservoir for the German protest against Christian civilization. But this complex is mobilized for the pragmatic goals of National Socialism and placed in the service of the technical rationality which guides the efforts to attain these goals. In transforming the mythological and metaphysical elements of the German mentality into instruments of totalitarian control and conquest, National Socialism destroys their mythological and metaphysical content. Their value becomes an exclusively operational one: they are made parts of the technique of domination. The apparently irrational philosophy of National Socialism

---

10 Karl Vossler, *The Spirit of Language in Civilization*, transl. Oskar Oeser, New York 1932, p. 82 f.
11 Ibid., p. 107 f.

actually represents the end of "German metaphysics," its liquidation by the totalitarian technical rationality.[12]

This process manifests itself in the syntactical form of the National Socialist language, in its vocabulary, and in the logical pattern of National Socialist "argumentation."

In its syntactical form, the National Socialist language shows a pervasive verbalization of nouns, a shrinking of the synthetical structure of the sentence, and a transformation of personal relations into impersonal things and events.[13] These features, far from characterizing a new "magic" language, rather demonstrate the adaptation of language to technological rationality.[14]

Instead of following up the linguistic analysis (which would require a separate study), we must here limit ourselves to a few general remarks on the relation between the technical and supra-technical language community. The supra-technical (mythological) language community is the reservoir of those forces which are most hostile and insusceptible to the spirit and language of Western civilization. Closer analysis will show, however, that National Socialism has "rationalized" these forces and given them a strictly pragmatic significance.

The National Socialist language obviously centers on "irrational" ideas such as folk, race, blood and soil, Reich. It must be noted that all these concepts, although their form is that of universals, actually exclude universality. They are used only as particular, even as individual concepts: they serve to distinguish the German folk, race, blood, and to discriminate against other folks, races, bloods. They designate singular "facts" and derive from such facts singular standards and values. Moreover, the facts which they designate are such "by nature," that is to say, they are placed outside the universal context of human civilization as something that belongs to a higher order. In this order, the "natural" inequality of men is more than their "artificial" equalization, the body more than the mind, health more than morality, force more than law, strong hatred more than feeble sympathy. We have previously mentioned that this entire "mythology" rests on a very definite empirical basis,[15] and that this basis is

---

12 Ernst Krieck, "Der deutsche Idealismus zwischen den Zeitaltern", in *Volk im Werden*, Leipzig 1933, no. 3, p. 4: "German idealism must therefore be overcome in form and content if we wish to become a political, an active nation." Oswald Spengler likewise proclaimed the end of German metaphysics; see especially *Jahre der Entscheidung*, chapter 1: "Der politische Horizont."
13 This has been shown in a paper by Henry Paechter.
14 The structure of a technological language has been outlined by Stanley Gerr: "Language and Science," in *Philosophy of Science*, April 1942, p. 146 ff.
15 *The Nazi Primer*, transl. H.L. Childs, New York 1938, p. 4: the National

to be found in the physiological and psychological preparation of German society for imperialist world conquest.[16] This policy required the destruction of all "universal" laws and standards which placed the German people in the context of international civilization, and the abolition of all (moral and legal) restraint implied in these laws and standards. The apparent irrationality of the National Socialist mythology emerges as the "rationality" of imperialist domination. We have furthermore mentioned that, in view of the situation of the German masses at the end of the Weimar Republic, the education to totalitarian imperialism could be successful only on the basis of immediate material compensations (full employment, participation in the spoils, controlled release of traditional taboos). The National Socialist mythology fostered rather than counteracted the extreme matter-of-factness with which the German people accepted this compensation for renouncing the democratic liberties. Paradoxically enough, education to cynical matter-of-factness is the spirit of this mythology. Note that its chief concepts substitute "natural" for social relationships (folk for society, race for class, blood and soil for property rights, Reich for state). The former seem to be more concrete and palpable than the latter. Folk and race are propagated as "facts," for birth by certain parents at a certain place is a fact, whereas class and mankind are abstract ideas. A healthy man must satisfy his healthy drives, this is a fact which supersedes the restraining claims of abstract morality. The Jew is a distinct and conspicuous outsider; even if he does not look and talk differently, he has different gestures and attitudes and, in any case, he is an unwelcome competitor. These "facts" are stronger than the standards of an abstract human equality.

It would be fatefully wrong, however, to explain the National Socialist mythology as a simple ideology of totalitarian imperialism, buttressed by the manifold material benefits which large strata of the population derive from the New Order. If this were the case, the breakdown of the imperialist expansion would almost automatically bring about the breakdown of the new German mentality. The actual relation between this mentality and the social and political structure is much more complicated. National Socialism has succeeded in imposing upon the German people the pragmatic rationality of totalitarianism because it has appealed to forces which belong to the deepest and strongest traits of the "German

---

Socialist outlook "is no theory, but adapts itself strictly to existing reality. The ideal of National Socialism is born of experience."

16 This is Hitler's own interpretation; see *My New Order*, New York 1941, p. 104 ff., and Robert Ley, *Neue Internationale Rundschau der Arbeit*, April 1941, p. 137.

character." These forces have been released in the mobilization of the mythological layer. They had been tamed and restrained by the process of Christian civilization, but they had continued to live under its cover, and their National Socialist emancipation constitutes the greatest threat to Western civilization.

Before we attempt to elucidate these forces, we wish to avoid two misunderstandings:

1 In talking of a "German character," we do not hypostatize a distinctive natural quality of "German man." We rather mean that, in the course of German history and under its specific conditions, the German people developed certain modes of thought and feeling which represent the distinct features of German culture.

2 Numerous studies have been made which trace the roots of National Socialism in German philosophy and literature since Luther, Herder or Nietzsche. If National Socialism is taken in its full scope and significance, the only result of such studies would the demonstration that the roots of National Socialism are to be found everywhere in German history since the Reformation. Apart from this demonstration, almost every German writer can be picked out as a precursor of some National Socialist conceptions, but almost every German writer can likewise be extolled as having contradicted these conceptions. The combing of German philosophy and literature for suitable quotations is without great value for the explanation of the psychological and emotional hold of the regime over the people.

5 THE PSYCHOLOGICAL FOUNDATIONS OF THE NEW MENTALITY

As a starting point, however, we may take Ernst Jünger's analysis of the "German character", perhaps the most intelligent National Socialist interpretation of the new mentality. In the opening sections of his book *Der Arbeiter*,[17] Jünger derives the decisive traits of the German character from the fact that the German has always been a "bad bourgeois," that the bourgeois standards of security, right and property have never taken roots in the German world, and that therefore the German cannot make any use of that form of liberty which has found its expression in the Declaration of the Rights of Man. Jünger proceeds to show that the ascent of National

---

17 Ernst Jünger, *Der Arbeiter*, Hamburg 1932.

Socialism signifies the truly German revolt against the bourgeois world and its culture (a world which, according to him, also includes Marxian socialism and the labor movement), a revolt which will replace the bourgeois by a new form of life, that of the "worker" who wields perfect power over a perfectly technical world, whose liberty is spontaneous service in the technical order, whose attitude is that of the soldier, and whose rationality that of totalitarian technology. Jünger's book is the prototype of the National Socialist union between mythology and technology, a book in which the world of "blood and soil" emerges as a gigantic, totally mechanized and rationalized enterprise, shaping the life of men to such an extent that they do with automatic precision the right operation at the right place and moment, a world of brute matter-of-factness without space and time for "ideals." But this totally technological world is born and fed by a supra-technological source which Jünger indicates by evoking the "anti-bourgeois" traits of the German character. Is there any justification for designating the mythological layer of the German mentality as anti-bourgeois?

It has always been noticed that the prototypical expressions of German culture stand antagonistic to the pattern of Western civilization. A qualitative difference prevails even within the same dimension: compare Luther with Calvin and the Puritans, German with French and Italian Gothic, Hölderlin with William Blake, German with French and British rationalism, the image of the medieval Kaiser with that of the French and British kings. The strange quality of German culture has been described by predicates such as transcendental, romantic, dynamic, formless, dark, pagan, *innerlich*, primordial. All these predicates seem to describe a pattern of thought and feeling that transcends the empirical reality, and transcends it on grounds which are themselves transcendental. It questions this reality by measuring it against a realm which is hard to grasp and define, a realm indicated by the specifically German concepts of nature, passion (*Leidenschaft*), *Seele*, *Geist*. In the clash between these two realms, the drives, impulses and actions of men become an explosive and destructive force, threatening the entire scheme of social restraint: friendship, loyalty, love, but also hatred and treachery assume elementary forms, and the heaven is strangely populated by Christian as well as ancient and pagan gods. The relationships among men and between men and nature are frightfully close and direct; it is as if all the intermediary social agencies are weakened and even abolished, and that these men, even if they don't talk in verses, talk a language which is foreign to threat of civilization. This in turn strengthens the metaphysical loneliness and longing prevalent in the representative works of German literature and art.

These traits are not confined to the works of art, literature and music, they may also be found in the actual behavior and customs of the German people. Here they appear in the still living remnants of folklore, in the predominance of the *Gemüt*, in the peculiar German attitude towards nature, in the proverbial German plainness and simplicity.[18]

The features we have just outlined may well contrast with the rationality, clarity, calculability and order which the Germans note as the "un-German" traits of Western civilization. And the German traits might even be classified as "anti-bourgeois" if we describe the bourgeois world in terms of its business philosophy, as a world of precariously balanced rights and obligations in which all subjective values are decidedly subordinated to the objective standards of supply and demand, exchange and contract. Jünger's emphasis on the anti-bourgeois elements of the German character, however, is nothing but an instrument of political propaganda, serving to placate the National Socialist order as an anti-capitalist revolution, and these traits must be interpreted on a quite different ground.

A rational justification for stressing the "anti-bourgeois" elements of the German character may be found in the fact that, up to the beginning of the twentieth century, the middle class has never integrally shaped the pattern of German society. The protracted rule of feudalism in Germany has brought it about that the forms of integration and control characteristic for middle-class society have never fully inculcated on the German population. Large sections of the German people were held under semi-feudal forms of integration and control: the relationships of domination and subordination were more direct, concrete and "personal" than under a system of integral commodity production and market economy. This might contribute to explain the "patriarchal" and authoritarian elements in these relationships. There was a strong inclination to regard government as a natural rather than social institution and to look upon it as something external to one's own personal life, something to which the individual could unconditionally submit without giving away his "personality." German individualism and authoritarianism, self-assurance and bureaucratism are two aspects of one and the same phenomenon: the restricted scope of middle class integration and control. As a consequence, the pragmatic and technological rationality typical for a developed middle class society was, prior to the rise of National Socialism, hardly representative for German society. Large sections of this society were never quite incorporated into the system

---

18 For the mythological layer of the German mentality and it concrete
     manifestations see the paper on "Private Morale in Germany," quoted above, and
     Max Horkheimer, "The End of Reason," in *Studies in Philosophy and Social
     Science*, vol. IX, 1941, no. 3, p. 383.

of rational domination and utilization of matter; they were not imbued with the "spirit of capitalism." An entire dimension of the German mind remained relatively free from the standards of utility, expediency and efficiency. This dimension became the resting place of the "soul," which retained a definite autarchy and autonomy as against the restrained and regimented social relationships.

A similar autarchy and autonomy was reserved to the realm of "nature." Nature plays a peculiar part in German thought and feeling. It is primarily viewed, not as mere matter to be mastered and utilized by man, nor as the mere environment or basis of the social process, but as the independent source of the most fundamental impulses, drives and desires of man. This rather pre-Christian, pagan conception of nature implies a strong protest against civilization: nature yields standards and values which frequently supersede those of civilization and thus constitute a sphere in which man lives "beyond good and evil." Man is as much nature as are the other organic beings, his "soul" is the token of his natural, sub-social essence. Compared with the "natural" realm of man, the entire network of social relationships becomes a rather secondary and foreign sphere. Man's true satisfaction spring from his natural essence, from the life of his soul which remains strikingly antagonistic to the life of civilization.[19]

Now this latent protest against civilization can easily be actualized and made the ferment of a social mass movement. In German history, we encounter time and again the strange merger between the "lower depths" of the soul and the lower depths of society, a merger which gives the numerous popular movements in modern German society their distinctive features. Such movements draw their force from the action, not of definite social groups which are united by a common rational interest, but of "masses" which are united on the basis of certain sub-social impulses and instincts. Ernst Krieck points to this fact when he says that National Socialism appealed to the "natural order" on which every social order rests, to the "instinctive depths" (*seelische Untergründe*) of folkdom, to the "lower regions of the soul" (*seelische Unterwelt*).[20] The appeal is to the physiological and emotional rather than the social status, and the masses which follow the appeal are constituted by cutting across the established lines of social stratification. Such a folkish movement is therefore easily manipulated and controlled "from above" and used for shifting the forms and weight of social domination without upsetting the prevailing scheme of

---

19 In *Mein Kampf*, Hitler uses the concept of nature almost exclusively for contrasting the "true" human relationships and institutions with their "perverted" forms in Christian civilization.

20 Ernst Krieck, *Nationalpolitische Erziehung*, Leipzig 1933, pp. 34, 37.

stratification. In forcing together the most diverging social groups, the folkish movement precludes the actualization of a definite social interest. Motivated by the desire to relieve the pressure of injustice and frustration, it is quickly diverted against other foes. For example, National Socialism incited the masses to fight against the Jews and the "capitalist plutocrats," but the extermination of the Jews and the decline of "finance capital" served to strengthen the hold of those industrial groups which were already predominant in German society.[21]

The manipulation of the folkish movement is rendered possible by the fact that the incited masses obtain an immediate compensation. The material compensations which we have already mentioned are supported and supplemented by not less important compensations for the frustrated impulses and instincts which carry the latent "discontent in civilization." They are released and satisfied in a form which perpetuates their frustration under aggravated forms of control. Their aggressive tendencies are directed against the feeble and the weak, the alien and the outsider, against the intelligentsia and the uncompromising critique, against luxury and conspicuous leisure. The quest for justice, liberty and happiness is perverted into revenge against those who seem to enjoy life, who don't toil, who are capable of expressing what they know and desire. The idea of human equality appears as the effort to level down what is above rather than to raise what is below. The National Socialist pageants imitate the grandeur of the heroic age of European society, or the glamour and pleasures of the pre-revolutionary French aristocracy which they extend in small doses to the little man. After each of these doses, he will more willingly perform his duties to the totalitarian state.[22]

All these gratifications are coupled with the emancipation of "nature" as against civilization. It is this appeal which makes them a ferment of aggression and, at the same time, an anodyne of submission. The "lower regions" are liberated from the restraint placed upon them by Christian civilization, but they are liberated in such a way that the released impulses strengthen the totalitarian forms of domination. The natural "right of the body" supersedes the claim of the intellect which threatens to penetrate the web of the "folkish community" and to discover its terroristic foundation.[23] The official care for health and beauty enhances the state's

---

21 Franz Neumann, *Behemoth*, p. 275; Hagen, *Will Germany Crack?*, p. 128.
22 For the utilization of the "new license" in the service of the National Socialist population- and labor policy see *Inside Germany Reports*, no. 19, 1941, p. 15, and *Juristische Wochenschrift*, LX, 1937, no. 48, p. 3057 f. With regard to the function of the National Socialist pageants, see E.R. Pope, *Munich Playground*, New York 1941, p. 40.
23 Hitler, *Mein Kampf*, Reynal and Hitchcock (ed.), p. 613 ff.

reservoir for labor and military power, and the "natural" attitude towards sex promotes the rise of the birth rate. The perversion of Christianity into a folkish religion gives man the good conscience for throwing off the moral restrictions on the struggle for life and power, for exterminating the weak and helpless, exploiting his fellow men and ruthlessly enlarging his living space.[24] But this neo-pagan naturalism performs an even farther-going function: it suppresses the desire to transcend the prevailing order to a juster and better one and delivers man in his entirety to the secular powers which rule over his life. It is this abolition of the faith into another order which is perhaps the most dangerous achievement of National Socialism and which makes the total offensive against this system on the psychological front a task requiring new and unusual weapons.

6 THE ABOLITION OF FAITH

From Italy come reports of a joke told about Mussolini. "He died and went to heaven, where a tremendous demonstration was given for him. . . . In the midst of this Signor Mussolini suddenly noticed that his crown was higher than God's and politely asked why. 'I gave your people one day of fasting a week,' God replied. 'You gave them seven. I gave them faith and you took it away. You are a greater man than I am.'" This joke might illustrate the psychological mechanisms which determine and perpetuate the morale in the Fascist countries. The last two sentences are more adequate to German than to Italian Fascism. Indeed, it was one of the most fundamental achievements of National Socialism, "to take away the faith from the people." Strange as it seems, the unabating loyalty of the human instruments of National Socialist domination rests, to a great extent, on the fact that National Socialism succeeded in abolishing their faith. We have mentioned the process of integral debunking and the cynical matter-of-factness which has gripped the German people. We may now attempt to interpret the significance of this process for the National Socialist morale.

The faith which National Socialism destroyed in order to build up its own system is not primarily religious belief. It is rather the faith in the standards and values of Christian civilization insofar as they have no immediate "cash value," that is to say, insofar as they have not been realized in the actual behavior of individuals, groups and nations. Not only the supreme tenets of Christianity, but also the avowed principles of secular ethics, business morale and politics belong to this category. It

---

24 *The Nazi Primer*, p. 73 f.

was the foremost undertaking of National Socialist propaganda to teach that the highly praised ideas of social justice, equality of opportunity, representation, international law and order are nothing but ideological manoeuvres, a thin veil behind which the interests of power and money continued to assert themselves.[25] National Socialism has hammered into the heads of its followers the idea that the world is an arena in which the most powerful and efficient competitor wins the race, and that he who wants to get along in this world can do no better than to forget about all transcendental ideas which hamper the efficient use of his means, and to orient himself to the brute matters of fact.[26] Ruthless utilization of all available means for getting a bigger share in the distribution of power – this, according to National Socialism, is the most adequate principle of individual as well as social and political action.[27]

In order to understand the rapid spread of this attitude among the German population, we must briefly consider the position of the labor movement. In Germany much more than in the Western countries this movement had gained its strength under the impact of Marxian theory and practice. The Social Democratic party and trade unions kept the fundamentals of Marxism in their program even when they abandoned them in practice. Under the Weimar Republic, Marxism had become an integral part of German culture: it was not only a faith but was also institutionalized in social and political organizations and operated in the home, family, youth movement, in the schools and even in the churches. Now if we compare the philosophy of the German with that of the American and British labor movement, we notice the extent to which the former was bound up with "transcendental" concepts and values. Dialectics, the notion of the inherent objective laws of capitalism and of the objective necessity of socialism, and the belief in the international solidarity of the proletariat had come to form a fixated conceptual and emotional structure. The pragmatic policy to fight for immediate advantages within the established social order never quite eradicated the "eschatological" hope for the

---

25 Hitler, *Mein Kampf*, p. 521 ff.; *My New Order*, p. 167; Alfred Rosenberg, *Der Mythus des 20ten Jahrhunderts*, München 1933, pp. 202 f., 540 f.
26 This attitude has been preached most convincingly by Oswald Spengler: "in the historical world there are no ideals, but only facts. There is no reason, no honesty, no equity, no final aim, but only facts, and anyone who does not realize this should write books on politics – let him not try to make politics" (*The Decline of the West*, transl. Charles Francis Atkinson, New York 1926, vol. II, p. 368). Accordingly the only thing that a nation needs in order to win in the international competition is "to be in form (in the sense of the modern sport)" – this is the very definition of the state (*Jahre der Entscheidung*, loc. cit., p. 24).
27 Hitler, *My New Order*, pp. 104 f., 200.

final realm of freedom. The more, however, the German labor movement was split into the labor aristocracy and bureaucracy on the one side, and the mass of the unemployed or temporarily employed on the other, the more the faith in the final realization of the goal gave way to the spirit of disillusioned matter-of-factness. In an economy with ten millions of unemployed, work turned from a right into a reward, conditioned upon efficient and compliant behavior. Moreover, through their actions, the leaders of the labor bureaucracy had promoted the process of debunking long before the National Socialists directed it. The ground was thus prepared for the National Socialist conquest: the plain facts of full employment and efficient control over the economic process apparently outweighed the remnants of the socialist faith.

As regards the farmers, the groups of small and middle business, the artisans and the white-collar workers, their susceptibility to the National Socialist matter-of-factness hardly needs any explanation. The Weimar Republic had not been able to halt or control the process of concentration which brought the weaker ever more rapidly under the power of the stronger. They had never been effectively influenced by the socialist movement, and they were ready to accept any constellation of facts which gave them security without expropriating their property.

Destruction of faith, however, is a purely negative process which might explain the dissolution of a system but hardly suffices to explain the construction and perseverance of a comprehensive order. And how can such a destructive process account for the building up and perpetuation of morale? Has not the abolished faith of the German people rather been replaced by another and even stronger faith, namely that in the charismatic leader and his unerring power? We shall take up the latter question first.

We may, of course, interpret the striking adherence of the German people to Hitler, and the even more striking coherence of the National Socialist system, by simply assuming an almost boundless faith in his person and regime. In doing so, however, we would obliterate the essential difference between the old and the new German mentality and inadequately describe the facts. Faith means trust beyond verification and compensation, trust which is not enforced and sustained from outside. The attitude of the majority of the German people shows none of these characteristics. True, they follow the regime also without direct terrorization, but they follow with a definite reservation. They trust the regime up to a certain point. This point is not the endurable limit of physiological and moral strain. It is rather the evident failure of the regime to keep the system of total regimentation going with full efficiency and capacity. Even so, however, the breaking point is not yet sufficiently defined. We must add an essential qualification: the breakdown of the regime must be concomitant with the actual chance to establish a democratic regime which can insure full employment and material security. We have mentioned this before and we come back to it time and again because it is the point at which the National Socialistic education comes to fruition. The disillusioned matter-of-factness and the destruction of faith here show forth as a powerful bond between the people and the regime. The people stands behind the regime on the ground of brute facts, not of ideals and promises. It will weigh the facts of the National Socialist order against the facts of that order which will follow the downfall of the regime. And the people will certainly prefer regimentation by its native rulers to regimentation by foreign rulers, and national independence to enslavement.[28]

That the strongest moral bond between the people and the regime is constituted by complete lack of faith rather than by faith is a fact pertinent to the question whether or not a distinction between the German people and the regime is justified. We must give this question a definite temporal qualification. At present, no clear-cut distinction is justified. To be sure, the regime functions only through institutionalized terror, but the majority of the population has accepted the language of facts and identified itself with the regime. The rest is done by integral organization. Identification, however, precisely because and insofar as it rests on the ground of brute matter-of-factness, can turn into hostility as soon as an actually new constellation of facts has been established. This turn might come in the form of a sudden shock, after which the National Socialist mentality appears eradicated and forgotten. But such a shock cannot be expected to come "by itself," it presupposes the creation of a new constellation of facts.

7   THE TRANSFORMATION OF MORALE INTO TECHNOLOGY

We may now attempt to answer the second question: how can the mere abolition of faith and a cynical matter-of-factness account for a morale which has so far insured the functioning of the National Socialist system and which has not broken down even under the extreme hardships and losses of the Russian war? The question must be approached without illusions and prejudices for it seems to lead to an answer which contradicts some of our most cherished ideas.

---

28 *Inside Germany Reports*, no. 15, 1940, p. 13; no. 21, 1942, p. 12 f.; Paul Hagen, *Will Germany Crack?*, p. 211.

What is called the morale or spirit of a people or an army apparently does not prevail on the German home and battle front. The available documents seem to warrant the conclusion that both fronts are permeated by the same disillusioned matter-of-factness. All the acts of utmost endurance and reliability, savage defiance and inhuman cruelty are performed with a likewise inhuman soberness, efficiency and smartness.[29] This is not faith in a "cause," although the "German cause" looms large in the struggle. But this German cause is like that of a giant machine or apparatus which constantly occupies the mind and feelings of its attendants, controls and dictates their actions and leaves them not the slightest refuge. In National Socialist Germany, all men are the mere appendices of the instruments of production, destruction and communication, and although these human appendices work with a high degree of initiative, spontaneity and even "personality," their individual performances are entirely adjusted to the operation of the machine (the sum total of their instruments) and timed and coordinated according to its requirements. And wherever men do not appear as the appendices of their instruments, they are the appendices of their functions (as deputy, *Gauleiter*, agent of the Gestapo, etc.) which have themselves been objectified and made a fixated part of the machine.[30] The system has a strictly *technical* structure, and its coherence is a strictly *technical* procedure. Morale has become a part of technology.

If we call the National Socialist morale a part of technology, we use the term technology in the literal sense. In technology, there is no truth and falsehood, right and wrong, good and evil – there is only adequacy and inadequacy to a pragmatic end. Accordingly, under National Socialism, all standards and values, all patterns of thought and behavior are dictated by the need for the incessant functioning of the machinery of production, destruction and domination. The leader and his supreme advisers form the board of directors, his deputies and generals are the owners and managers, the terror is the inevitable instrument of discipline, and the rest of the

---

29 See the report in the *New York Times*, March 15, 1942 on the diary of a German soldier on the Russian front: "I'm surprised it didn't affect me more to see a woman hanged. It even entertained me. Spent birthday digging up bodies and smashing in their faces. My sweetheart will say 'yes' when she hears how I hanged a Russian today."

30 Hans Frank, the German Governor General of Poland, has himself compared the National Socialist state with a perfectly functioning machine. According to him, the functioning of the state machine is a "matter of technique," and the entire realm of the state can be interpreted and understood in terms of "mathematical–physical method" (Technik des Staates," in *Zeitschrift der Akademie für Deutsches Recht*, 1941, no. 1, p. 2). This is far more than an analogy; it is an adequate description of the foundational mechanisms of the National Socialist state.

population makes up the vast army of the employees and workers. Within the whole, all parts are thoroughly synchronized; the enterprise is the only going enterprise, so no other possibility of living exists. There is actually no loophole for transgression and escape – neither physically nor mentally. Faith, ideals, morale in the traditional sense are things that can be dispensed with. The entire philosophy of blood and soil, of the folk and the leader has a strictly operational meaning. The new philosophy and religion is a highly flexible system of mental techniques and procedures, serving to prepare, announce and adjust the policy of the enterprise as well as its work methods, and to "sell" them in the most effective manner. It might thus be compared with a gigantic advertisement campaign and it is handled with the skill, logic and language of such a campaign. Of course, there is nothing to sell that has not to be bought anyway, but there are enough competing interests within the enterprise, and enough injustice and inequality in the distribution of earnings and spoils. Constant readjustment, compromise and bribing are therefore necessary.

The National Socialist transformation of moral standards and ideas into technical concepts and procedures was necessitated by the specific situation of German society after the First World War. In organizing the nation into a ruthlessly expanding industrial enterprise, National Socialism faced the task of making up, in a few years, for decades of backwardness. To be sure, the industrial apparatus of German industry did not lag behind that of the Western countries, on the contrary, already prior to the ascent of National Socialism, this apparatus was probably the most thoroughly rationalized and mechanized system in Europe. But this apparatus was constantly hampered by extreme difficulties of utilization, not only because of the economic crisis, but also because of the social legislation of the Republic and the pervasive "anti-capitalist" attitude of the population. We have tried to explain the latter by pointing to the abortive middle class revolution in Germany and the "anti-bourgeois" mentality prevalent among large strata of the German population. National Socialism has overcome this resistance by mobilizing the mythological layer of the German mind, which constituted the vast reservoir of the German protest against Christian civilization, and in doing so, it has made this protest one of the most powerful instruments for training in technological rationality.

The rationalization of the irrational (in which the latter preserves its force but lends it to the process of rationalization), this constant interplay between mythology and technology, "nature" and mechanization, metaphysics and matter-of-factness, "soul" and efficiency is the very center of the National Socialist mentality. It is this pattern which also determines the technicalization of morale. We may illustrate this by the shifting of taboos, which has been noted as a characteristic feature of National Socialism.

The destruction of the family, the attack on patriarchalic and mono-gamic standards and all the similar widely heralded undertakings play upon the latent "discontent" in civilization, the protest against its restraint and frustration. They appeal to the right of "nature," to the healthy and defamed drives of man, to the calamity of his monadic existence under the money system, to his longing for a true "community" in a world dominated by profit and exchange. They claim to reestablish the "natural" and direct rapports among men. They invoke the "soul" against soulless mechan-ization, folkish solidarity against paternal authority, the open air against the smugness of the "bourgeois home," the strong body against the pale intellect. This inevitably implied the granting of easier opportunities for satisfaction, but the new liberties are just as many duties to the population policy of the Reich; they are rewarded contributions to the campaign for a larger supply of labor and war power. Personal satisfaction has become a controlled political function, and its dangerous impact has been turned into a force of coherence. Racial restriction, the confinement and super-vision of leisure, the abolition of privacy, and the request for "purity" dilute and regulate the permitted pleasure. The omnipotent Party is a more effective authority than the *pater familias* and the moral law.[31]

The new authorities and taboos do not only operate as an external power, but have taken root in the very character of men and in their spon-taneous behavior. Men take what is offered to them and make the best of it. Here again, the cynical matter-of-factness of the new mentality plays into the hands of the National Socialist regime. In its school, men have learned to be shrewd, secretive and suspicious. They have no time and energy for sticking to their own thoughts and feelings. In a world where everyone works day and night on the instruments of conquest and des-truction, love, passion and faith are senseless and ridiculous. Educated to consider his body as the most precious source of that energy which feeds these instruments, the good Nazi treats the satisfaction of his drives as an act of mental and physiological hygiene, as a productive and profitable technique. His thought and emotions are turned into technical tools.

In view of the decisive role played by psychological and emotional mechanism in the technicalization of morale, it would be wrong to say that under National Socialism moral coherence has been replaced by

---

31 For the interpretation of the National Socialist abolition of taboos see the paper on "Private Morale in Germany," quoted above, and my paper "State and Individual under National Socialism."

organizational coherence. To be sure, without its omnipotent organization, National Socialism would immediately break down. This organization, however, is itself built up and perpetuated by psychological and emotional mechanisms which converge on the abolition of faith and training in cynical matter-of-factness. They have facilitated men's surrender to the all-embracing machinery of expansion and domination. Men are compelled to think, feel and talk in terms of things and functions which pertain exclusively to this machinery. They are forced into an existence which at any moment depends on the correct performance of required operational functions. The present has absorbed the past and the future. National Socialism has proclaimed the millennium of the Third Reich, but this millennium has constricted itself to the given moment, the here and now in which it can be finally conquered or finally lost. Men must concentrate on this given moment; the rest is up to "fate." History is condensed into the hour of National Socialism; everything else is either pre-history or fate. The notion of fate plays an increasingly important part in National Socialist propaganda:[32] it makes the regime the executioner of destiny itself, and the future of mankind depend on the all-out effort to utilize the weapons which the regime has provided.

8   THREE STAGES OF COUNTER-PROPAGANDA

Whereas the deadly opposition between National Socialism and Western civilization has been abundantly emphasized, adequate account has not been taken of the fact that the new German mentality with its cynical matter-of-factness and totalitarian technological rationality constitutes a not less fundamental break with the traditional German culture, which is regarded as a mere "swindle."[33] This is of extreme importance because the German people, which, for a decade, has been prevented from thinking in any other logic and talking in any other language than that of their masters, will not be accessible to the appeal of its traditional logic and language. The attack on the National Socialist mentality must therefore develop new forms of infiltration, forms which dissolve this mentality by responding to it.

---

32 Cf. Hitler's and Goebbel's speeches after the German setbacks in Russia.
33 Ernst Krieck, "Kulturpleite," in *Volk im Werden*, no. 5, 1933, pp. 69 and 71: "Radical criticism makes it clear that so-called culture has become completely inessential and never represents a higher value." "Finally, let us see simply, truly and accurately here too, so that the growing strength and health of the nation should not be vitiated by this swindle, culture."

In the following sections, we shall make a few suggestions for the development of such a counter-language. We shall attempt to sketch its outline at three different stages of the attack:

1 the language of facts,
2 the language of recollection,
3 the language of re-education.

1 The Language of Facts

The notion that the present war is primarily a war between ideologies and philosophies is detrimental to any effective counter-propaganda. In the long process of integral debunking, the German people have been trained to consider everything that is not corroborated by plain facts as an ideology in the sense of an intentional distortion of facts by vested interests. Consequently, the appeal to the Rights of Man, the democratic liberties, the dignity of man, the laws of morality, etc. is, to the German ears, just as suspicious and strange as the National Socialist philosophy is to our ears. What the German people understands and acknowledges is facts, and it craves for facts and factual achievements. This brings the German mentality much closer to the Western mind than it has ever been and builds the first bridge of communication between the two hostile worlds.

The counter-propaganda must speak the pragmatic language of facts, and, fortunately, there are enough facts to be used against the facts of National Socialism. The productive capacity and the war potential of the United Nations, their standard of living, their effective control over prices and profits, the way in which they have conquered unemployment and transformed the economic system without crushing the labor movement – all this can be brought to the knowledge of the German people in such a manner that it dwarfs and indicts the National Socialist "achievements." Statistics is not the right method for transmitting such facts, brief first hand reports on incidents in the factories, shipyards, streets and shops, on military and economic actions will do the job much better.

Everything, however, depends on the setting in which the facts are placed, that is to say, on what is to be made of them in the progress and after the termination of the war. This, of course, at present goes beyond the language of facts and belongs to another stage in the development of counter-propaganda which we shall try to indicate later on. But since the general setting of the facts must naturally also determine their presentation, we wish to mention here at least one decisive factor.

We have said that, at present, a clear-cut distinction between the German people and the regime is not yet justified. Insofar as the counter-propaganda is directed to the majority of the German people and not to particular social groups (the latter form must be discussed separately), it must take this majority as it presently is, namely, as tied up with the regime. Consequently, there must not be the slightest doubt that the United Nations are all out to wage the war until National Socialism is finally destroyed, together with the entire system which it set up. In other words, there must not be the slightest doubt that no shift within the system, but only the abolition of the system itself will end the war. And here, the question which alone matters to the German people is, what will happen after the war? Will they only exchange one form of oppression and regimentation for another one? We have pointed to the catastrophic fatalism in which the National Socialist matter-of-factness culminates: the only alternative is complete annihilation. The more the war progresses, the more is the German mind possessed by this conception, and the last speeches of the National Socialist leaders were strikingly dominated by it. It is perhaps the strongest anti-toxin against any counter-propaganda. At present, only a negative treatment might be possible: the official refutation of all imperialist programs, the extension of the principle of self-determination and representative government, the fight against monopolistic appropriation of raw materials and markets.

Obviously strong "anti-capitalistic" feelings prevail among the majority of the German population. The slogan of the "proletarian nations" and the war against the "plutocrats" is probably the most popular National Socialist parole.[34] To be sure, the regimentation of the German war economy hardly conceals the fact that the German "plutocrats" have retained and even strengthened their power, and the National Socialist propaganda is carefully confined to the "capitalism" in other countries. Moreover, the anti-capitalist feelings of the majority of the German people (in contrast to those of the active opposition) are restricted to large scale property and "finance capital" and are not at all hostile to private property. On the contrary, they dream of the restoration of small scale property into its former right and of the abolition of monopolistic "expropriation." Here, the counter-propaganda may again hold facts against facts. Without any form of terror, economic development in the Western countries

---

34 The early National Socialist propaganda against the treaty of Versailles and the "November Criminals" was skilfully linked with an appeal to the anti-capitalist tendencies among the German population (Hitler, *Mein Kampf*, p. 530 ff.). Hitler has resumed the anti-capitalist propaganda with his speech of December 10, 1940 (*My New Order*, p. 873 ff.).

tends to diminish the import of finance and merchant capital in favor of industry. "Wall Street" is no longer the symbol of the actual distribution of power. And, most important, the democratic government itself has taken up the struggle against detrimental monopolistic concentration and practices. The reports of the Congressional investigation committees, and the measures taken and proposed by the various governmental agencies provide the adequate framework for the presentation of facts that may counteract the National Socialist assertions. They can be used to show that the democratic countries are more efficient in their fight against the encroachment of monopolistic interests upon the general welfare than the Fascist countries.

The Germans still fear and respect American efficiency as perhaps the only adversary of equal worth. The union between superior efficiency and democracy must be the central proposition of the logic and language of facts. It can be verified not only on the battle – but also on the home front. The extent of liberty and satisfaction open to the democratic peoples in the midst of total war can be strikingly documented (photographs, newspapers). These liberties and satisfactions should be contrasted with the regimented "purity" and poverty of National Socialist "pleasures." It can be furthermore shown how, in the democracies, they join forces with military strength, full capacity and a better standard of living, and how they are not reserved to a few privileged groups.

2   The Language of Recollection

The second step in the development of a counter-language might be characterized as a gradual softening up and disintegration of that cynical matter-of-factness which binds the German people to the regime. This step can only be made on the ground of matter-of-factness itself, that is to say, it presupposes a steady increase in the war efforts of the United Nations and in the difficulties and setbacks of the National Socialist regime. Then, the language of facts can be supported and supplemented by another language which we might call the language of recollection or remembrance.

Recollection of the past was one of the strongest psychological implements of National Socialist propaganda. We have said that, in National Socialist Germany, the present has absorbed the past, but the latter has been preserved in the former which styles itself as the final conquest of the past. The proverbial Fourteen Years which Hitler hammered time and again into his audience was more than a trick. This magic formula opened the gates through which the frustrations, miseries and defeats of the past broke into the present so the people sought refuge with him who consecrated the past. We have mentioned the catastrophic conception of the future in National Socialism, we now encounter a likewise catastrophic conception of the past. The present is ground between these two catastrophes, and that is why the German people seems to be blind to what is actually happening. We have pointed to the fact that National Socialism has created an outlet for the discontent in the past and turned this discontent into a ferment of cohesion and control. The Fourteen Years is the most concrete and effective symbol of discontent, the more effective because it discredits, not authoritarian, but democratic government.

The grip of the past over the present might provide a lever which might help to break up the present. Used as such a lever, remembrance has the function to resurrect images which lighten up the present terror. For the past was not only frustration and misery, but also the promise of freedom. Unnumbered scores or Germans have given their blood to make good this promise. The German people has not forgotten, neither the traitors nor the martyrs of freedom. Their names are defamed, and loyalty to them is punished by death and torture. But there might be another form of liberating the living memory, namely, the form of art. To lighten up the reality by the promise of freedom and happiness has always been an essential function of art, and in the present struggle, this function might obtain a new significance.

The role of art in political propaganda is one of the most difficult problems, and a wrong conception might do more harm than the refusal to use this weapon. Weapons are so scarce, however, that it might be allowed to venture a few suggestions. The broadcasting of "classical masterpieces" probably has very little effect. Apart from the fact that there are excellent performances of such works even in National Socialist Germany, these works do not speak the language of recollection to the German ears. To the new German mentality, they have no "truth value": they are not apprehended as images of real promises and potentialities. Moreover, they do no longer possess that quality of "estrangement" which is constitutive for the political function of art. To fulfill this function, the work of art must be alien to the reality which it indicts, alien to such an extent that it cannot be reconciled with the reality, but at the same time, it must appeal to those who suffer from the reality and speak their undistorted language. Today, the "political" work of art must illuminate at one stroke the absolute incompatibility of the prevailing reality with the hopes and potentialities of men. Classical art, however, has been made part and parcel of the official "culture" in National Socialist Germany, and in this process, the "classics" have been domesticated and reconciled with the prevalent pattern of thought and feeling. Insofar as they have withstood the process of domestication, they have been killed by the spirit of matter-of-factness which accepts art as a prescribed stimulant and recreation. It is significant that Hitler's "philosophy of art" centers around this special expediency value of art.[35] He uses it as a tonic and adornment of submission.

The power of art to serve as an anti-Fascist weapon depends on the strength with which it speaks the truth, unconditionally and without compromise. This simple fact implies a fundamental change in the form structure of art. Art can no longer "depict" reality, for the latter has passed beyond the reaches of adequate "aesthetic" representation. The terror as well as the sufferings of those who resist it is greater than the force of artistic imagination. But the laws which govern this reality, and the promises and potentialities which they have destroyed can be revealed in another form, and this form too belongs to the domain of art. For they can be most adequately represented when they are represented in all their phantastic "irreality." Our language and our senses were tuned to a world in which the notion "reality" comprised the dark as well as the light sides of existence, freedom as well as frustration, hope as well as despair. In this sense, our language and our senses transcended reality even if they described it. In contrast, National Socialism has done away with the transcending elements in thought and perception; consequently, its world cannot be represented and reproduced in the traditional forms. In terms of these forms, the world of National Socialism is an "irreal" world. The whole truth on this world can be told only in a language not loaded with the reconciliatory hopes and promises of culture, or, in a language which contains these hopes and promises in precisely that satanic form in which National Socialism has realized them. For example, the true story of Hitler's ascent to power may be brought out most effectively in the form of a cheap gangster melodrama with a Shakespearean plot of collusion, murder, treachery and seduction (the German poet Bertolt Brecht has made such an attempt).

3 The Language of Re-education

The light that the language of recollection can flash upon the past and the present can only have a supporting value but can neither create nor

---

35 *Die Reden Hitlers am Parteitag der Freiheit 1935*, München 1935, pp. 36, 40.

transform the facts on which everything depends. The same holds true for the third step in the development of a counter-language, namely, re-education.

Responsible American and British statesmen have frequently expressed the view that the mere restoration of the status quo would not insure the annihilation of National Socialism. Henry Wallace's statement that the "revolution of the past 150 years has not been completed," and that "this revolution cannot stop until freedom from want has actually been attained," and Sumner Welles' declaration that "the age of imperialism is ended" take account of this fact.[36] It must not be overlooked that National Socialism has done what it could do in order to destroy the very notion of the status quo in the mind of the German people, and the effects of this undertaking can hardly be obliterated.[37] At this point, the break between the old and the new Germany is perhaps the sharpest. Germany cannot go back, even if she wants to – not only because of the objective conditions of the international economic development. The National Socialist education to technological rationality and efficiency has – much more than the loudly heralded shifting of traditional taboos – changed the thought and behavior pattern of men in all strata of the population. The traditional German "inwardness" and "romanticism" which also expressed the political immaturity of large sectors of the population have been destroyed by their National Socialist mobilization.

Under the impact of that integral politicalization to which National Socialism subjects them, the German people may become ripe for political self-determination – quite against the will of its rulers. The people has seen how easy it was for the National Socialist gang to take over and perform the administrative functions which had been the privilege of a firmly entrenched privileged group, especially trained in performing these functions. The governed masses have experienced how effectively this gang has "planned" and regimented the productive and distributive process, handled the threat of inflation and other economic disturbances, and geared the industrial apparatus to full capacity. National Socialism has deprived the supreme administrative activities of the exalted qualities which removed them from the eyes and hands of the governed population, and has made them a normal business. To be sure, National Socialism has at the same time reserved this business to its own racket, but this reservation is a matter of mere power, not of special ability and ingenuity. And this power can be broken. Moreover, the matter-of-factness in which the people has been

---

36 *P.M.*, May 10, 1942; *New York Times*, May 31, 1942.
37 Paul Hagen, *Will Germany Crack?*, p. 246.

trained may sharpen its mind for the striking contradiction between the rationalized industrial apparatus and its totalitarian restriction, between the gigantic productive power and the use to which it is put, between the potential wealth and the actual terror.

It might happen, however, that all this knowledge and insight are choked to death. Without adequate means for their realization, they must remain powerless. It is a vain hope to wait for the self-dissolution of the National Socialist system. If the new German mentality contains any liberating forces, they can be released only in the successful struggle against the regime. Re-education, that is, the emancipation and cultivation of these forces, is itself an element in this struggle.

National Socialism perpetuates its power by playing off real security against potential freedom. To the German masses, totalitarian security was more real than the democratic liberties they had enjoyed under the Weimar Republic. It has been a fundamental principle of National Socialist propaganda to teach the incompatibility between (democratic) liberty and security, between the Rights of Man and full employment, between equality of opportunity and equality of power. Democracy, liberty, unemployment and poverty have been welded together into one terrifying entity. Consequently, the appeal to democratic freedom appears as equivalent to the appeal to insecurity and unemployment. The spokesmen of the United Nations have taken this fact into account and oriented their appeal to the notion of "general security" as the standard of the post-war order. In line with this policy, any re-education of the German masses must aim at severing the psychological link between security and authoritarianism, full employment and totalitarian regimentation. The submissive and authoritarian character of man under the Nazi system is not an unchangeable natural property but a historical form of thought and behavior, concomitant with the transformation of large scale industry into a directly political dominion. This character will therefore dissolve when the social forces are defeated which are responsible for the transformation of industrial into authoritarian society. In National Socialist Germany, these forces are clearly distinguishable: they are the great industrial combines on which the economic organization of the Reich centers, and the upper strata of the governmental and party bureaucracy. The breaking up of their dominion is the prerequisite and the chief content of re-education.

Re-education is thus more than the traditional idea of education which "reflects the truth of a preceding age rather than the coming age."[38] Re-education is primarily to teach people "to produce more food and more

---

38 Henry Wallace, in *P.M.*, June 7, 1942.

goods," and to produce them for consumption. This is indeed something that must be taught and learned. For in indoctrinating the masses with the philosophy of irrational sacrifice, toil and privation, National Socialism has rationalized the economy of scarcity which it perpetuates. Economic reconstruction must therefore be accompanied by education to "freedom from want," which, in National Socialist society, has again become a nonsensical idea.

9 DIFFERENTIATION OF COUNTER-PROPAGANDA

We have so far not differentiated our discussion of counter-propaganda according to the various groups of the German population to which it should be directed. We have said that the enforced "unification" of the German people allows of a large range of undifferentiated propaganda, but the more the war progresses and with it the internal antagonism of National Socialist society, the more will such a differentiation be imperative.

Two groups are from the beginning to be excluded from the objects of counter-propaganda, namely, the social pillars of the regime among large scale industry, and the governmental bureaucracy. They will lose everything with the downfall of the regime, and they can expect no gains from any other regime. To be sure, they will try to "adjust" themselves, but under any form of government, they will form the nucleus of totalitarianism.[39] Apart from this group, the active opposition to the National Socialist system likewise stands outside the reaches of propaganda in the strict sense. This opposition knows what to do. The only things it can get from outside are factual information on matters beyond their own experience, and instruments for sabotage and counter-terror.

There remain the groups of middle and small business, the free professions, the farmers and large strata of the workers. Partly overlapping with them, but constituting a rather firmly coherent mass of followers is the lower party bureaucracy and the actual party members. It is in these groups that the new mentality has taken its deepest roots, and it can be dissolved only by appealing to their most immediate and material interest.

National Socialism has destroyed the independence of small and middle business and transformed its members into minor officials, employees or workers.[40] In these positions, they participate in the new security. In

---

39 Paul Hagen, pp. 244–7.

view of the progressing technological rationalization in all industrial countries, their restoration into their former independent position appears as a retrogressive policy. What they mostly dread, is their decline into the "proletariat." They might even prefer authoritarian security to the insecure freedom of small scale enterprise. They know that the old "normalcy" cannot return. They want to see that the democratic plan for a post-war economy does not deliver them to the dominion of large scale industry nor make them proletarians, that they are not to be submerged in the "free flow of economic goods". A planned economy in which they have their definite place will appeal to them much more than the promise of old normalcy and "business as usual."

In the free professions, however, freedom was much more than an "ideological" value: it constituted the very essence of the profession itself. Consequently, free professions do not exist in National Socialist Germany, and in their case, the standard of general security must be supplemented by the appeal to their former freedom. They are the democratic professions par excellence, wholly dependent on freedom of speech, research, and freedom of the press.

As regards those strata of the working population (including the farmers) which do not belong to the active opposition, the strongest appeal is full employment and a higher standard of living. National Socialism, while carefully avoiding lowering the latter too conspicuously, has been compelled to combine full employment with a steady intensification and extension of work. Counter-propaganda can emphasize the contradiction between the "folkish community" and the privileged position of the small ruling groups which made their enslavement necessary, but it can do little to insure the German workers that a democratic peace economy will be able to sever the link between full employment and enslavement. The problem of full employment, however, is not only an economic but also a political one. The United Nations have declared time and again that the post-war world must be a "planned" world. The content and the functioning of the new plan will depend on the new distribution of power and on the form of government which the liberated people obtain. If the German workers believe that they will have an adequate share in the new distribution of power, that they will be the subjects and not only the objects of the plan, then a decisive step has been made to win them to the cause of democracy.

---

40 Franz Neumann, *Behemoth*, p. 264 f.; *Inside Germany Reports*, no. 10, 1940, p. 10.

SUPPLEMENT ONE†

The following remarks are based upon the assumptions outlined in my memorandum on the New German Mentality, in the memorandum on *Stimmung* and *Haltung*, and in your memorandum on *German Popular Psychology And Its Implications for Propaganda Policy*.

Nothwithstanding the essential differences between your interpretation and mine, we agree in that we recognize a specific Nazi mentality which requires a specific new approach in propaganda. The term *Haltung* might be a useful abbreviation for characterizing this mentality. I think we further agree that the basic element in the new propaganda approach must be the *"language of facts"* as opposed to appeals to "morale," anticipations of gratification and punishment, promises, and so on. The point may now have been reached where the language of facts may be supplemented by other appeals, but it must still remain their actual basis. To speak the language of facts does not mean to restrict propaganda to news broadcasts, but it means that all broadcasts must be built around "fact symbols." The samples of the *German Labor Show* which you made available to me contain numerous examples of a perfect use of the "language of facts." (I mention only the striking contrast between the American and the German working hours and the excellent treatment of the problem of foreign workers.) Furthermore they avoid the cardinal mistake of taking the Nazi ideology seriously and refuting it on an objective level. At the same time, however, they frequently contradict their own standard and fail to reach the vulnerable spots of the Nazi mentality.

---

† This text is without title and date in the Marcuse archives (#119.02). It mentions his report on "The New German Mentality" and other memoranda, and is presumably part of his work with the Office of War Information between 1942 and March 1943.

The broadcasts are full of sentences such as "Der Tag rückt unerbittlich und unaufhaltsam näher . . . ," "Das muss vereitelt werden! Die Kriegs-verlängerungspläne Hitlers müssen zunichte gemacht werden," "Der Tag der Abrechnung ist nicht mehr fern." This purely anticipatory language renounces all possible effect on the German workers because it is entirely a language of assurances and expectations which are neither implemented nor mediated by facts and fact symbols. To the German workers, it might all too easily appear as wishful thinking and, what is worse, as the same kind of wishful thinking as they themselves indulge in without being able to realize their wishes. This might make us their partners in weakness rather than strength.

We may assume that the Nazi *Haltung* has been imposed upon the German workers just as well as upon the German middle classes and the German youth. The bulk of the German workers have accepted the Nazi system; they try to put up with it and "to stick it out." They still feel that "they are all in the same boat;" they wait for whatever is going to happen. This attitude is probably perpetuated by brute terror, but it still prevails,[1] and it cannot be destroyed by appeals and exhortations to freedom and by picturing the blessings of democracy. For the German workers think of democracy chiefly in terms of the Weimar Republic, that is to say, in terms of incessant parliamentary feuds, internal strife, inflation, unemployment and insecurity. And the memory of their former rights and liberties has no liberating appeal to them as long as these are known and understood in terms of the past. Nor can they become symbols of liberation if they are presented as gifts of the future, for the facts of the past will overshadow the future until these promises have become a reality.

If I speak of the "bulk" of the German workers, I exclude those groups which keep alive the *Marxian* tradition of German labor. We know nothing about their strength, but however great it might be, these groups do not need any propaganda in the sense in which it can be directed to the other strata. The only broadcasts that, to them, might be worth listening to are perhaps those transmitting factual information on events and measures beyond their range of experience and knowledge (for example, details on the connection between big business and the Nazi party, German investments abroad, the conditions in the occupied countries).

I shall venture a few suggestions on the propaganda approach to the German workers by singling out some passages from the samples at hand.

---

1 The fact that there has been no noticeable decline in German production is in itself sufficient evidence for this assumption, which is also corroborated by reports from Germany and by the terror of Nazi propaganda.

The broadcasts frequently contrast social progress and social legislation in America and Germany. To the German workers, this must appear as crude and false propaganda. The German papers are full of descriptions of American home conditions (mostly taken from American newspapers and magazines). They know of the housing conditions in the new war centers, the discrimination against Negroes, the lack of a comprehensive social insurance. On the other hand, Nazi Germany maintains a general social insurance system, and the housing conditions of German workers have certainly not deteriorated. A sentence to the effect "dass es in Deutschland unter Hitler abwärts ging" is perhaps for most of them without any meaning. They have had full employment ever since 1934. Of course, food is scarce; they can't buy anything, and they work 10, 12 and 14 hours a day, but they think they are in a war for their very existence. Under these circumstances, the contrasting of social progress in America and social decline in Germany cannot provoke anything but a hostile or cynical reaction.

The broadcasts call upon the German workers to help the United Nations to overthrow the Hitler regime and to liberate Germany from the "tyrant." They talk about the "*Mission*" of the German workers. But this is what Hitler keeps telling them all the time! We should be most careful *not* to exhort the German workers to revolt or even to help us in defeating Hitler, because this might easily provoke the answer that it is a poor trick to call for revolt from a safe port 3000 miles away. And the request for "help" might easily meet the reply that we did not do anything to help the German workers in 1933–34 and have therefore no right to expect their help now.

We should furthermore avoid talking about the "Volk, das unter dem eisernen Joch der Hitlerschen Diktatur seufzt," and about the "Mächte der Unwissenheit der Unduldsamkeit, der Sklaverei und des Krieges," which we want to destroy "ein für allemal." This language suggests the holiday speeches of the old *Bonze*; its vocabulary can only evoke laughter or horror. The listener might not even understand what we are talking about. We encounter here one of the most serious problems involved in broadcasts to Nazi Germany. We cannot a priori operate on the assumption that, to the average Aryan German citizen, the Hitler regime and the Gestapo convey the same terror that they convey to us and to the active opposition in Germany. To them, the Gestapo is hardly more real or terrifying than the F.B.I. is to the average American citizen. They know that the Hitler regime is a dictatorship, but it has for them no more connotations of terror than the Republic which had free elections and organizations, but also unemployment and inflation.

This leads immediately to the question of the *war and peace aims*, and how to formulate them so that they might appeal to the German workers. The democratic liberties would not do. Nor would the "Zusammenschluss der Arbeiter in freien Gewerkschaften." Apart from the fact that, in the minds of the German workers, the trade unions are inseparably linked with a system that could not prevent the rise of Nazism and could not give them security, it is doubtful whether the trade unions will be the best symbol for the future democratic society in Germany. The German workers have been constantly fed with stories about the "racketeering" and the spoils system in the American unions, and their belief in these stories cannot be shaken by simply picturing the American unions as a model of freedom. All peace aims are necessarily vague anticipations of the future which can carry little weight with the German worker who is entirely preoccupied with the totalitarian impact of present facts. There is only one way to break this preoccupation, namely, to activize their desire to end the war as quickly as possible. And this, again, cannot be done by promises of invasion and exhortations to help, but only in the "language of facts," by showing them that the Hitler regime is bound to continue the war because it is bound to defend and perpetuate the economic exploitation and spoliation of the European continent in the interest of Nazi big business. Such a demonstration could destroy the conviction that the German workers fight for the independence and freedom of the German *people*, and that they will enjoy security and a rising standard of living.

To achieve this purpose, the demonstration must proceed strictly in terms of factual information. The material available is abundant. Three main lines could be followed:

1 show the actual expansion of Nazi big business in the occupied and controlled countries, the investments in the East, in the Balkans, in Western Europe; give detailed information on the rapid growth of the Dye Trust, the Continental Oil Corporation, the textile industry;
2 show that Hitler's economic policy and, to a great extent, even his political and social measures increasingly serve to strengthen and enlarge the dominion of Nazi big business;
3 show the ever increasing amalgamation between the Nazi party and big business; show that the "heroic" party and S.S. leaders have acquired substantial business interests.

By this method, the image of the war as one for Germany's national existence might slowly and gradually be transformed into the image of a war for securing the riches of the bosses in the Nazi party and in big business, and the belief in the *Volksgemeinchaft* (which may still exist among large strata of the German masses) might turn into a realization of the inevitably growing inequality of sacrifices and rewards. (It is unfortunate that the broadcasts, in their treatment of the Total Mobilization, did not seize upon the striking facts which demonstrate this inequality.)

SUPPLEMENT TWO[†]

An analysis of the internal conditions in Germany seems to warrant the assumption that all those social groups which do not directly benefit from the Nazi policy (e.g. the party bureaucracy, the big industrialists and landowners, the military) have lost their faith in the New Order. This does not mean a breakdown of German morale. Apart from the fact that the Nazi regime can, to a great extent, dispense with public and private morale (which has been replaced by technological and organizational coherence), the population is bound to the regime by "being in the same boat," and as long as the boat is afloat, opposition would simply be suicidal. But the change in the attitude of the German population indicates how this population can be mobilized for active collaboration with the United Nations after the military defeat of the Nazis.

We are here concerned with only one aspect of this problem, namely how the presentation of the enemy to the American people could prepare and expedite such mobilization. This is not a matter of the far future, for the willingness of the German people to collaborate with the United Nations will greatly depend upon the attitude of the American people toward Germany during the decisive stages of the war.

The attitude of the German masses toward the Americans is ambivalent – they fear them as their most dangerous enemy, but they also admire them and are ready to emulate them. The reason for this is that, during the last

† This text is without title and date in the Marcuse archives (#129.00). The text is typed in a script similar to other Marcuse manuscripts of the period, is close in content to "The New German Mentality," and describes projects that Marcuse was involved in, thus it is fair to conclude that the text is by Marcuse. It mentions his report on "The New German Mentality" and was written presumably as part of his work with the office of War Information between December 1942 and March 1943.

decade and despite the obvious ideological conflict, the gap between German and American "culture" has been increasingly bridged. The Nazi regime itself, with its technocratic and pragmatic policy, has accelerated this process. We may safely assume that large strata of the German population are anxiously looking to the Americans, watching for every sign that might reveal whether and how the Americans understand their situation and what policy they intend to follow. The American people, on the other hand, seems not sufficiently aware of the nature of an enemy who might – almost overnight – become a prospective ally in the struggle against Nazism. They either identify the German people with the Nazis, or regard the Nazis as "accidental" foes, or make distinctions which are far too narrow and do not correspond to the facts. Consequently, there is, on the one hand, a tendency of objective and impartial appraisal which neutralizes the terror of the enemy and hampers the resolution to destroy him with all available means, a psychological aloofness which grants the Nazis more than even the Germans grant them, and, on the other hand, a tendency to extend Nazism indiscriminately to everything that is German, fostering an attitude which likewise fails to meet the real enemy.

The following paragraphs venture a few suggestions on how the presentation of the enemy to the American people might counteract these tendencies.

1 The significance of a **supreme symbol** of the enemy can hardly be over-rated. The more complicated and diffuse the actual fronts in the global war are (Bolshevist Russia and the victims of "imperialism" in the same camp as the "imperialist plutocracies"), the more imperative it is to have a striking symbol designating the real enemy. Such a symbol must be as much as possible loaded with the full terror and strength of the enemy, and at the same time clearly define scope and dominion as against his "coordinated" victims. The term "axis" is too technical and emotionally neutral; "totalitarianism" has the same disadvantage and is too abstract and vague. "Dictatorship" obliterates the difference between Germany and Russia. "Tyranny" and "Despotism" shift the emphasis from the social and economic reality to a narrow political form and acquit the social groups and forces which support and sustain the political form. "Nazis" and "Nazism" (*not* National Socialism) still seem to be the most adequate symbols. They contain in their very sound and structure something of that barbaric hate and horror which characterize their referents. Moreover, they are free from the national and socialist illusions which their unabridged form still might convey. The disadvantages of this symbol are obvious: it lacks comprehensiveness since it is confined to the German regime. But

Italy and France are even more openly Nazified and will certainly be knocked out of war with the defeat of Germany. With regard to Japan, the term "Japs" offers a neutral analogy.

2 The supreme symbol is of little effect if it is paralyzed by **conflicting symbols**. The Russians are frequently presented as "Reds," although to many this term conveys the same feelings as "Nazis" (whereas the term "Red Army" has by now acquired a different connotation). Furthermore, the Reich, to speak of the Führer or Leader, the Elite Guard, the Labor Front, etc., likewise amounts to paralyze the enemy symbols by using conflicting symbols which take over the Nazi ideology instead of denying it. They should be replaced by terms which refer to the reality of Nazism, for example, Hitler, his terroristic gang or bodyguard, the compulsory labor organization, etc.

3 The most serious shortcoming of the terms "Nazi" and "Nazism" lies in the fact that they do not allow of any **differentiation** between the regime, its followers, and its objects. In reporting on the enemy, the symbol must therefore be broken down into more concrete terms designating the actual components of Nazism. Such a differentiation must fulfill the double purpose of (a) singling out those social groups which are, by virtue of their conditions and interest, the nuclei of post-war reconstruction, and (b) concentrating the hate against the enemy and the resolution to destroy him on those groups which form the backbone of Nazism. In both cases, the differentiation must clearly indicate the policy the United Nations intend to follow concerning post-war Europe.

A differentiating presentation of the enemy along those lines is furthermore complicated by the fact that the distinction between the active supporters of Nazism, the followers, the masses, and the active opposition cuts across the demarcation lines of social stratification. Apart from the big industrialists and the top strata of the party and state bureaucracy amalgamated with them, none of the traditional social groups can be desig-nated as definitely Nazi or anti-Nazi. The regime has certainly accelerated the polarization of society into the ruling cliques (which are not identical with the old ruling class) and the regimented and manipulated masses, but the latter have little in common with the conception of a proletarian opposition. The former "labor aristocracy" has been transformed, greatly expanded, and absorbed into the Nazi bureaucracy. Except for the active underground opposition, the workers are bound to the regime by the ties of terror, security and fear. Those groups of the middle classes which have not been dissolved by the process of concentration and rationalization have been coordinated, economically as well as psychologically, with the policy of the regime, but they cannot be counted among its "natural" supporters.

The easiest method of differentiation seems to be that of singling out the *Nazi party* as the actual criminal. This method is fallacious, however, for three reasons: (1) The anonymity of the party covers up the strongest and most active forces behind the regime, namely, the big industrialists and the remnants of the old political bureaucracy. (2) Party membership as such does not testify to active Nazism since it was in many cases a matter of expediency or compulsion. (3) With the downfall of the regime, the party will disappear so quickly and so thoroughly that it will be hard, with the exception of the well known top figures, to identify a single party man. And conversely, many people who did not play any role in the party but who are bound to the social and economic foundations of Nazism will style themselves as anti-Nazi.

Under these circumstances, the only firm ground for a discriminating presentation is provided by the social and economic structure of Nazism itself. This means that the presentation should, at every possible occasion, expose the real beneficiaries and instigators of Nazi policies, measures and decrees. Such a procedure would apply the policy of "divide and conquer" to those who handled it so skilfully against the democracies, and since, under the thin veil of the folkish community, the social antagonisms in Germany are much more fundamental than in the democratic countries, the exposure of these antagonisms promises to be most effective. We want to give only two examples: (1) In reporting on the measures against the Jews, almost exclusive emphasis was laid on the part played by the S.S. and the party, on their cruelty, and on the passive resistance of the masses. But at least as much space should be devoted to showing that the actual beneficiaries of these measures were, not the small merchants and traders, but big business itself. Concrete instances could easily be given. It would then become manifest that the Nazi policy serves to expropriate and enslave entire strata of the "Aryan" population, and the more or less hidden sympathy many Nazi measures have found outside Germany could be destroyed. (2) American newspapers have frequently heralded the restrictions placed by the Nazi regime upon the freedom of capital, investment and profit, but it has rarely been shown how, despite these restrictions, the position of the "economic royalists" has been strengthened rather than weakened, and that they still hold the key jobs in the Nazi economy. A comparison between the earnings of the big German corporations and the real wage level would provide good illustrative material. This is one of the cases where the presentation, in order to fulfill its purpose, must be made in terms of the institutions involved rather than in terms of certain persons or agents. The Nazi policy might hit the latter, restrain their movement, curtail their influence, while nevertheless enhancing the power of the great combines, trusts and cartels.

4 The presentation of the **German arms** offers a special problem. We have elsewhere pointed to the detrimental effect of "glamorizing" the might of the German army, the marvels of its organization, and the ingenuity of its generals (a method especially practised by *Time* magazine). Here, we want to draw attention to the conspicuous reports on rifts between the old officer corps on the one side, and Hitler and the S.S. or the Nazi party on the other. Differences undoubtedly exist, and clashes have undoubtedly occurred. It would be fateful, however, to present them in such a way that the American people would come to see in the German army a potential spearhead in the fight against Nazism. The army might eventually turn against Hitler and his gang, it might even now try to "isolate" him in order to offer itself to another regime when the time is ripe, but under no circumstances will it be won over for any democratic reconstruction. For the German army is in its entire structure and philosophy tied up with the interests and requirements of imperialist expansion. The army and the party are two heads of the same monster. Conflicts between the army and the party should be presented as what they are: struggles between two competing cliques, fighting for the most efficient and profitable methods of controlling the German people and securing the dominion of its masters. In the occupied territories, the German army has endorsed, instigated and exercised every kind of atrocity, torture, oppression and exploitation. These acts should be contained in the picture of the army offered to the American mind.

5 In recording and analyzing **speeches and writings** of prominent Nazis, the American press seems to be guided by the standards of academic objectivity and exactness. Hitler's utterances are combed down to the most intimate detail for signs of anxiety and weakness, and the translation gives them an aura of rationality and coherence which is distinctly lacking in the German text. Such a procedure makes the Nazi chiefs into oracles whose words spell hope and anxiety to the world; they perpetuate the legend of the "Führer". We don't need a complicated interpretation of Hitler's speeches in order to find out whether he feels pessimistic or optimistic. Instead of giving them a broad and dignified publicity, the Nazi speeches should be treated with a kind of contemptuous superiority. While it would be detrimental to ridicule the actual efforts and power of the Nazis, their speeches and their ideological promulgations are most adequately presented in an atmosphere of spiteful absurdity.

6 Public opinion in this country sees in Nazism a predominantly German or at least European affair, and the war has greatly strengthened this interpretation. Now however we may define the social structure of the system, whether it be state socialism or state capitalism, it unquestionably has **international implications and ramifications** which go beyond the present fronts of the war. Military expansion and invasion of foreign territories are not the only tokens of the international aspect of Nazism, and psychological warfare is not its only "peaceful" inroad into the democracies, although these are almost exclusively featured. The decisive steps towards fascism in the democratic countries are taken by natives of these countries and the driving forces emanate from the key positions of big business. Isolationism was wrong not only from the military but also from the social point of view. Even if any form of invasion were technically impossible or highly improbable, the fight against Nazism would still be a fight for one's own home and soil, for the most primitive rights and liberties of men in their own country. This aspect should be adequately brought out in the presentation of the enemy. The fact that Americans fight abroad, thousands of miles from their unassailable mother country, has always facilitated the defamation of the war as a matter of "imperialism." Emphasis on the social character of the war might help to counteract the possible effects of such propaganda on the American mind.

7 It has been frequently stated that one of the most serious drawbacks in the prevalent presentation of the enemy is the absence of sufficiently **concrete formulations of war-and-peace aims,** formulations which strikingly contrast the enemy and his world with the world the United Nations are fighting for. Here too, the question is for catching symbols rather than for academic explanations. "Freedom," still used as the supreme symbol in this sphere, seems to be losing its appeal to the extent to which its meaning is absorbed into that of security and full employment. The latter may be achieved without the maintenance of freedom, and they function as the chief assets of Nazi propaganda. Moreover, with a large part of the population in the democratic as well as in the fascist countries, freedom and security seem to have become mutually exclusive symbols, and preference seems to be distinctly for security. The trend in public opinion from freedom to security cannot be reversed by propaganda, for it is deeply rooted in the structural transformation of society from a market economy to a planned economy. One of the most impressive attempts to weld "freedom" and "security" together into a new symbol of free security is Henry Wallace's "era of the common man." The contrasting symbol for the enemy's New Order would be the "era of economic overlords," for example.

8 The problem has still a more general aspect which pertains to the systematic foundations of content analysis, namely what **type of symbols** may be most effectively used for the presentation of the enemy. The question can only be answered on the ground of a thorough analysis of the social situation in the enemy country and of the tendencies operative in this situation. For the symbols should appeal not only to the American people but also to those groups of the population in the enemy countries which can be broken away from the regime and taken as the nuclei of future reconstruction. They should find the enemy presented in such a way that they can identify him as their own enemy, that they can recognize their own interests and goals in the present war, as distinguished from the interests and goals of the regime.

From the available material, one principle can be derived as the clue for the selection of effective symbols: *demand symbols must be consistently subordinated to and as much as possible replaced by fact symbols*. We have attempted to justify this principle in our memorandum on "The New German Mentality." Equally strong facts support the validity of the principle for the American scene. The era of mass production and consumption, with its technological rationality and pragmatic matter-of-factness, has changed the attitude of men towards the slogans and ideals of the liberalistic periods: they interpret these slogans and ideals in terms of the brute facts of the social reality, and if the facts do not correspond to the ideals, they adjust their thoughts and actions to the former, and not to the latter. The piece of critical realism implied in this attitude makes the facts a much higher authority than even the most highly cherished values. In view of this increasingly growing appeal of fact symbols, we have suggested that, in presenting the enemy, the brute facts of the Nazi reality should be stripped of their mystical or rational veil and exposed in their true significance for the "common man."

It is much more difficult, of course, to find fact symbols for the presentation of war-and-peace aims, for statements on these aims will naturally have the form of "expectations" and refer to future events and values. Nevertheless, the future policy may well be reflected in the present, and in this way fact symbols may become the bearer of a warranted expectation. The treatment of "Quislings" in the liberated territories provides a good example, and the symbol "Quisling" is loaded with expectations.

With regard to the enemy, the post-war order should be spoken of in terms of present institutions, agencies, relations and organizations. This means, negatively, that it should be as clearly as possible stated which institutions, etc., will be definitely destroyed and abolished. It means, positively, that the outline of the order which is proposed to replace them should be in terms of day-to-day material interests rather than of world-wide blueprints.

SUPPLEMENT THREE [†]

On Psychological Neutrality

The present war has fundamentally changed the traditional attitude of the civilian population towards the enemy. They do not haste, they are not swept by passionate enthusiasm and determination: they simply appreciate, sober, indifferent, and in a matter-of-fact way. The recent Nazi pleas for deeper hate and deeper egoism which "overrules the desire to be unbiassed and just" testify to the prevalence of this desire in Germany.[1] It is not confined to Germany, however. The technological character of the war and its social and economic setting have fostered a state of "psychological neutrality" in the democratic countries too. And the Nazis, who fight this attitude violently among their own population, have done everything to use it for undermining the morale of their enemies.

This has been abundantly proven in the case of France where the psychological neutrality among large strata of the population became the instrument for spreading defeatism and resignation. The dangerous implications of this attitude go far beyond the special case of France, however. The pragmatic matter-of-factness of every day life which characterizes the behavior of men in the technological era tends to interpret the concrete issues, the fate of every single individual which is actually at

---

[†] A text with the title "On Psychological Neutrality" with no author or date was found in the Marcuse archives (#129.01). It mentions Marcuse's report on "The New German Mentality" and presents similar ideas in a similar style, thus the manuscript appears to be part of his work with the Office of War Information between December 1942 and March 1943.

1 Goebbels, quoted in the *New York Times*, September 3, 1942.

stake, in terms of objective forces, machines, and institutions. Man thus discharges himself psychologically of the almost unbearable burden that has been placed upon him. Such rationalization not only protects him from the impact of events which threaten his very existence, but also from the relentless determination to fight this threat at every moment of his existence. The war becomes "so reasonable that it is hard to get excited about it."[2] This lack of excitement, far from making men see the facts, rather blinds them against the facts. They do not believe in atrocity stories when the reality has become more atrocious than the most fantastic story. "The people . . . whose indignations were (in the first World War) prostituted in the interests of military victory, today protect themselves neurotically against such exploitation by failing to react when confronted with authentic atrocities."[3] Under the present circumstances, however, hatred and belief in atrocity stories even without documentation come closer to the truth than the most reasonable and dispassionate appraisal. The terror which Hitler's New Order spreads over the world defies all reasonable appraisal and calls for hatred and faith beyond reasonableness as the only adequate reaction. Such a reaction is also more human than the "desire to be unbiassed and just," for it makes sympathy with the victims and the unerring will to liberate them the supreme motive of thought and action.

The German plea for hate and enthusiasm demonstrates that these psychological factors also have a direct bearing upon the technical conduct of the war. They make man capable of forcing a situation in which reasonableness would soon resign, of seeing possibilities which are beyond the reaches of unbiassed appraisal, of coping with the unexpected and unknown, of inventing weapons and finding solutions at a moment's instance, of mastering the "art of improvisation." The Germany army captain who praised these qualities of the Russian soldier[4] has recognized that lack of enthusiasm and abundance of reasonableness may prove a very material shortcoming even in the most technological of all wars. According to this expert, they were greatly responsible for the failure of the Nazis to gain the decisive victory in Russia. Indeed, the Nazis showed themselves true masters in the art of achieving the impossible only there where they actually hated, namely, in their extermination of the enemy within, in their persecution of the helpless and feeble, in their ghettos and concentration camps.

---

2 Edmond Taylor, *The Strategy of Terror*, Pocket Book Edition, p. 234.
3 Ibid., p. 169.
4 The *New York Times*, September 5, 1942.

The problem offered by the widespread psychological neutrality of the population is twofold:

1 To sharpen the unbiassed matter-of-factness among the population in the Fascist countries up to the point where it comes to grip with the true matters of fact of the National Socialist regime and its chances [contrasted to] the United Nations. This problem has been discussed elsewhere (in the memorandum on "The New German Mentality").

2 To break up the psychological neutrality prevalent among the population of the democratic countries insofar as this attitude threatens to impede the all-out struggle against the Axis. It would be fateful, of course, to adopt Fascist methods of propaganda and education to hate. The passionate determination to destroy Fascism is the exclusive quality of free people and can be created and preserved only in the determinate fight against Fascism in all its forms and on all fronts. Every step that insures freedom, justice, and the equality of sacrifice at home will automatically strengthen the will to wipe out Fascism abroad.

This basic policy should be supplemented, however, by a campaign against some forms of influencing public opinion which, trifles though they may seem, are instrumental in fostering a reconciliatory attitude towards Fascism. We mention only the following instances:

1 The seemingly impartial and objective presentation of National Socialism in the press, in the movies, in literature, and over the radio. The question is not whether some accomplishments of the regime are good, or whether some individual Nazis are "not so bad." The system is such that it does not allow of any exemptions: even its achievements turn into destruction, and everyone who participates also shares its horror. The truth is that the horror is so great that the few cases which "might not be so bad" can never balance or alleviate the all-present bestiality. The only truly objective and impartial presentation is that which reveals this bestiality in operation: in the acts of the German soldiers on the front, in their treatment of the civilian population in the occupied territories, in the extermination of the helpless and sick.

2 The tendency to reconcile the war with the standardized comfort and entertainment of peace time normalcy. This tendency finds its worst manifestation in the styling of commercial advertisements as national proclamations, in the juxtaposition of "cuties" and heroes, in the mobilization of night clubs for the war effort. Such a policy of "relaxation" might have buttressed public morale during the First World War, but the conceptions which were valid at that time no longer correspond to

the present situation. As the war goes on, the gap between the life at home and the life at the front will become increasingly detrimental.

3 The depreciation of the issues at stake by minimizing the enemy. Cartoons, stories and pictures which "make fun" of the Nazis only serve to alleviate the terror of their regime. The result is that the mind, when confronted with the reality of National Socialism and its world, suffers a shock which might make it incapable to react properly. In order to be a weapon of defense, satirical presentation must reveal the true nature of its object. In the case of National Socialism, this means it must retain the unalleviated horror. But this is beyond the reaches of comics.

4 The trend to glorify and "glamorize" the achievements of the German army, especially of its generals (this trend is particularly obvious in the reports of *Time* magazine on Rommel, on Bock, Raeder, etc.). Such a presentation is instrumental in sustaining the legend of German superiority. Certain groups among the population of the democratic countries are all too readily inclined to marvel at the efficiency of the Nazi machine in dealing with internal problems (labor trouble, rationalization, overall control of production, distribution and consumption, elimination of waste and of subversive activities, etc.). They may be tempted to seize upon any opportunity to contrast these German "achievements" with the conditions in their own country, and to draw the conclusion, that, after all, Nazism did some useful things.

VI

Herbert H. Marcuse
4609 Chevy Chase Blvd.
Washington, 15, D. C.

Description of Three Major Projects[1]

Project No. I

A. Project Synopsis

1. Title or Subject - (a) Civil Affairs Handbook Germany, especially Section 1A. (b) Civil Affairs Guides Germany, especially "Dissolution of the Nazi Party and its Affiliated Organizations," and "Policy toward Revival of Old Parties and Establishment of New Parties in Germany."

2. Location - (a) Headquarters, Army Service Forces, and OSS. (b) War Department and OSS.

3. Number of Professional Workers - 20.

4. Scope and Plan - See Note.

5. Principal Sources - See Note.

6. Adequacy of Data - See Note.

7. Research Methods Used - Collection, analysis, and evaluation of historical, political, economic, and statistical data

8. Length of Study - 3-4 months.

9. Findings and Conclusions - See Note.

10. Use Made and Influence of Study - The Handbook and the Guides were to be used for determining and implementing occupation policy in Germany, and for background information for Civil Affairs Officers.

11. Publication - Headquarters, Army Service Forces, 1944. War Department, 1944.

12. Names and addresses - Eugene N. Anderson, Department of State Hajo Holborn, Yale University

1. Note: The Projects described here are classified. They are available in the State Department for inspection by authorized personnel.

† There is no date on the manuscript, but it was evidently written between 1946–7, as it notes the publication date for one of the projects as May 27, 1946, and lists a forthcoming book "to be published" in fall–winter 1947 on his selected publications list, a book that was apparently never published. The document has the name "Herbert H. Marcuse" on the top righthand corner and lists his address as 4609 Chevy Chase Blvd, Washington, 15, D.C.

DESCRIPTION OF THREE MAJOR PROJECTS†1

PROJECT NO. I

A Project Synopsis

1 Title or Subject – (a) *Civil Affairs Handbook Germany*, especially Section 1A. (b) *Civil Affairs Guides Germany*, especially "Dissolution of the Nazi Party and its Affiliated Organizations," and "Policy toward Revival of Old Parties and Establishment of New Parties in Germany."
2 Location – (a) Headquarters, Army Service Forces, and OSS.
   (b) War Department and OSS.
3 Number of Professional Workers – 20.
4 Scope and Plan – See Note.
5 Principal Sources – See Note.
6 Adequacy of Data – See Note.
7 Research Methods Used – Collection, analysis and evaluation of historical, political, economic and statistical data.
8 Length of Study – 3–4 months.
9 Findings and Conclusions – See Note.
10 Use Made and Influence of Study – The Handbook and the Guides were to be used for determining and implementing occupation policy in Germany, and for background information for Civil Affairs Officers.

---

1 Note: The Projects described here are classified. They are available in the State Department for inspection by authorized personnel.

11 <u>Publication</u> – Headquarters, Army Service Forces, 1944.
                         War Department, 1944.
12 <u>Names and addresses</u> – Eugene N. Anderson, Department of State.
                              Hajo Holborn, Yale University.

B   Participation in Project

1 <u>Formulation</u> – Participated in the discussions of the formulation, organization and implementation of the entire project, completed several
   parts of it independently.
2 <u>Development of Techniques and Procedures</u> – Determined sources, procedures and techniques to be used for all parts of the project assigned
   to me.
3 <u>Analysis of Data</u> –
   (a) Collected data myself with the help of several assistants, on the
   basis of the available intelligence material.
   (b) (1) I used in the analysis and interpretation of data empirical
   as well as theoretical (deductive) methods. The latter were applied
   wherever the empirical data were falsified by the fact that they were set
   within the framework of a totalitarian state. In these cases, the data
   had to be evaluated in terms of the fundamental structure and aims of
   the totalitarian state. The deductive interpretation was tested against
   the facts of the implementation of policies in the various fields of social
   life in Germany, Austria and the German-occupied territories.
        (2) Insofar as such relationships were pertinent at all to the
   project, I discussed their determination with statistically trained
   members of the staff.
4 <u>Conclusion</u>
   (a) On the basis of this analysis and evaluation, policy suggestions
   were drafted by me and discussed with the planning staff.
   (b) The parts of the projects assigned to me were written by me. Final
   editing was done by the branch editor. Charts and graphs were suggested by me and supplied by the presentation section after discussion
   with me.
5 <u>Supervision</u>
   (a) About 6–10 professionals participated in the collection, organization and evaluation of data.
   (b) They were responsible for the work assigned to them, subject to its
   integration into my part of the project.
   (c) Most of them were trained specialists. Supervision thus applied

only to the last phase of their work. I directed the less trained personnel in all phases of the assignment.

6 Project Promotion – I participated in the promotion of the project and interpreted my part of it to the planning staff.

PROJECT NO. II

A   Project Synopsis

1 Title or Subject – The Social Democratic Party of Germany.
2 Location – Office of Strategic Services, Research and Analysis Branch.
3 Number of Professionals – Four.
4 Scope and Plan – The traditional policies and attitudes of the Social Democratic Party, its composition and strength, its prospective development and strategy under the occupation.
5 Principal Sources – See Note (Project I).
6 Adequacy of Data – See Note (Project I).
7 Research Methods Used – Collection, analysis and evaluation of historical, political, economic and statistical data.
8 Length of study – Two months.
9 Findings and Conclusions – See Note (Project I).
10 Use Made and Influence of Study – The political studies on Germany were to be used for determining American occupation policy toward the various social and political groups in Germany.
11 Publication – OSS, Research and Analysis Branch (R&A No. 1549), September 1, 1945.
12 Names and Addresses – Frederick Burkhardt, President, Bennington College, Vermont; Franz L. Neumann, Columbia University, New York.

B   Participation in Project

1 Formulation – I formulated the project and drafted the outline, which was then discussed with the staff.
2 Development of Techniques and Procedures – I determined the use of sources and data, and discussed their evaluation with the staff.
3 Analysis of Data –
(a) Data were collected jointly by the field staff, the members of the section participating in the project and myself.

(b) (1) Data were selected, processed and evaluated on the ground of a historical and sociological analysis of the role of the Social Democratic Party in national and international policy.

(2) Insofar as much relationships were pertinent at all to the project, I discussed their determination with statistically trained members of the staff.

4   Conclusion –

(a) I was responsible for drawing conclusions, which were then discussed with the staff.

(b) I wrote the entire report. Final editing was done by the branch editor.

5   Supervision –

(a) Four professionals helped in the collection and organization of data.

(b) They were responsible for the work assigned to them, subject to its integration into my part of the project.

(c) Most of them were trained specialists. Supervision thus applied only to the last phase of their work. I directed the less trained personnel in all phases of the assignment.

6   Project Promotion – I promoted and interpreted the project.

PROJECT NO. III

A   Project Synopsis

1   Title or Subject – Status and Prospects of German Trade Unions and Works Councils.

2   Location – Department of State.

3   Number of Professionals – Four.

4   Scope and Plan – Strength, political affiliations, tactics and policies of organized labor in the various zones of occupied Germany. Prospects of the German labor movement in relation to US policy and to the international scene.

5   Principal Sources – See note (Project I).

6   Adequacy of Data – See note (Project I).

7   Research Methods Used – In addition to the procedures outlined in answer to Project No. II, A, 7, economic and socio-psychological analysis was used in order to determine the tendencies prevalent in the German labor movement.

8   Length of Study – 6–7 weeks.

9 Findings and Conclusions – See note (Project I).
10 Use Made and Influence of Study – The study was to report on the development of the policy of the four occupying powers and on the German implementation of and reaction to these policies. The study was to contribute to the discussion of possible changes in US policy toward organized labor.
11 Publication – Department of State, Office of Research and Intelligence, No. 3381, May 27, 1946.
12 Names and addresses – H. Stuart Hughes, DRE, Department of State.

B   Participation in Project

1 Formulation – Project was formulated in the meetings of the branch staff. I was responsible for the organization and completion of the entire project.
2 Development of Techniques and Procedures – I determined the use of sources and data, and discussed their evaluation with the staff.
3 Analysis of data –
(a) I collected and organized the data used in the project on the basis of the intelligence material sent in from the field (covert and overt).
(b) (1) Empirical methods of sociological, historical and political analysis; comparative analysis of the tendencies prevalent in Western and Eastern trade unionism.
    (2) Insofar as such relationships were pertinent at all to the project, I discussed their determination with statistically trained members of the staff.
4 Conclusion –
(a) I was responsible for drawing conclusions and incorporating suggestions made by members of the section staff.
(b) I wrote the report with the exception of some parts dealing with the Eastern Zone. These parts were reviewed by me. Final editing was done by the Branch editor.
5 Supervision –
(a) Three professionals. One wrote the parts of the project mentioned under 4 (b), the others participated in the collection and organization of data.
(b) They were actually responsible for their part of the work. Integration of the results into the report was done by me.
(c) I supervised the use, selection and organization of the intelligence material.

6 <u>Project Promotion</u> – I participated in the promotion of the project and
   interpreted it to interested agencies.

SELECTED PUBLICATIONS

A   Books

Reason and Revolution: Hegel and the Rise of Social Theory. Oxford University
   Press, New York, 1941.
(co-author) *Authority and the Family: Sociological Studies*, ed. Institute of Social
   Research, Paris, 1938 (in German).
(contributor) *Germany under Military Government*. Edited by E. Mason and Franz
   L. Neumann. To be published by Oxford University Press, fall–winter 1947.

B   Articles

"Some Social Implications of Modern Technology," in *Studies in Philosophy and
   Social Science*, New York, 1941.
"Liberalism and Totalitarianism," in *Zeitschrift für Sozialforschung*, 1934 (in
   German).
"The Concept of Labor in Economics," in *Archiv für Sozialwissenschaft und
   Sozialpolitik*, 1933 (in German).

VII

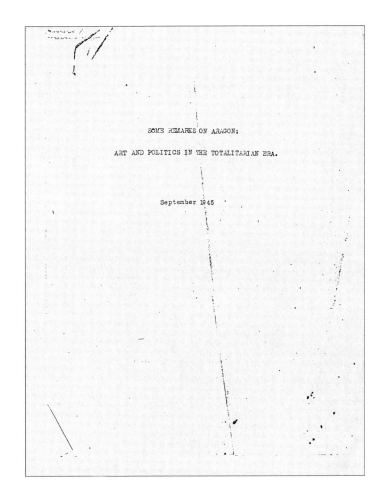

SOME REMARKS ON ARAGON:

ART AND POLITICS IN THE TOTALITARIAN ERA.

September 1945

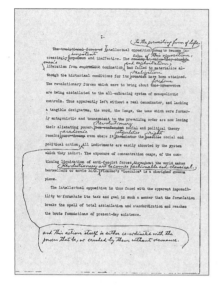

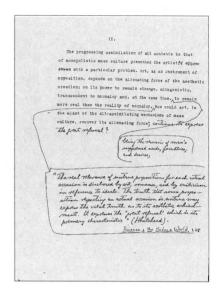

---

† The title page of the text contains the date "September 1945" (#8.38). But the first page is typed on a different typewriter from the subsequent 30 pages and perhaps condenses seven pages of an earlier, now apparently lost, manuscript, since pagination jumps from page 1 in section I to a section II starting on a page 8. The first two typed pages are heavily edited and contain hand-written inserts which seem to reflect Marcuse's later language and which might have been intended for insertion in texts like *Eros and Civilization*, or his final work *The Aesthetic Dimension*. Thus, it appears that Marcuse wrote the opening, introductory section of the essay at a later date, at which time he also added some comments to Section I, while Sections II–IV are relatively unedited. The text published here is as printed in *Theory, Culture & Society* (London, Newbury Park and New Delhi: Sage), vol. 10 (1993), 181–95.

SOME REMARKS ON
ARAGON†

<hr>

Art and Politics in the
Totalitarian Era

I

Intellectual opposition to the prevailing form of life seems to become increasingly impotent and ineffective. The aim of this opposition: man's liberation from domination and exploitation, has failed to materialize although the historical conditions for its realization have been attained. The revolutionary forces which were to bring about freedom are being assimilated to the all-embracing system of monopolistic controls. Thus apparently left without a real denominator, and lacking a tangible designatum, the word, the image, the tone which were formerly antagonistic and transcendent to the prevailing order are now losing their alienating power. Revolutionary social and political theory remains academic, even where it stipulates the right social and political action, and this action itself is either co-ordinated with the powers that be, or crushed by them without resonance. All indictments are easily absorbed by the system which they indict. The exposure of concentration camps, of the continuing liquidation of anti-fascist forces throughout the world makes bestsellers or movie hits. Revolutionary art becomes fashionable and classical. Picasso's *Guernica* is a cherished museum piece.

The intellectual opposition is thus faced with the apparent impossibility to formulate its task and goal in such a manner that the formulation breaks the spell of total assimilation and standardization and reaches the brute foundations of present-day existence.

II

The progressive assimilation of all contents to that of monopolistic mass culture presented the artist with a particular problem. Art, as an instrument of opposition, depends on the alienating force of the aesthetic creation: on its power to remain strange, antagonistic, transcendent to normalcy and, at the same time, being the reservoir of man's suppressed needs, faculties and desires, to remain more real than the reality of normalcy.

> The real relevance of untrue propositions for each actual occasion is disclosed by art, romance, and by criticism in reference to ideals. The truth that some proposition respecting an actual occasion is untrue may express the vital truth as to its aesthetic achievement. It expresses the 'great refusal' which is its primary characteristic.
>
> (Whitehead 1926: 228)

How could art, in the midst of the all-assimilating mechanisms of mass culture, recover its alienating force, continue to express the great refusal?

If all contents are *gleichgeschaltet*, incorporated and absorbed into the monopolistic way of life, the solution may be found in the form. Free the form from the hostile content, or rather make the form the only content, by making it the instrument of destruction. Use the word, the color, the tone, the line in their brute nakedness, as the very contradiction and negation of all content. But this shock, too, was quickly absorbed, and the subconscious which it involved became easily a part of the official consciousness. The surrealistic terror was surpassed by the real terror. The intellectual avant-gardists joined the Communists, split on the issue of Stalinism, fought with the Resistance forces. Now, in France, the avant-gardists of the 1920s and early 1930s, who then worked and lived for "le scandale pour le scandale," worshiped de Sade and Lautréamont and made a mockery of the "génie français," celebrate the severe classical style, praise the true love, life and death for the Fatherland.

The avant-gardistic negation was not negative enough. The destruction of all content was itself not destroyed. The formless form was kept intact, aloof from the universal contamination. The form itself was stabilized as a new content, and thus came to share the fate of all contents: it was absorbed by the market. The problem of formulation remained unsolved. The work of the Resistance writers represents a new stage of the solution.

Their world is the reality of totalitarian fascism. This determines the totality of their art. Its raison d'être is the political. The political is the absolute negation and contradiction. But to present the political directly would mean to posit it as a content, thus to surrender it to the monopolistic system. The political must rather remain outside the content: as the artistic a priori which cannot be absorbed by the content but which is itself absorbing all content. The political will then appear only in the way in which the content is shaped and formed.

The content as such is irrelevant, can be everything (for everything is today the object of totalitarian domination and therefore of liberation) but it must be shaped in such a manner that it reveals the negative system in its totality and, at the same time, the absolute necessity of liberation. The work of art must, at its breaking point, expose the ultimate nakedness of man's (and nature's) existence, stripped of all the paraphernalia of monopolistic mass culture, completely and utterly alone, in the abyss of destruction, despair and freedom. The most revolutionary work of art will be, at the same time, the most esoteric, the most anti-collectivistic one, for the goal of the revolution is the free individual. The abolition of the capitalist mode of production, socialization, the liquidation of classes are only the preconditions for the liberation of the individual. And this liberation is achieved only when everyone receives according to his needs. This ultimate principle of socialist theory is the sole absolute negation of the capitalist principle in all its forms. Only the brute materialistic content of freedom negates all repression, sublimation, internalization of class society. Such freedom is the realization of the fully developed needs, desires and potentialities of man, at the same time his liberation from the all-embracing apparatus of production, distribution and administration which today regiments his life.

To present this goal already means to distort it. Its actuality is so obvious, its possibility so real, its necessity so pressing that its mere formulation appears ridiculous. The goal is realistic to such a degree that it can no longer be a matter of theory, of presentation, definition and formulation.

By the same token, there can be no artistic salvation of the goal. Art is essentially unrealistic: the reality which it creates is alien and antagonistic to the other, realistic reality which it negates and contradicts – for the sake of the utopia that is to be real. But liberation is realistic, is political action. Consequently, in art, the content of freedom will show forth only indirectly, in and through something else which is not the goal but possesses the force to illuminate the goal.

The oppositional, the negating power of art will appear in the form, in the artistic a priori which shapes the content. The latter may then be victimized by the assimilating mechanisms of the prevailing order; it may perish (like all forms of freedom in an unfree society) – still, in perishing it will reveal the goal which was enchained rather than materialized in the content.

The artistic form, in the sense of the artistic a priori, is more than the "technical" implementation and arrangement of the work of art: it is the "style" which selects the content and which prevails throughout the work, in setting the central point that determines the relationships among the component parts, the vocabulary, and the rhythm and structure of each sentence.

Sensuality as style, as artistic a priori, expresses the individual protest against the law and order of repression. Sensual love gives a "promesse du bonheur" which preserves the full materialistic content of freedom and rebels against all efforts to canalize this "bonheur" into forms compatible with the order of repression. Baudelaire's (1989) "Invitation au voyage" is indeed, in the face of a society based on the buying and selling of labor power, the absolute negation and contradiction, the "great refusal," "le scandale pour le scandale," and, at the same time, the utopia of real liberation.

> Mon enfant, ma soeur,
> Songe a la douceur

rejects the entire order of toil and efficiency by taking its promises and potentialities seriously:

> C'est pour assouvir
> Ton moindre désir . . .

Sensuality is the unpolitical *kat' exochen*, but in its unpolitical character it preserves the goal of political action: liberation. Baudelaire has defined the task of poetry in these terms:

> C'est une grande destinée que celle de la poésie! Joyeuse ou lamentable, elle porte toujours en soi le divin caractère utopique. Elle contradit sans cesse le fait, à peine de ne plus être. Dans le cachot, elle se fait révolte; à la fenêtre de l'hôpital, elle est ardente expérience de guérison; dans la mansarde déchirée et malpropre, elle se pare comme une fée du luxe et de l'élégance; non seulement elle constate, mais elle répare. Partout elle se fait négation de l'iniquité.
>   Va donc à l'avenir en chantant, poète providentiel, tes chants son le décalque lumineux des espérances et des convictions populaires!

By virtue of this "promesse du bonheur," love, as an artistic form, becomes a political a priori. Thus it reappears in the artistic opposition of the 1920s.

With such "promesse du bonheur," love becomes the political a priori of the artistic opposition. Aragon writes in 1924:

> Je ne pense à rien, si ce n'est à l'amour. Ma continuelle distraction dans les domaines de l'esprit . . . trouve dans ce goût unique et incessant de l'amour sa véritable raison d'être. Il n'y a pour moi pas une idée que l'amour n'éclipse.

And fifteen years later, at the outbreak of the war, during the fight against fascism:

O mon amour, o mon amour toi seule existe
A cette heure pour moi du crépuscule triste . . .

In 1943 Paul Eluard publishes the clandestine edition of "Les Sept Poèmes d'Amour en Guerre" (Eluard, 1968), with the lines:

. . . nous apportions l'amour
La jeunesse de l'amour
Et la raison de l'amour
Et l'immortalité.

To these political poets and active communists, love appears as the artistic a priori which shapes all individual content, first and foremost the political content: the artistic counterblow against the annexation of all political contents by monopolistic society. The artist counteracts by transposing these contents (which are his own and art's own) to a different sphere of existence, thereby negating their monopolistic form and rescuing their revolutionary form. France, the fatherland, resistance, liberation – they are not the objective and end of this poetry (although it tells of nothing other than them) but its medium, that is, the medium of love as the artistic–political a priori. Bluntly speaking: the fatherland, resistance, liberation become artistic contents only in so far as they are preconditions for the fulfillment of the "promesse du bonheur." Love and liberty are one and the same. Eléonore, "reine des cours d'amour," shows her true face:

Mais ce ne fut enfin que dans quelque Syrie
Qu'ils comprirent vraiment les vocable sonores
Et blessés à mourir surent qu'Eléonore
C'est ton nom Liberté Liberté chérie.

Or, the beginning and the concluding stanza of the last of the 'Sept Poèmes d'amour en guerre' (Eluard, 1968: 1186–7):

Au nom du front parfait profond
Au nom des yeux que je regarde
Et de la bouche que j'embrasse,
Pour aujourd'hui et pour toujours

Il nous faut drainer la colère
Et faire se lever le fer
Pour préserver l'image haute
Des innocents partout traqués
Et qui partout vont triompher.

Between these two stanzas, the poem comprises all the terror of fascism and all the hope of the revolution, interspersed with the lines:

> Au nom des rires dans la rue
> De la douceur qui lie nos mains
> Au nom des fruits couvrant les fleurs
> Sur une terre belle et bonne

which retrieve the image of the "Invitation au voyage" in the midst of the Resistance.

Neither La Patrie nor La Résistance nor La Libération are ends in themselves; they are only the media for the "promesse du bonheur." The posited content is thus at the same time negated, and its negation rescues the true content, the revolutionary goal. The political is being depoliticized, and in this way becomes the true political. Art and politics find their common denominator.

> Du point de vue surréaliste, action politique (révolutionnaire) et action créatrice ne soient que le partage arbitraire d'une même volonté fonda-mentale ayant pour fin de remettre l'univers en question.
>
> (*Poésie* 45, no. 24, p. 36)

That the political content demands an "unpolitical" form of presentation was one of the earliest problems of surrealism. In 1935, during the bitter political discussion among the French surrealists, Breton (1935: 33) cited Courbet and Rimbaud in order to show how the political content evokes in the artist a strictly "technical" reaction:

> La préoccupation centrale [with the political] qui s'y fait jour est manifestement encore d'ordre technique. Il est clair . . . que la grande ambition a été de traduire le monde dans un langage nouveau.

The language of the Resistance poetry revives the traditional, the classical vocabulary of love, suggesting the well-known, long-practised paraphernalia and rituals:

> Je suis à toi seule J'adore
> La trace de tes pas le creux où tu te mis
> Ta pantoufle perdue ou ton mouchoir Va dors
> Dors mon enfant craintif Je veille C'est promis

Nothing could apparently be farther from avant-gardism, opposition, resistance than this language. At the same time, it expresses a sensuality which does not allow the sublimation of the promise:

> Ecoute dans la nuit mon song bat et t'appelle
> Je cherche dans le lit ton poids et la couleur

Or Paul Eluard:

> La source coulant douce et nue
> La nuit partout épanouie
> La nuit où nous nous unissons
> Dans une lutte faible et folle
> Et la nuit qui nous fait injure
> La nuit ou se creuse le lit
> Vide de la solitude
> L'avenir d'une agonie

In the night of the fascist terror appear the images of tenderness, "douceur," calmness and free fulfillment; the agony of the Gestapo becomes the agony of love. As a mere juxtaposition, this would be romanticism, cheap escapism. But as an element of the a prioristic artistic form of this poetry, the language of love emerges as the instrument of estrangement; its artificial, unnatural, "inadequate" character is to produce the shock which may bare the true relationship between the two worlds and languages: the one being the positive negation of the other. The beloved is "enfant craintif," "soeur" and *Geliebte*; her free weakness, laxity and compliance evokes the image of the victim as well as the conqueror of the fascist order, of the sacrificed utopia which is to emerge as the historical reality. As the language of estrangement, the paraphernalia of love and sensuality thus are part of the political form of these poems.

Estrangement, as an artistic–political device, is furthermore increased by constraining the poetic language in the strict system of classical versification.

The return of avant-gardistic art to the laws and rules of classical poetic metrics is perhaps the most surprising aspect of the Resistance poetry. Aragon himself has explained the return to the classical rules by the necessity to rescue language from its utter destruction, to make it again an instrument for "faire chanter les choses." They must be made to sing since they can no longer be made to talk without talking the language of the enemy. The artistic opposition cannot talk the language of the enemy but must contradict his language together with its content. The classical system of versification, in the form of estrangement, has perhaps most directly preserved the immediate sensual "ordre de la beauté," the "promesse du bonheur."

Moreover, the classical system of versification provides perhaps the most adequate form for the shaping of the political content in the medium of the artistic a priori (love). The welding together of the "promesse du bonheur" with the agony and terror of the fascist world is, on the strictly technical level, achieved by the use of the rhyme. The rhyme is reintroduced in its original function as the concord (*Zusammenhang*) of two or more ideas. In its new usage, the rhyme drives the welding together of the dream and the reality almost into an immediate identification:

> Une fille rêvait sur le pont d'un bateau
> Près d'un homme étendu mais moi-même rêvais-je
> Une voix s'éleva qui disait A bientôt
> Une autre murmurai qu'on mourait en Norvège.

Or:

> Et tes lèvres tenaient tous les soirs le pari
> D'un ciel de cyclamen au-dessus de Paris.

Or:

> Je me souviens des yeux de ceux qui s'embarquèrent
> Qui pourrait oublier son amour à Duncerque.

The seamless juncture of the different verses and ideas is also accomplished by the device of the "rime enjambée" which spreads one component of the rhyme over the end of the one and the beginning of the next verse. Aragon's own example:

> Ne parlez plus d'amour. J'écoute mon coeur *battre*
> Il couvre les refrains sans fil qui l'ont grise
> Ne parlez plus d'amour. Que fait-elle là-*bas*
> *Tr*op proche et trop lointaine ô temps martyrisé.

A highly artificial technicality which, however, "précipite le mouvement d'un vers sur l'autre," makes the rhyme the concord of complex ideas rather than of isolated words or sounds, and increases the estrangement of poetic language, its alienation from the language of monopolistic culture.

III

Aurélien, the novel, like the poetry, returns to the classical form (Aragon, 1945). Classical in the twofold sense of a revival of the strict traditional rules characteristic of the artistic form of the novel during the nineteenth century, and of a revival of the old, long since obsolete and dusty paraphernalia of the "roman." *Aurélien* follows the familiar standards of the "*Gesellschaftsroman*": it gives the picture of a whole epoch in its repercussions on the representative strata of society, and reflects the historical fate of the epoch in the personal story of the hero and the heroine, Aurélien and Bérénice. This pattern seems so faithfully applied that the impression of an intentional accumulation of old-fashioned paraphernalia is almost unavoidable. For example, the plot: a young petty-bourgeois wife from the provinces comes to Paris, is caught in the glittering, decadent, immoral life of the metropolis, falls in love with a formidable playboy, feels herself betrayed by him, escapes with an avant-gardistic inhabitant of Montmartre, eventually returns to her husband in the provinces, meets, after twenty years, her true love again, and dies in his arms from the bullets of the German invaders. Moreover, the erring heroine is the wife of a stuffy pharmacist!

Aurélien is the third volume of a series which Aragon calls *Le Monde Réel*. In his story of the "*Monde Réel*" between 1922 and 1940 there is hardly any indication of social and political problems; the stage is almost exclusively filled with the members of the well-to-do bourgeoisie (and a few crazy artists), and the almost exclusive trouble is woman trouble. In the case of Aurélien and Bérénice, the trouble develops into a love tragedy.

"Bérénice," the name, evokes in Aurélien the strange memory of the Roman Orient, of decaying imperial grandeur and luxury. Bérénice could be an image of *La Vie Antérieure*:

> J'ai longtemps habité sous des vastes portiques
> Que les soleils marins teignaient de mille feux
> . . .
> Au milieu de l'azur, des vagues, des splendeurs
> Et des esclaves nues, tout impregnés d'odeurs,
> Qui me refraichissaient le front avec des palmes,
> Et donc l'unique soin était d'approfondir
> Le secret douloureux qui me faisait languir.

Their love becomes a "*Krankheit zum Tode*" which absorbs their entire life, makes them incapable of any solution, and is the more desperate as Bérénice refuses to sleep with Aurélien (as all the others around them do) – for no ostensible reason. Then, however, after weeks of terror, during which circumstances separate him from Bérénice, after a drunken night spent with a prostitute, upon his return home, he finds Bérénice waiting in his bedroom. She had waited for him there all night, New Year's night. She begs him to let her rest for a while, and while he goes to prepare some food, she disappears. She disappears not only for him, but also for her husband, her friends. She writes Aurélien that she will never see him again, and he knows it is the truth. She lives a few months in hiding somewhere in the country near Paris, with a boy whom she does not love (and with whom she sleeps). Then she leaves him and returns to the provinces, to her husband and his pharmacy.

However, Aurélien does see her again before her return, by a mere accident. He takes Rose Melrose, the famous actress, for a visit to Claude

Monet's country home. While Rose interviews the master, Aurélien strolls
in the garden, and meets Bérénice (whose hiding place is close to Claude
Monet's house). This meeting, the artistic culmination of the novel, is of an
almost unbearable tenderness, sorrow and desperation. There are attempts
to ask and to answer, to explain and to understand. But there is no
explanation. The shock remains unabated, the shock caused by the fact
that in 1922 (or 1944), a love should break and, breaking, destroy two
lives just because, in a drunken night, the lover slept with a prostitute
– something that bourgeois as well as anti-bourgeois morality considers as
perfectly normal.

The shock may be an artistic device for revealing what bourgeois as well
as anti-bourgeois morality conceals: the revolutionary promise of love. The
fate of Aurélien and Bérénice transcends in its very nature all essentially
'normal' relationships, including all the other serious and easy, smart and
tragic, sensual and romantic love affairs described in the novel. All the
others live with and without their love; it is fulfilled within the established
order (or, if not fulfilled, replaceable within it). In contrast, Aurélien's
and Bérénice's relationship binds itself to a "promesse du bonheur" which
transcends the happiness of the others as much as a free order of life
transcends all liberties within the established order of life. And because it
does, it must end at once, automatically, when it is adjusted to the normal
state of affairs.

"Faithfulness," the physical impossibility to substitute for somebody
anybody else, is, in an order of universal exchangeability, the token of
transcendence, of absolute contradiction. The act of substituting cancels
that contradiction once and for all and marks the triumph of normalcy
and legality over an essentially abnormal and illegal relationship. The
separation of love from sensuality, the right to enjoy the latter without
damaging the former, belongs to the sacred liberties of the bourgeois
individual. By taking this liberty, he testifies for the society to which it
belongs. (In the image of the "Invitation au voyage," sensuality *is* love.
Aurélien substitutes sensuality for love – or for its failure. This liberty is the
necessity of bourgeois society: universal exchange relationships. The first
two lines of the "Invitation au voyage" are quoted in *Aurélien*: they are
attributed to the woman who most happily practises the liberties of love as
sanctioned by bourgeois society: Rose Melrose. And she comments on the
image which these lines consecrate with one word: "Merde!")

It is its essential illegality, its transcendence over the established order of
life which makes love a political and at the same time artistic a priori.
Illegality is the common denominator of Resistance action and Resistance
art. In *Aurélien*, the illegality of love lies in its incompatibility with all

normal relationships (business, "social life," incorporation into the life of the "community"), in its disproportionate character which absorbs all other contents, in its impossibility to adjust itself to the requirements of sanity and reasonableness.

The brief Epilogue, resuming the story eighteen years after the events described in the novel, concludes the fate of Aurélien and Bérénice by letting them share the fate of France in 1940. Far from being a mere epilogue appended to the story, this chapter rather makes explicit the a priori of the whole book: the artistic negation of the political content. It is the only chapter in which politics enter in a decisive role: Aurélien flees southward with a contingent of the beaten and disorganized French army, he comes to the town where Bérénice lives, he billets himself in her house. At the dinner table, with the pharmacist and the members of the household, the political situation is discussed. Bérénice has become active for the left: she protects and sponsors a Spanish Loyalist refugee. Alone with Aurélien, politics stand between them. They don't speak the same language anymore, or, the language of politics silences the language of their dead love which they still try to speak. She is a new, a strange Bérénice – not the ghost of the beloved one. Then follows the weird drive into the night, into the dark country, with the pharmacist's half-drunken party, in an old automobile. There is more drinking in an isolated mountain cottage. On the way home, in the overcrowded car, Aurélien is pressed against Bérénice on the front seat. For the first time, he holds her tight in his arms – but he does not feel her: she is a strange and cold person. From the dark, the Germans strafe the road with their bullets. Aurélien is slightly wounded, but only after a while does he notice that he is embracing a dead Bérénice.

Their love, which has been destroyed before, dies in politics. Not from without: it is dead when Bérénice speaks the language of politics, which Aurélien does not understand. Nothing, apparently, can be more alien, more hostile to the "promesse du bonheur" than this language and the activity which it denotes. The call for political action is the negation of the "Invitation au voyage." But the negation reveals at the same time the true relation between the two realities: their final identity. This identity is in Bérénice, and in the dead Bérénice. Political action is the death of love, but the goal of political action is love's liberation. This goal is the same world which was meant from the beginning of their fate: the world in which the "promesse du bonheur" finds its fulfillment.

"Bérénice avait le goût de l'absolu." The absolute is that which is essentially unrelated, which finds its realization in itself and by itself, independent of other forms of life. The absolute is independence, freedom. "Le goût de l'absolu" is therefore incompatible with happiness, which is by necessity fulfillment within the prevailing, unfree form of life. To Bérénice, her love had the characteristics of the absolute, and because of that, it was destroyed when it was adjusted to the prevailing form of life. After eighteen years, when they meet again for the last time, Aurélien must again talk about their love – there is nothing else. But Bérénice talks about the collapse of France, the Marshal, the necessity to resist, to continue the fight against the Germans. Aurélien interrupts:

> Qu'est-ce que nous sommes là à dire?
> Et Bérénice:
> "Nous disons les seules choses quil y ait a dire aujourd'hui . . . cette nuit . . . ne protestez pas, ne dites pas que vous auriez à me parler damour . . . comme autrefois?"

But the poet had demanded:

> Mais si Parlez d'amour encore et qu'amour rime
> Avec jour avec âme ou rien du tout parlez
> Parlez d'amour car tout le reste est crime

Aurélien does not understand that, then and now, she is speaking the same language. In the Epilogue, the absolute appears in the disappearing image of the political. It is the reflex of the "Monde Réel" in the collapsing reality. Just as, in the poems, freedom appears in the figure of the beloved, so, in the novel, the face of the dying Bérénice appears as the face of France, *la patrie*. But this fatherland is not *La Grande Nation*: it is the liberated earth on which the "promesse du bonheur" finds its fulfillment. The historical coincidence which made the revolutionary fight against the prevailing order a fight against the foreign invaders makes the fight for absolute liberation appear as a fight for national liberation. This illusionary identification is corrected by the true identification of the fatherland with the "promesse du bonheur." Only rarely has art dared to dissociate the idea of the fatherland from all patriotic context and to make it the symbol of ultimate human fulfillment:

> Es gibt in unserm Vaterland so manchen Pfad, du Liebe,
> Der uns zusammen Hand in Hand noch zu durchwandern bliebe

IV

Art may well try to preserve its political function by negating its political content, but art cannot cancel the reconciliatory element involved in this negation. The "promesse du bonheur," although presented as destroyed and destroying, is, in the artistic presentation, fascinating enough to illuminate the prevailing order of life (which destroys the promise) rather than the future one (which fulfills it). The effect is an awakening of memory, remembrance of things lost, consciousness of what was and what could have been. Sadness as well as happiness, terror as well as hope are thrown upon the reality in which all this occurred; the dream is arrested and returns to the past, and the future of freedom appears only as a disappearing light. The artistic form is a form of reconciliation:

> Ihr glücklichen Augen,
> Was je ihr gesehn,
> Es si wie es wolle,
> Es war doch so schön!

This reconciliatory element seems to be the intrinsic curse of art, the curse which links it inseparably with the prevailing form of life; it seems to be the token of art in an unfree world. The work of art, by giving the content an artistic form, isolates this content from the negative totality which is the historical world, interrupts the terrible stream, creates artificial space and artificial time. In the medium of the artistic form, things are liberated to their own life – without being liberated in reality. Art creates a reification of its own. The artistic form, however destructive it may be, stays and brings to rest. In the artistic form, all content becomes the object of aesthetic contemplation, the source of aesthetic gratification. The aesthetic element transforms the content as well as the form, for the latter forms the given matter; even if this matter is absolutely negated, it participates in the triumph of the form. The artistic presentation of the total terror still remains a work of art; it transforms the terror into another world – a transformation which is almost a transfiguration. If the Guernica picture, in spite of such transfiguration, still preserves the fascist terror unmitigated, how much of this is due to the fact that the picture is explicitly designated as *Guernica*, thus evoking the knowledge and associations which this historical event carries? In other words, how much of this is due to an extra-artistic means, outside the realm of art and aesthetics? The picture itself seems rather to negate the political content: there is a bull, a slaughtered horse, a dead child, a crying mother – but the interpretation of these objects as symbols of fascism is not in the picture. Darkness, terror and utter destruction are brought to life by grace of the artistic creation and in the artistic form; they are therefore incomparable to the fascist reality. (They appear in the picture as the individualization of universal forces and as such they transcend the fascist reality into a "supra-historical" order. They have a reality of their own: the artistic reality. That is perhaps the reason why Picasso refuses to call them "symbols." They are "signs," but signs for a bull, a child, a horse, etc. – not for fascism.)

Art does not and cannot present the fascist reality (nor any other form of the totality of monopolistic oppression). But any human activity which does not contain the terror of this era is by this very token inhuman, irrelevant, incidental, untrue. In art, however, the untruth may become the life element of the truth. The incompatibility of the artistic form with the real form of life may be used as a lever for throwing upon the reality the light which the latter cannot absorb, the light which may eventually dissolve this reality (although such dissolution is no longer the function of art). The untruth of art may become the precondition for the artistic contradiction and negation. Art may promote the alienation, the total estrangement of man from his world. And this alienation may provide the artificial basis for the remembrance of freedom in the totality of oppression.

References

Aragon, L. (1945) *Aurélien*. Paris: Gallimard.

Baudelaire, Charles (1986) "Invitation au voyage," Poem LIII in *The Complete Verse*, Volume I, edited by F. Scarfe. London: Anvil Press.

Breton, A. (1935) *Position politique du surréalisme*. Paris: Editions du Sagittaire.

Eluard, Paul (1968) "Les Sept Poèmes d'amour en guerre," *Oeuvres complètes*. Paris: Gallimard.

Whitehead, C.N. (1926) *Science and the Modern World*. New York: Macmillan.

VIII

febr. 1947

I. Teil

Thesen:

1. "Nach der militärischen Niederlage des Hitler-Faschismus
(der eine verfrühte und isolierte Form der kapitalistischen
Reorganisation war) teilt sich die Welt in ein neo-faschi-
stisches und sowjetisches Lager auf. Die noch existierenden
Ueberreste demokratisch-liberaler Formen werden zwischen
den beiden Lagern zerrieben oder von ihnen absorbiert.
Die Staaten, in denen die alte herrschende Klasse den
Krieg ökonomisch und politisch überlebt hat, werden in
absehbarer Zeit faschisiert werden, die anderen in das
Sowjet-Lager eingehen."

2. "Die neo-faschistische und die sowjetische Gesellschaft
sind ökonomisch und klassenmässig Gegner und ein Krieg
zwischen ihnen ist wahrscheinlich. Beide sind aber in
ihren wesentlichen Herrschaftsformen anti-revolutionär
und einer sozialistischen Entwicklung feindlich.) Der Krieg
mag den sowjetischen Staat zu einer neuen radikaleren
"Linie" zwingen: eine solche Wendung wäre äusserlich,
dem Widerruf ausgesetzt, und würde, wenn erfolgreich,
von der ungeheueren Machtsteigerung des Sowjetstaates
aufgehoben werden."

† The manuscript which I am calling "33 Theses" was found in the Max Horkheimer archive with no title, and a handwritten "H. Marcuse. febr. 1947" in the top righthand corner. In the center of the page, "Teil I." (Part I) is written. The manuscript contains 33 theses on the current world situation which were intended as a contribution for a possible relaunching of the Institute journal *Zeitschrift für Sozialforschung*. Although an October 17, 1947 letter to Horkheimer (see page 257) indicates that Marcuse is working on the theses, this manuscript has not been found. Thus we are publishing the February 1947 draft found in the Horkheimer archive. Thanks to Gunzelin Schmid Noerr for making accessible this document.

33 THESES[†]

Translated by John Abromeit

1 After the military defeat of Hitler-Fascism (which was a premature and isolated form of capitalist reorganization) the world is dividing into a neo-fascist and a Soviet camp. What still remains of democratic–liberal forms will be crushed between the two camps or absorbed by them. The states in which the old ruling class survived the war economically and politically will become fascistized in the forseeable future, while the others will enter the Soviet camp.

2 The neo-fascist and the Soviet societies are economic and class enemies and a war between them is probable. But both are, in their essential forms of domination, anti-revolutionary and hostile to socialist development. The war might force the Soviet state to adopt a new, more radical "line." This type of shift would be superficial and subject to revocation; if successful, it would be neutralized by the massive increase of power of the Soviet state.

3 Under these circumstances there is only one alternative for revolutionary theory: to ruthlessly and openly criticize both systems and to uphold without compromise orthodox marxist theory against both. In the face of political reality such a position would be powerless, abstract and unpolitical, but when the political reality as a whole is false, the unpolitical position may be the only political truth.

4 The possibility of its political realization is itself a part of marxist theory. The working class and the political praxis of the working class, and changing class relations (at the national and international level) continue to

determine the conceptual development of theory, as they in turn are determined by it – not by the theory without praxis, but by the one which "seizes the masses." Realization is neither a criterion nor the content of marxist truth, but the historical impossibility of realization is irreconcilable with it.

5   The position alluded to in thesis #3 acknowledges the historical impossibility of its realization. Outside the Soviet camp there is no workers' movement "capable of revolution." The social democrats have become more rather than less bourgeois. The Trotskyist groups are divided and helpless. The communist parties are not willing (today), and thus also not capable of revolution, but they are the only anti-capitalist class organization of the proletariat and thus the only possible basis for revolution (today). But they are at the same time the tools of Soviet politics and as such hostile to the revolution (today). The problem lies in the unity within the communist parties of forces potentially capable of revolution with others hostile to revolution.

6   The total subordination of the communist parties to Soviet politics is itself the result of changed class relations and the reorganization of capitalism. Fascism, as the modern form of the class dictatorship of capital, has completely changed the conditions of revolutionary strategy. Capital has created (not only in the fascist states) a terroristic apparatus with such striking power and ubiquitous presence, that the traditional weapons of proletariat class struggle appear powerless against it. The new technology of war and its strict monopolization and specialization turns the arming of the people into a helpless affair. The open identification of the state with the economy, and the integration of the union bureaucracy into the state, both work against political strikes, particularly the general strike – perhaps the only weapon against fascistized capital. This development has led to the fact that the only possible way to successfully oppose the massive military–political apparatus of capital is to construct and implement an at least equally powerful military and political counter-apparatus, to which the traditional revolutionary strategy is subordinated. The Soviet Union will be seen as this kind of counter-apparatus.

7   The question, whether or not the rulers in the Soviet Union are even still interested in revolution, was secondary in the context of this argument. The argument was upheld, even when it was assumed that a subjective tie no longer existed between Soviet power and the revolution. Soviet power would, so it was said, inevitably be forced into an increasingly heated conflict with the capitalist states - even if they were only representing and

pursuing national interests. The Soviet Union would be the most dangerous and seductive object of the imperialist politics of capital and as such the given enemy, who sooner or later would be forced to take up arms. The common opposition against capital would be the basis for a future reunification of revolution and Sovietism – just as the current alliance of capitalism and Sovietism is the basis for the separation of revolution and Sovietism.

8   This justification of the communist line is open to the objection, that education in anti-revolutionary, national politics makes the working class hopelessly incapable of revolution – even if it is mere "tactics." It creates "vested interests" which have their own dynamic and come to determine tactics. It undermines class consciousness and strengthens submission to national capital. It contravenes the unity of economy and politics and subsumes class relations under political dictates.

9   The rejection of the political justification of the subordination of revolutionary strategy to Sovietism is only the first step in returning the problems to their actual sphere – that of real class relations. The communist line points back behind its own political justification to these relations: it is the expression and result of a structural change within the working class and in its relation to the other classes. The transformation of the form of the domination of capital (upon which the political justification of the communist line is based) should be understood in terms of this structural change as well.

10   It has found its most obvious expression in the fact that Social Democracy has victoriously survived Fascism (whose rise to power it facil-itated), that it has once again monopolized the entire organized workers' movement outside of the communist parties, that the communist parties are becoming more social democratic themselves, and that up to now no revolutionary workers' movement has emerged from the collapse of Hitler-Fascism. Thus, Social Democracy seems to be the adequate expres-sion of the non-communist workers' movement. Social Democracy has not radicalized itself either, but has instead essentially followed its pre-fascist politics of class-cooperation. The non-communist workers' movement is a bourgeoisified [*verbürgerlicht*] (in the objective sense) workers' movement, and workers' voices against the communist parties are voices against the revolution, not just against Sovietism.

11   The bourgeoisification, or the reconciliation of a large part of the working class with capitalism cannot be explained by pointing to the (growing) "workers' aristocracy." The workers' aristocracy and the factors

which make it possible have certainly played a decisive role in the development of Social Democracy, but the depth and breadth of bourgeoisification goes far beyond the level of the workers' aristocracy. In Germany and France the carriers of bourgeoisification in the post-fascist period are not by any means primarily exponents of the workers' aristocracy. The depth and breadth of bourgeoisification cannot be explained with the domination of the bureaucracy over the organizational apparatus (of party and unions) either. The organizational apparatus was dismantled by Fascism, and yet the vacuum which defeated fascism left behind has not been filled by a counter-movement, rather this same bureaucracy is back in power again.

12 One of theory's most urgent tasks is to investigate bourgeoisification in all its manifestations. To say it again: bourgeoisification must be seen as an objective class phenomenon, not as the Social Democrats' insufficient will to revolution or their bourgeois consciousness, but rather as the economic and political integration of a large part of the working class into the system of capital, as a change in the structure of exploitation. The basis of this investigation can be found in Marx's references to surplus profit and the monopolizing position of certain producers and spheres of production. The development results on the one hand in the direct fusion of the state with capital, and on the other in state-administrative regulation of exploitation, which leads to the replacement of the free labor contract with binding public collective contracts. These factors define the boundaries within which the economic integration of the working class is proceeding. With it the working class's portion (quantitative and qualitative) of the social product is growing to such an extent, that opposition to capital is being transformed into extensive cooperation.

13 In the course of this same development the full weight of exploitation falls upon groups which occupy a marginal or alien position within society, those "outsiders" excluded from the integrated part of the working class and its solidarity, and, in the extreme case, "enemies." They are the "unorganized," "unskilled workers," agricultural and migrant workers, minorities, colonized and half-colonized, prisoners, etc. Here war must be seen as an essential element of the capitalist process as a whole: rapacious reproduction of monopoly capital through plundering of conquered countries and their proletariat; creation of foreign concentrations of surplus exploitation and absolute impoverishment. The fact that the rapacious plundering makes use of the most advanced modern technology and strikes highly developed capitalist countries strengthens the power of monopoly capital and its victorious state to a previously unheard of degree.

14 The economical and political identification of the integrated part of the workers with the capitalist state is accompanied by a no less decisive "cultural" integration and identification. The thesis of the legitimacy of the existing society, which, even though poorly, does after all maintain and provide for the whole, should be applied to all spheres of social and individual life. Its validity has been strongly confirmed by the obvious refutation of its opposite in the development of the Russian revolution. The fact that the first successful socialist revolution has not yet led to a freer and happier society has contributed immeasurably to reconciliation with capitalism and has objectively discredited the revolution. These developments have allowed the existing society to appear in a new light, and the existing society has understood how to use this to its advantage.

15 The phenomenon of cultural identification demands that the problem of "cultural cement" (*Kitt*) be discussed upon a broader basis. One of the most important factors involved here is the leveling of formerly avantgarde–oppositional forces with the cultural apparatus of monopoly capitalism (the transformation and application of psychoanalysis, modern art, sexuality, etc. in the work and entertainment process). First and foremost the effects of "*Kitt*" within the working class should be investigated: "scientific management," rationalization, the interest of the worker in increased productivity (and with it, in the intensification of exploitation), strengthening of nationalistic sentiments.

16 The communist strategy of party dictatorship is the reply to the bourgeoisification of the working class. If the revolution can only be brought about by the working class, which has, however, through its integration in the system of capital, been alienated from its task, then the revolution presupposes the dictatorship of the revolutionary "avant-garde" over the integrated working class. This turns the working class into the object of revolution which can develop into a subject only through party manipulation and organization. The communist dictatorship over the proletariat becomes the first step toward dictatorship of the proletariat.

17 The only alternative would be the objective reversal of bourgeoisification, the breakdown of integration caused by the unfolding contradictions of capitalism, which would also necessarily undermine the economic foundation upon which capital maintains integration. But in the coming crises capital will appear as fascistized or once again as fascist capital: at its highpoint the working class in America is already largely disempowered, its organization broken, and the military and police apparatus omnipresent. If England does have an independent development then the anti-revolutionary trade union socialism will set up a middle class society there that will make bourgeoisification even more perfect. France still has the possibility of developing in any of the three ways: the fascist, the trade union socialist, or the Soviet. And Germany will remain suppressed in the near future, as the object of these three forces. The developing contradictions of capitalism tend toward fascism or anti-revolutionary state socialism – not toward revolution.

17a The trade union socialism dominant in England (and emerging in Germany) is not yet state socialism. The partial socializations, which are undertaken primarily for "economic" reasons (increased productivity, rationalization, ability to compete, centralization of administration) or as political punishment, have allowed the decisive positions of capital (the steel and iron industry, the chemical industry in England) to remain intact. The stage of state socialism is not reached until the government has assumed and legalized control of industry as a whole and has taken over ownership from private capital. The government, the state – not the unified producers, the working class.

18 The societal tendency of state socialism is anti-revolutionary. Power over the means of production has been transferred to the state, which exercises this power through the employment of wage labor. The state has also assumed the role of the direction of capital as a whole ("*Gesamt-kapitalisten*"). The direct producers do not control production (and with it their destiny) any more than they do in the system of liberal-democratic capitalism. They remain subordinated to the means of production. The domination of humans mediated by the means of production continues to exist. The universal interest, for which the planned economy is designed and implemented, is the existing apparatus of production, the existing form of the social division of labor (national and international) and the existing social needs. They have not been fundamentally changed; change is supposed to come about gradually, as a consequence of planning. But in this way state socialism maintains the foundation of class society. The abolition of classes, the transition to a free society *presupposes* the change, which state socialism sets as its goal. The difference in time signifies a *qualitative* difference.

19 The production apparatus developed under capitalism, propelled by wage labor within the existing form of the division of labor, perpetuates the existing forms of consciousness and needs. It perpetuates domination and exploitation, even when control of the apparatus is transferred to the state, i.e. to the universal, which is itself one of domination and exploitation.

Prior to the revolution the universal is not a factor in socialism: its domination is not freer and not necessarily more rational than that of capital. Socialism means a determinate universal: that of free persons. Until developed communist society has become real, the universal can only take the form of the domination of the revolutionary working class, because only this class can negate all classes, it alone has the real power to abolish the existing relations of production and the entire apparatus that goes with it. The first goal of the communist dictatorship over the proletariat (see #16) must be to surrender the production apparatus to the proletariat: the council republic.

20   This goal, and all the politics that go with it, is not in the program of any communist party today. It is irreconcilable with social democracy. In the given situation it is advanced only as pure theory. This separation of theory and practice is demanded by practice itself and remains oriented towards it. That is to say, negatively, theory does not ally itself with any anti-communist group or constellation. The communist parties are and remain the only anti-fascist power. Their denunciation must be purely theoretical. It knows that the realization of theory is only possible through the communist parties and that it needs the help of the Soviet Union. This consciousness must be contained in all of its concepts. More: in all of its concepts the denunciation of neo-fascism and social democracy must outweigh that of communist politics. The bourgeois freedom of democracy is better than total regimentation, but it has been literally purchased with decades of prolonged exploitation and delayed socialist freedom.

21   Theory itself is faced with two main tasks: the analysis of bourgeoisification (#12–15) and the construction of socialism. The reasons which moved Marx to omit this type of construction must be reconsidered in light of the harm being done by the spurious and semi-socialist constructions. The construction of socialism is faced with the task of rethinking the two-phase-theory or the difference between socialism and communism, which dominates the discussion today. This theory itself already belongs to the period of bourgeoisification and social democracy, as an attempt to draw this phenomenon into the original conception and to rescue the conception from it. It presupposes that the socialist society will "emerge" from the capitalist, and that the latter will work its way into socialism. It accepts, for the first phase, the continuation of the subordination of labor to the division of labor, the continuation of wage labor and the domination of the production apparatus. It remains oriented toward the necessity of technological progress. It can strengthen the dangerous view that, regarding the development of the forces of production

and efficiency, socialism is an intensified capitalism, and that the socialist society has to "surpass" capitalism.

22 The two-phase-theory gained historical justification in the Soviet Union's struggle against the surrounding capitalist world, and in the necessity to "construct socialism in one country." It justifies the non-existence of socialism in this situation. Beyond this it is false. By accepting capitalist rationality, it plays out the weapons of the old society against the new one: capitalism has better technology and greater wealth (technological); this foundation allows capitalism to let people live better. Socialist society can imitate and outdo this only if it forgoes the costly experiment of abolishing domination and imitates and outdoes the capitalist development of production and the productivity of labor, i.e. the subordination of wage labor to the production apparatus. The transition to socialism becomes *rebus sic stantibus*[1] pointless.

23 In contrast to this, the two-phase-theory can only project a change into the future. Its value is very small for European and American workers in the grip of trade union ideology; positivism has triumphed here as well. And the value becomes smaller the longer the "first phase" lasts. Its extension breeds a spirit of submission and accommodation in the affected workers, who themselves uphold the perpetuation of the "first phase" and extinguish revolutionary desires. Under these circumstances, the end of the "first phase" and the transition to communism can appear only as a miracle or as the work of external, foreign forces (see #7).

24 The construction of socialism should place its difference, not its "emergence" from capitalism in the center of discussion. The socialist society should be presented as the determinate negation of the capitalist world. This negation is not the nationalization of the means of production, nor their better development, nor the higher standard of living, but rather the abolition of domination, exploitation and labor.

25 The socialization of the means of production, their administration by the "immediate producers" remains the precondition of socialism. This is its first distinguishing characteristic: where it is missing, there is no socialist society. But the socialized means of production are still those of capitalism: they are objectified domination and exploitation. Not only in the purely economic sense. What was produced with them bears the mark of capital-ism: it is also stamped upon the consumer goods. Certainly, a machine is only a machine; the process of wage labor first makes it into capital. But

---

1 Things being this way.

as capital the given means of production have also formed people's needs, thoughts and feelings, and determined the horizon and content of their freedom. Socialization as such changes neither the horizon nor the content: if production continues uninterrupted, what was there before the moment of socialization will also be reproduced. Habituated needs continue to influence the new conditions and the socialized means of production. Socialization of the means of production becomes socialism only to the extent that the method of production itself becomes the negation of its capitalist counterpart.

26 This includes, to begin with, the abolition of wage labor. The bureaucratic-state administration of the means of production does not do away with wage labor. This does not become the case until the producers themselves directly administer production, i.e. themselves determine what, how much, and how long objects are produced. This step is, under the conditions of the modern economy, probably tantamount to the transition to anarchy and disintegration. And precisely this anarchy and dis-integration is probably the only way to break capitalist reproduction in socialism, to create the interregnum or even the vacuum, in which the change of needs, the birth of freedom can take place. The anarchy would testify to the abolition of domination, and the disintegration would eliminate the power of the production apparatus over humans, or at least mean the greatest chance for a total negation of class society.

27 When the workers take production into their own hands (and do not immediately submit themselves again to a new bureaucracy of domi-nation), perhaps they will abolish wage slavery first, i.e. shorten working hours. They might also decide what to produce, whatever appears most important to them in various locations. This would lead automatically to the dissolution of the national economy in its integrated form; the production apparatus would disintegrate into separate parts, in many instances the technical machinery would remain unused. A backwards movement would begin, which would not only break the national economy out of the world economy, but would also bring poverty and affliction. But the catastrophe signals that the old society has really ceased to function: it cannot be avoided.

28 This would mean that the leap into socialism would entail a leap into a lower standard of living than that reached in capitalist countries. Socialist society would begin at a technologically "surpassed" level of civilization. The starting criterion of socialist society is not technological – it is progress in the realization of the freedom of producers, which expresses itself in a qualitative change in needs. The will to abolish domination and exploitation appears as the will to anarchy.

29 The beginning of socialism at a "surpassed" level of civilization is not "backwardness." It differs from the beginning of Soviet society in the fact that the setback is not an economic necessity (determined by the technical level of production), but rather an act of revolutionary freedom, a conscious interruption of continuity. The present production and distribution apparatus is suspended by the workers, not fully utilized, perhaps even partially destroyed. If the proletariat cannot simply "take over" the state apparatus, then the same is true for the modern production apparatus. Its structure demands specialized and differentiated bureaucracy, which necessarily perpetuates domination, and mass production, which leads necessarily to standardization and manipulation (regimentation).

30 The problem of preventing a state-socialist bureaucracy must be seen as an economic problem. Bureaucracy has its social origins in the (technological) structure of the production apparatus; the removal of its heteronomous form presupposes changing this structure. A general socialist education would certainly make specialized roles interchangeable and thus break the heteronomous form of bureaucracy, but this type of education cannot succeed in an established bureaucracy of domination. It has to precede the functioning bureaucracy – not replace it. Such an education is only possible when the heteronomously structured production apparatus is surrended to the producers for "experimentation." The rational authority, which has to lead this experimentation, must remain under the direct control of the producers.

31 The revolutionary disintegration of the capitalist production apparatus will also disintegrate workers' organizations, which have become a part of this apparatus. The unions are not only organs of the status quo, but also of the maintenance of the status quo in the new forms of state socialism and Sovietism. Their interests are bound to the functioning of the production apparatus whose (second-rate) partner they have become. They might exchange masters, but they need a master to share their interest in the taming guidance of the organized-workers.

32 While the unions in their traditional structure and organization represent a force hostile to revolution, the political workers' party remains the necessary subject of revolution. In the original Marxist conception the party does not play a decisive role. Marx assumed that the proletariat is driven to revolutionary action on its own, based on the knowledge of its own interests, as soon as revolutionary conditions are present. In the mean time monopoly capitalism has found the ways and means of economically, politically and culturally leveling [*gleichschalten*] (#12–15) the majority of the proletariat. The negation of this leveling *before* the revolution is impossible. The development has confirmed the correctness of the Leninist conception of the vanguard party as the subject of the revolution. It is true that the communist parties of today are not this subject, but it is just as true that only they can become it. Only in the theories of the communist parties is the memory of the revolutionary tradition alive, which can become the memory of the revolutionary goal once again; only its situation is so far outside the capitalist society that it can become a revolutionary situation again.

33 The political task then would consist in reconstructing revolutionary theory within the communist parties and working for the praxis appropriate to it. The task seems impossible today. But perhaps the relative independence from Soviet dictates, which this task demands, is present as a possibility in Western Europe's and West Germany's communist parties.

IX

Max Horkheimer

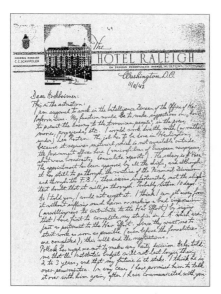
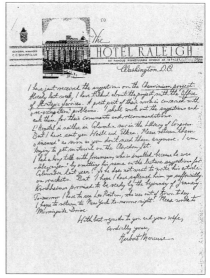

† These letters from Marcuse to Horkheimer were found in the Horkheimer archive. Unfortunately, most of Marcuse's letters written during the 1940s appear to have been lost. A wider selection of the Horkheimer/Marcuse correspondence can be found in Volumes 16–18, Max Horkheimer, *Gesammelte Schriften* (hereafter *GS*) edited by Gunzelin Schmid Noerr, Frankfurt: Fischer Verlag, 1995–6. Thanks to Schmid Noerr for permission to publish these letters and to Benjamin Gregg for translating the letters, originally written in German.

LETTERS TO
HORKHEIMER[†]

October 15, 1941

Dear Horkheimer:

Yesterday I had an improvised yet quite thorough discussion with Lynd.[1] In fact I had really only wanted to say hello, but he immediately took off on a nearly one-hour speech about the Institute. Basically the same old story: that we had wasted a great opportunity. That we had never achieved a true collaboration in which we might have confronted our European experiences with conditions in America, for example to analyze monopoly capitalism, fascist tendencies and so forth. That our first "fatal mistake" was to have published the *Zeitschrift* for years in German, and that when we finally published it in English, we failed to change the design and format.[2]

I told him we felt his objections were basically directed at our abstract, theoretical approach. He took strong exception to that, saying there was quite enough concrete, empirical research in America, and that what was missing was precisely a grand and vital theoretical perspective, but that such a perspective would have to be presented in a way that would make it relevant to the Americans and would make sense to them. He said he had the greatest respect for your theoretical undertakings and had, even back then, encouraged you to publish them, but that you were always apprehensive about being viewed as a Marxist and therefore had always presented your thoughts in an incomprehensible, garbled manner. When I asked him if perhaps the final volume was somewhat more in line with his expectations, he said he was just now beginning to read it, but that its paper and format alone would put any reader off. He said we should use *Social Research* as a model, including its design and format.[3]

Every time I tried to get him to be more concrete he countered that it really didn't matter *what* we actually studied and wrote about if we would just be truly collaborative in our work. He also said we shouldn't always wait for American aid and impetus but rather should first create something on our own, by our own efforts.

Even though he said this all in the friendliest manner and in a tone of genuine concern, I felt his enmity was not to be overcome, indeed not even neutralized. Irrational hatred is doubtless involved. I see no way to really win Lynd over. At most we might take the edge off his attacks – though I wouldn't know how.

Pollock suggested I give a talk in English on the "State and Individual under National Socialism."[4] Perhaps the work of preparing the talk could then be re-used for my article – in which case it would be worth the effort. It might provide a concrete standpoint from which to reveal the bourgeois individual as he really is and to show that National Socialism constitutes his fulfillment much more than his demise.

In recent days I've been working on a small presentation I shall make next Friday here at the Institute on the notion of a linguistic critique of fascism. I could re-use this material as well. Please let me know what you think.

The committee meeting, at which we were supposed to discuss our lectures, has been postponed until next week.[5]

One of Lynd's first questions, by the way, was when you were to return. I told him: in the coming weeks.

With cordial greetings to you and your wife,
Yours, Herbert Marcuse[6]

---

1 Robert Lynd, Professor of Sociology at Columbia University, was author of the renowned studies (with Helen Merrell Lynd) *Middletown* (New York: Harcourt, Brace & World, 1956 [1929]), *Middletown in Transition* (New York: Harcourt, Brace & World, 1937), and his own *Knowledge for What?* (Princeton: Princeton University Press, 1967 [1939]). He presented himself as a "friend" of the Institute of Social Research, but was often critical of the Institute for its failure to carry out collective research projects and better integrate itself into American academic life.

2 *Zeitschrift für Sozialforschung* was the official journal of the Institute of Social Research published in German from 1932 until the last several issues in 1940–1. Lynd and others urged the Institute to publish in English and to broaden its authorship to engage a broader American audience and in its last four 1940–1 issues it did indeed do so.

3 *Social Research* is the journal published by the New School for Social Research from January 1934 to the present. Initially conceived as a publication for the faculty of the New School, it reached out and published prominent social theorists and researchers. The journal had an attractive format and a respectable readership, aiming at a broad audience in the social sciences. The New School was founded and run by a rival school of German emigrant scholars and their journal *Social Research* represented more empirical, less critical and a more pluralistic approach to social theory and research than the Institute's. On the New School and its

journal *Social Research*, see Claus-Dieter Krohn, *Intellectuals in Exile: Refugee Scholars and the New School for Social Research*. Amherst: University of Massachusetts Press, 1993.

4 Marcuse did indeed give a talk on the topic of "State and Individual Under National Socialism" in October 1941, and a revised version of the lecture, prepared for possible publication, is published on page 69f. The study "Some Social Implications of Modern Technology" (page 41f.) also takes up the theme of the fate of the individual in modern society.

5 A Committee of the Sociology Department at Columbia University was considering Institute lectures for the following seminars and eventually approved a lecture series by Horkheimer which became his book *Eclipse of Reason* (New York: Herder and Herder, 1974 [1947]).

6 Translated by Benjamin Gregg.

November 11, 1941
[New York]

Dear Horkheimer:

I was very pleased by your telegram. I see that in fact I didn't misunderstand you after all. Long distances are such a nuisance.[1]

I shudder at the thought of having to stay here even longer. I can accept the material deprivations (I came here with one and half suits, and in the long run a sofa in the Institute is hardly a bed). But I really would like very much to begin to work with you. I know something will come of it, and that it will come quickly. On the other hand I realize it unfortunately will have to be a long-term work, and that its preconditions will need more than ever to be fulfilled. We can no longer afford this fragmentation of energy. I now see from my own experience that it can't go on any longer. So we need to wipe the slate here clean. How I should love to say: forget Columbia and just leave this nonsense behind. But I still can't bring myself to say that. I'm just not one for leaving "messages in a bottle."[2] What we have to say is not just for some mythical future. I have observed you often enough in discussion and know the kind of response you can elicit. That, too, obliges. Your book must be a "success":[3] I know exactly what I'm saying. We can formulate our problems by arguing them back and forth – which can only do them good.

All this seems to me more important than political protection. We can no longer achieve the kind of isolation to really enjoy peace and quiet.

I constantly argue with myself and in a dark place in my soul I almost hope that MacIver on Wednesday gives me just the answer that would allow me to leave. I would ask for your concurrence. Otherwise – if I again have the impression that the matter will be pursued and really has a chance, I will stay on.

I hope to be able to complete my essay here.[4] I take consolation in the fact that you will be occupied with your essay still for some time.[5] I ordered a book for you by the American historian Carl L. Becker: *The Heavenly City in Eighteenth Century Philosophy*. It is a slim volume on utopias of the Enlightenment (which appeared already in 1939) and is supposed to be good.

I feel sorry for my family, to which after all I also belong.

With cordial greetings, also to your wife,
Yours,
Herbert Marcuse[6]

---

1 The reference is to Horkheimer's plan to, on one hand, work toward downsizing the Institute of Social Research, and, on the other hand, to try to secure lectures or a more profitable institutional affiliation with Columbia University.

2 The term "message in a bottle" was Adorno's idea of preparing texts for future generations who might accidentally and fortuitously discover the Institute texts. Marcuse wanted to publish work in the present for a more contemporary audience, addressing topics of current interest as well as more esoteric theoretical issues.

3 The "book" refers to the text that became *Dialectic of Enlightenment* (New York: Herder and Herder, 1972 [1947]). Marcuse hoped to be a major collaborator on the book, but that task fell upon Adorno who emerged as Horkheimer's closest collaborator and sole co-author of the planned work that in 1941 involved Marcuse.

4 This refers to Marcuse's studies of the "Social Implications of Modern Technology" (see pages 41f.).

5 Horkheimer's article on reason appeared as "The End of Reason," in *Studies in Philosophy and Social Science* (the new name for the *Zeitschrift für Sozialforschung*, now published in English), Vol. 9, Nr. 3 (1941): 366–88.

6 Translated by Benjamin Gregg.

November 11, 1942

Dear Horkheimer:

This is the situation:

I am supposed to work in the Intelligence Bureau of the Office of War Information.[1] My function would be to make suggestions on "how to present the enemy to the American people," in the press, movies, propaganda, etc. I would work directly with (or rather under) Leo Rosten.[2] The job has to be done in Washington, because it requires material which is not available outside the government offices here (microfilms of European newspapers, short wave broadcasts, Consulate reports). The salary is $4600 – The appointment has been approved by all the chiefs, and although it has still to go through the routine of the Personnel Division and through the F.B.I., there seems unfortunately not the slightest doubt that it will go through. Probably within 10 days. As I told you, I would not accept it. I think I can get away from it without suffering much harm or making a bad impression (unwillingness to contribute to the War Effort) by saying that I have first to complete my studies in L.A. which are just as pertinent to the War Effort. Since they want me to start work as soon as possible (even before the formalities are completed), this will end the negotiations. Pollock has urged me not to make any hasty decision.³ He has told me that the Institute's budget will not last longer than 2 to 3 years, and that my future is at stake I think he is over-pessimistic. In any case, I have promised him to talk it over with him again, after I have communicated with you.

I have just received the suggestion on the *Chauvinism project*.⁴ Already last week, I have talked about the project with the *Office of Strategic Services*. A great part of their work is concerned with "re-occupation" problems. I shall work out the suggestions and ask them for their comments and recommendations.

L'Hôpital is neither in Columbia nor in the Library of Congress. But I have sent you Weil and Elkan. Please return them "insured" as soon as you don't need them anymore. I am trying to get material on the Avedon Set.⁵

I had a long talk with Grossmann, who is insulted because he was "übergangen" [passed over] by omitting his name on the lecture suggestions for Columbia last year!⁶ So he does not want to write his article on rackets. But I hope I have softened him up sufficiently. Kirchheimer promised to be ready by the beginning of January. To-morrow I have to see Leo Rosten, who was out of town today. I hope to return to New York to-morrow night! Please write to Morningside Drive.

With best regards to you and your wife,
Cordially yours,
Herbert Marcuse

---

1 Marcuse is referring to the job just offered to him by the U.S. government in which he was engaged for the following years. His report on "how to present the enemy to the American people" appears on page 179f.
2 Leo Rosten became Marcuse's boss in the Office of War Information and he also later reported to him during his work with the Office of Strategic Services, as Marcuse notes in an April 18, 1943 letter to Horkheimer (page 243), where Marcuse describes Rostan as "a very decent and intelligent person."
3 Frederick Pollock was one of Horkheimer's closest friends who was the Institute economist and in charge of administering the finances of the Institute of Social Research. Marcuse had gone out to California to work with Horkheimer in May 1941 and hoped that the Institute of Social Research would support him on a sufficient level to enable him to work on the envisaged book on dialectics with

Horkheimer and live in California where he had rented a house in Santa Monica for his family. Upon arriving in California, however, Horkheimer had told him that due to the worsening finances of the Institute, Marcuse's monthly stipend would have to be cut from $330 to $300 and then $280 per month (Horkheimer to Pollock, May 30, 1941 in Max Horkheimer, *GS*, Vol. 17. Frankfurt: Fischer 1996: 46). Horkheimer also warned Marcuse that the Institute was not sure how much longer they would be able to support him at all and Pollock later suggested that he should seriously consider the U.S. government job which he did indeed accept; see the following letters.

4 The Institute had drafted a "Report on German Chauvinism" and Marcuse gave a copy of the project to Edward Hartshorne, of the OSS, who in a letter of December 7, 1942 thanked Marcuse for the study, remarked that he felt "confident that the line of research indicated is not only well worth-while but highly urgent" and suggested some changes. Evidently, the Institute did not, however, pursue this project further.

5 *L'Hôpital*, Weil and Elkan and material on the Avedon Set refers to texts that Marcuse searched for in libraries to send to Horkheimer for work he was doing.

6 Henryk Grossmann, Institute economist, was a very orthodox Marxist who frequently feuded with Horkheimer, Pollock and others in the Institute, but seemed to get along with Marcuse. Grossmann was angry that he was not included in the 1941 lecture series on National Socialism at Columbia and he eventually broke off relations with the Institute, returning to Germany in 1948 when he received a Chair at Leipzig University, in the German Democratic Republic.

November 15, 1942

Dear Horkheimer:

Thanks for your letter of Nov. 10.

I know that, unfortunately, all "rational" argumentation speaks for my accepting the position in Washington. But it seems to me that you somewhat underrate my desire to continue the theoretical work we have been doing. In spite of my opposition to some of your conceptions, I have never and nowhere concealed my conviction that I know of no intellectual efforts today which are closer to the truth, and of no other place where one is still allowed and encouraged to think. It might be good to say this at this moment, and to tell you that I shall not forget what I learned with you. When I so strongly insisted on my trip to Washington, it was because I wanted to prolong this relationship as much as possible – and not because I was afraid of being inducted, as you indicated.

Only if you say that, on account of the Institute's financial situation, this relationship will anyway come to an end within a very short time, and that my position in Washington would make it possible to continue our common work after a relatively short interruption – only then would the rational argumentation harmonize with my rather "irrational" desire to continue our theoretical studies. I am too much of a materialist as to bring and make sacrifices without good reasons, and the contrast between the living and working conditions in Washington and in California is so striking that the extent of the sacrifice becomes clearer every day!

The work I would have to do in Washington seems to be respectable and perhaps even interesting, but I could consider it merely as a contribution to the War Effort and as an investment for the future. It might also be helpful for the Institute. However, I still subordinate these aspects to the prospects of our theoretical work. I should like to suggest that we postpone the decision until the "routine procedure" has been completed, and the offer becomes definite. Yesterday, I received a wire from the O.W.I. that I shall have definite word by Tuesday.[1]

The *Memorandum on German Chauvinism* is with the Office of Strategic Services, Psychology Division.[2]

I am working a little on my *Operationalism*.[3]

With best regards to your wife,
Cordially yours,
Herbert Marcuse

---

1 Marcuse indeed received the position in the Office of War Information (OWI) and began working there in December 1942, as his letter to Horkheimer of December 2, 1942 (below) indicates.
2 On the *Memorandum on German Chauvinism*, see note 4 of the November 11, 1942 letter to Horkheimer (page 234).
3 Marcuse's critique of operationalism refers to studies he was doing of behaviorism, operationalism and what he later called "one-dimensional thought." The manuscript on operationalism was frequently referred to in Marcuse's 1940s letters to Horkheimer, but did not appear in his archives. The critique of operationalism eventually emerged in *One-Dimensional Man*.

December 2, 1942

Dear Horkheimer:

Last week Saturday afternoon, I received a telephone call from Washington, asking me to attend a conference at the Office of War Information, to be held on Monday. The topic of the conference (which was attended only by 9 people) was to determine which groups, persons and institutions of Nazi Germany should be actually branded as The Enemy. During the conference, I received the message that my appointment has been approved and that I should take the oath of office tomorrow. Next morning, I went to see Dr. Pettee, the head of the division in which I am supposed to work. He told me that he expected me to start work at once. I replied that I could not possibly do this, since I had not yet made up my mind and not yet consulted the director of the Institute with respect to the new situation. I finally succeeded in obtaining a time limit of Sunday night.

I don't have to tell you how I feel about it. Your wire of congratulation strengthens my impression that you think I acted illoyal to you and our common work. I must tell you that I am deeply affected by this reproach. I was not making phrases when I wrote you that I would lose everything if this common work would stop "indefinitely." You are the only one with whom I could do some real work. This means more to me than anything else. And it is precisely the maintenance of our future collaboration which made me go to Washington and proceed according to your suggestions. I thought I had convinced you of the sincerity of my wishes. I still want to believe I have.[1] You and Pollock have supported my argumentation in strong terms; and Pollock has urged me – for the reasons well known to you – to accept the position as a leave of absence from the Institute. This I would be willing to do, for I know that my stay in Washington will by no means be "indefinite." This at least you will grant me: that I do not care about the legal and administrative aspects of the case, but I do care very much that I continue to be a member of the Institute, or rather, your collaborator. Even in my position in Washington, I would have plenty of opportunity actually to function as a member of the Institute: not only because of the connections I will make, but more specifically because I could regularly turn to you for advice, suggestions, etc. The nature of my work there would be such that this collaboration could be very close, very logical, and even to some extent "official." I feel strongly that I shall need such collaboration in the future just as much as I needed it in the past, and that I could be of much compensating service to the Institute in many respects. I would be a kind of liaison man between various offices, particularly between the Office of War Information and the Office of Strategic Services. In both, we are well known, and I would like to develop and utilize this asset. But I would not hesitate to reject the position if you have any bad feelings about it, and if you would no longer consider me as belonging to you.

I would like to write you more, but I want you to have this letter on time.

Cordially yours,
Herbert Marcuse

---

1 In a letter of December 4, 1942 to Marcuse, Horkheimer makes it clear that he did not in any way think that Marcuse had acted disloyally and that he indeed

supported Marcuse's decision to work for the U.S. government. In fact, Horkheimer was relieved that the Institute was disemburdened of the responsibility to support Marcuse with its dwindling funds (see Horkheimer's letter to Löwenthal, November 8, 1942 in *GS*, Vol. 17, op. cit., 378). In any case, Marcuse makes clear his continued desire to maintain contact with Horkheimer and to continue working on Institute projects, which he was really not able to do as he became more and more immersed in his wartime work.

———

December 11, 1942
2920 – 38 St. N.W.
Washington, D.C.

Dear Horkheimer:

I have just received your letter of Dec. 4, which was forwarded to my new address. I am sorry for having misunderstood your wire; you will realize that I was rather nervous at the unexpected turn of the situation. I feel a little better now (not much).

You are quite right: my family should stay in L.A. for the next months. This is extremely hard for me, and the only comfort is your offer to help her there. But (1) I must wait until I see the developments here (the F.B.I. investigation has not yet started), and (2) living conditions here are on the border-line of *kulturelle Verelendung* (cultural impoverishment). The newcomer cannot even be sure of finding a house outside the District, 10–15 miles from downtown. And the furnished rooms are horrible. Fortunately I found a rather secluded place in the basement of a one-family house, one-hour streetcar ride to the office! But fortunately again, Anderson lives in the same neighbourhood and he and some of his colleagues take me in their car.[1] This might become a regular institution.

In the office, I am making myself familiar with the material, as they call it: reading microfilms of the European press and transcriptions of short wave broadcasts, etc. I hope to start on my first reports next week. It is highly improbable that I can go to New York over the weekends: (1) I work until 2 p.m. Saturdays (maybe longer), and (2) it is too expensive. Maybe once a month.

As I wrote you, I had discussed the *Memorandum on German Chauvinism* with some people in the Office of Strategic Services. I enclose the reply which I received today. In view of the fact that it is extremely difficult to get a written statement from any of the top War Agencies, the letter of the O.S.S. seems very useful and important.[2] I shall see Hartshorne next week and suggest to tell him that the project now will be exclusively carried out by the Los Angeles group of the Institute. Please *let me know* whether you want to follow up this connection and, if so, in how far you want to work on the project. It might be advisable to do so, but it would take too much of the time for real work.

Please keep me informed on *your work*: it will be my only opportunity for *thinking*, and I still need badly such opportunity. Please look after my family. I urged my wife a week ago to give up her job at once since it is now too much strain for her.

I am afraid that it will be too much even if she can go by car regularly.

How are all the others out there? I envy you and all of them.

Best regards to you and your wife,
Cordially yours,
Herbert Marcuse

Mail sent to my *office* must pass censor and will be considerably delayed. Please write to home address.

---

1 Eugene Anderson, Professor of History at the American University who had been very friendly to the Institute of Social Research during its sojourn at Columbia, helping them to prepare a Rockefeller Foundation proposal to study "Cultural Aspects of National Socialism." See Roderick Stackelberg, "Cultural Aspects of National Socialism: An Unfinished Project of the Frankfurt School," *Dialectical Anthropology* 12 (1988): 253–60. Marcuse worked with Anderson in government service in Washington and he had a very high opinion of Marcuse. See Eugene N. Anderson, *History of the European Section*, February 17, 1945, National Archives Record Group 226; discussed in Alfons Söllner, editor, *Zur Archäologie der Demokratie*, Volume 1. Frankfurt: Fisher, 1986: 30f. See also Söllner's interview with Anderson in *Zur Archäologie*, Volume 2: 22–58.
2 The reply from Edward Hartshorne to Marcuse on December 7, 1941 indicated OSS interest in the project (see note 4 to Marcuse's November 11, 1942 letter to Horkheimer, page 234). In a January 1, 1943 letter (below) Marcuse comments on Hartshorne's recommendations. Although there was some more discussion concerning the German Chauvinism project among Institute members in 1943, they were more focussed on developing projects on anti-semitism which were to be funded by the American Jewish Committee (AJC) and never undertook the studies of German chauvinism.

January 1, 1943
2920 – 38 St. N.W.
Washington, D.C.

Dear Horkheimer:

I postponed the answer to your letter of December 19 until I had talked to Hartshorne again.[1]

It is *by no means* necessary that you follow H[artshorne]'s suggestions very closely. The more we write on the basis of our own experience and knowledge, the better it is.

You should not concentrate the study on items 1 and 2 of H's suggestions. They have here plenty of reports on pre-Nazi and Nazi Germany. True, these reports are largely collections of facts. But I am afraid that precisely the lack of factual material at your disposal there will, in the eyes of the people here, diminish the value of your study. It is amazing what an abundance of material they have here (for example, complete sets of German newspapers and periodicals up to 1942). I would therefore suggest that you orient the work on the probable situation at the end of the war, and the items 3 ff. in H's letter. This would give you a high degree of freedom in the choice of your concepts and methods. I doubt that I can send you any material. They are terribly fussy here with the designation "confidential" and "secret." But I shall be glad to "paraphrase" any kind of document that you need, and to get all the information for you that pertains to the problem.

The study should be as extensive as possible. It is hard to say anything about time. In any case, reconstruction problems apparently come increasingly in the center of interest here. Next week I shall meet R. Turner, the chief of the German section of the Cultural Relations division in the State Dpt. I shall report as soon as I have seen him. He is director of the re-education studies in Germany.

Operationalism: I have tried to work on it as much as possible.[2] But: the Office of War Information "discourages all outside publications on controversial matters." Which means that the paper must be read and "cleared" by at least two chiefs of the bureau. What is your opinion?

What you write about your work makes me jealous. But couldn't you send me once in a while a copy? In this way I could at least keep in contact with the progress of your work.

I am working hard. We are now writing weekly reports on German home conditions and shifts in the German propaganda line.

With the best wishes for 1943,
Cordially yours,
Herbert Marcuse

---

1 On the German Chauvinism project and Hartshorne, see Marcuse to Horkheimer, November 11, 1942, note 4 (page 234), and Marcuse to Horkheimer, December 11, 1942, note 2 (page 239).
2 On the Operationalism project, see note 2, Marcuse to Horkheimer, November 15, 1942 (page 236). In fact, Marcuse did not publish anything during World War

Two and only published a couple of articles and reviews during his government service from 1942–50.

━━━━━━━━━━

March 4, 1943
2920 – 38 St. N.W.
Washington, D.C.

Dear Horkheimer:

Since long I wanted to congratulate your on your letter to Grossmann.[1] Pollock showed it to me in New York, and I was quite excited about it. I have rarely seen such a comprehensive summary of our standpoint in these matters. I agree with every single word. If you can spare a copy, please let me have one.

I was quite surprised to learn that my wish to see you here would be fulfilled. Pollock told me that you would be in New York next Fall at the latest. I was very happy about your lectures, and I hope that you are not too unhappy about the interruption of the work.[2] I still think it will be a good "investment." With respect to the Antisemitism project, I am of a different opinion. Unless the main work is done by you or at least under your constant active collaboration, it will be unworthy of the labor and the money.[3]

In the meantime, I had the first political differences. I was supposed to find Bolshevik tendencies in the Nazi system, which I could not do. Another difference of opinion arose re Russia. I related the details to Pollock, who will perhaps write you about it. In any case, I have seen and I am learning every day that our diagnosis of the tendencies prevalent in this country was terribly correct – except on one point: it was much too optimistic. The identity of the opposites (in this case, of the opponents) is unbelievably solid and perpetuates itself with a degree of consciousness which is sometimes amazing even to me.

The domestic branch of the Bureau of Intelligence will be severely curtailed in the next months since Congress has drastically cut the budget of the OWI and of other Government agencies. However, I shall probably be retained, and if not, I shall not be too unhappy.[4]

Hoping to hear from you soon,

With best regards to your wife,
Cordially yours,
Herbert Marcuse

1 In a letter from Horkheimer to Grossmann of January 20, 1943 Horkheimer
  developed in detail a critique of Grossmann's orthodox Marxist political economy
  and outlined his own perspectives; see Horkheimer to Grossmann, *GS*, Vol. 17:
  398–415.
2 Horkheimer gave lectures at Columbia University in Spring 1943 that became the
  basis of his later book *Eclipse of Reason.*
3 The anti-semitism project refers to studies undertaken with the sponsorship of the
  American Jewish Committee which were collected in *Studies in Prejudice* some
  years later. Although Horkheimer was indeed Director of the project many of the
  research projects did not really reproduce his own theoretical and political
  positions and his letters of the period present many conflicts with officials of the
  American Jewish Committee and his own conflicted opinion of their work and
  publications.
4 Marcuse was in fact transferred to the Office of Strategic Services (OSS), as his
  letter to Horkheimer on April 18, 1943 (below) confirms.

April 18, 1943
2920 – 38 St. N.W.
Washington, D.C.

Dear Horkheimer:

Thanks for your letter of April 3. I realize the necessity of carrying
out the Antisemitism project, and the much worse necessity of your
taking a large part in it. I only hope that you can carry over enough of
your theoretical work, and that you can resume our true task as soon as
possible.

You will have heard that I have decided to go to the OSS. The latest
reorganization has furthermore weakened the position of the OWI, and
this agency seems increasingly bound to become the prey of newspapermen
and advertising agents. Apart from this fact, I have seen that the OSS has
infinitely better material, and that I could do much more useful work there.
The OWI did not want me to go, and made it a condition that I could
continue to work for Leo Rosten (who is a very decent and intelligent
person). This has been arranged, and the agreement is to be concluded this
week.[1]

Pollock has shown me your notes on the project. If you want to
collaborate with Renso Sireno, let me know. He is a very good friend of
mine, and indeed a very able and sympathetic man.[2]

Please read Georges Bernanos, *Lettre aux Anglais.* It is a great book, and
it comes closer to the truth than any other I have seen in many years. It gave
me the only encouragement I have found here. I am doing my work and I
am supposed to do it well (it will amuse you as much as it did amuse me
that I received the "efficiency rating" excellent, a rare mark), but I have not

the slightest illusions, and it is very hard for me to keep going in the face of what is happening around me and in the world. I wished I could talk all this over with you.

My family was in St. Louis already on the 17. I am most happy to have them here. I was long enough alone.

Wish best regards to your wife,
Cordially yours,
Herbert Marcuse

---

1 In March 1943, Marcuse transferred to the Office of Strategic Services (OSS), working until the end of the war in the Research and Analysis Division of the Central European Branch. Marcuse and his colleagues wrote reports attempting to identify Nazi and anti-Nazi groups and individuals in Germany and drafted a *Civil Affairs Handbook Germany* that dealt with de-Nazification.
2 Renso Sireno was a close friend of Marcuse's about whom nothing more is known.

———

July 28, 1943
6600 Luzon Ave. N.W.
Washington 12, D.C.

    Dear Horkheimer:

I was very glad to receive your letter; I sometimes thought that you had forgotten about me. True, Pollock sent me the New York papers on the project, but I have not yet received the Los Angeles contributions. In order to keep my mind on theoretical problems, I have tried to work up my own ideas on anti-Semitism. So I can at least use the more or less exclusive material I get here for the common cause. Although your letter does not reveal the concrete pattern of your studies, I think I can see their general direction, and I seem to be working along the same way.

Perhaps I wrote you already that the "spearhead" theory in the form in which we formulated it originally seems to me inadequate, and this inadequacy seems to increase with the development of fascist anti-semitism.[1] The function of this anti-Semitism is apparently more and more in the perpetuation of an already established pattern of domination in the character of men. Note that in the German propaganda, the Jew has now become an "internal" being, which lives in Gentiles as well as Jews, and which is not conquered even with the annihilation of the "real" Jews. If we look at the character traits and qualities which the Nazis designate as the Jewish elements in the Gentiles, we do not find the so-called typical Jewish traits (or at least not primarily), but traits which are regarded as definitely

Christian and "human." They are furthermore the traits which stand most decidedly against repression in all its forms. Here, we should resume the task of elucidating the true connection between anti-Semitism and Christianity (which so far has not been followed up in the project). What is happening is not only a belated protest against Christianity but also a consummation of Christianity or at least of all the sinister traits of Christianity. *Der Jude ist von dieser Welt*, and *diese Welt* is the one which fascism has to subject to the totalitarian terror.[2]

As far as the socio-economic aspects of anti-Semitism are concerned, it seems to me that we should place more emphasis on anti-Semitism as an instrument of *international* fascism. With the eclipse of the Hitlerian stage of fascism (which, as we see now, was only a preparatory stage), anti-Semitism becomes more and more a weapon for the "coordination" of the diverging national fascism, or, a bid for the negotiated peace. Here again, we have to correct our earlier conception. I mean that of the "sham war." In the last analysis, the conception holds true. But the *Scheinhäftigkeit* [illusoriness] of the war demands rather than excludes the utter defeat of Germany and rests in the ends rather than in the means to achieve the ends. However, I do not believe a minute that the fascist stabilization will succeed in "integrating" the actual conflicts for any length of time. I do not believe so against all facts and common sense. The most depressing aspect of Mussolini's exit is that all this happened without any excitement, rebellion, hate. After more than twenty years of terror, the fascist party dissolves itself like a *Kegelklub* [bowling club]. Nobody really cares. Life goes on. Nothing has happened. A sign, not of a more mature consciousness, but of a totalitarian apathy, fatigue, indifference. Can you imagine Hitler and his gang just resigning and handing over business to a new management (partly new), but staying on in Germany unmolested and enjoying undisturbed privacy? I think this goes even beyond our most audacious predictions, and still, it might happen.

Sometimes, it is too much even for *unsereiner* [our group]. I have now snatched a week's vacation which we spend in Virginia, in a nice and quiet place with good swimming and bad food.

It is about time that you come East and we have a real talk.

Heartiest regards to you and your wife,
Cordially yours,
H.M.

Many thanks for your birthday congratulations.[3]

---

1 The "spearhead" theory of anti-semitism discussed by the Institute of Social

Research saw anti-semitism as a "spearhead" to incarcerate other groups, such as Communists, Social Democrats, anarchists and other political enemies of National Socialism. Marcuse goes on to develop some of his ideas on anti-semitism. Eventually, Horkheimer and Adorno developed a series of perspectives on anti-semitism in *Dialectic of Enlightenment*, refusing to privilege any one position.

2   "The Jew *is of this world*, and *this world . . .* "

3   Marcuse's birthday was July 19; he was born in 1898.

September 24, 1943
6600 Luzon Ave. N.W.
Washington 12, D.C.

Dear Horkheimer:

I should like to go through your paper On the Sociology of Class Relations[1] sentence for sentence, but I feel that this can be done only in personal discussion. I am waiting for this discussion, but since I'm afraid I have to wait too long, I want to comment at least on some major points of your paper:

As the paper is organized, the emphasis of the racket conception is placed on labor.[2] In view of this fact, you must be especially careful to avoid the impression that you take the "transformation of the class struggle into class adaptation" as a fait accompli and as the whole story. Although you say at several places that the labor racket comprises only the vast bureaucracy or the trade unions, and that underneath this stratum the victims of the unabated class struggle continue to live their miserable existence, the full weight of your argument falls upon the role and function of this top stratum. However, I think you will agree with me that the coordination of the working class as a whole with the apparatus of monopolistic society has not been successful, not in this country, certainly not in Germany and France, probably not in Great Britain. And the class struggle has not only been transformed into a means of class adaptation, but also in national and international war all over the earth. Here too, the monopolistic merger of economic and political factors asserts itself. If you would a little further develop this "counterevidence against social pessimism," it would also become clearer why the workers "become a more and more disquieting factor by their very assimilation."

I would furthermore suggest that you indicate how the coordination of so large a part of the working class with the ruling groups has come about. I think we are able to give an economic-political explanation (supporting the analysis in terms of "mass culture"), and it seems to me that the old established concept of the "labor aristocracy" could be retained and re-interpreted. (Economic and political origin of the labor aristocracy: monopolistic and technological rationalization; increased efficiency and increased dependency.) On page 30, you say that today the misery of the losing competitor and of the vanquished opponent can no longer be ascribed to objective anonymous processes, as it could under the market system. Here I must make a question mark. It seems to me that today more than ever before the triumph of the more efficient and more powerful enterprise can be attributed and is being attributed to objective anonymous processes, namely, to the iron laws of technological rationality, laws of which the monopolistic racketeers appear only as the obedient executors.

You can easily imagine how happy I was to read a paper which talks a language which I understand and which deals with the problems which are *the* problems. Congratulations. Let me just pick out a few passages that I consider especially good and far-reaching; your analysis of the "pragmatic totalities" of present day society, the interpretation of the role of the party and of the locus of theory, the development of the concept of mimesis, the social content of technocracy.

If the paper should be published, the English should be thoroughly revised, and some passages should be clarified (our old trouble). If you want me to do it, I shall be glad to designate these passages. Thanks for your letter of September 11. I wished I could occupy myself with all these things. Sometime I succeed in utilizing an evening, but that is all. Please send me as soon as possible your notes on the articles in the *Partisan Review*.[3]

With most cordial greetings to you and your wife,
Yours,
Herbert Marcuse

---

1 Horkheimer's "Sociology of Class Relations" is found in Max Horkheimer, *GS*, Vol. 12: 75ff.
2 Horkheimer's "racket conception" suggested that ruling groups were like gangs or "rackets," organized for their personal profit and power. For some years, he and others in the Institute of Social Research used the concept to describe both German fascism and monopoly capitalism, but never systematically developed the concept and eventually dropped it. Horkheimer's study of "rackets" that Marcuse read was never published.
3 In a September 11, 1943 letter from Horkheimer to Marcuse, he mentioned that he was planning to write a response to three articles in the *Partisan Review*, Vol. X, Nr. 1, 1943, by Hook, Dewey and Nagel. His comments eventually made it into Chapter II, "Conflicting Panacea," in *Eclipse of Reason*. New York: Oxford University Press, 1947.

October 25, 1943
6600 Luzon Ave. N.W.
Washington 12, D.C.

Dear Horkheimer:

Thanks for your letter of Oct. 11. You ask me to expand on the problem of the labor aristocracy and its relation to the rest of the workers.[1] I am thinking and even writing quite a lot about it, but I am far from clear. You know that Marx explained the rise of the labor aristocracy by the surplus profit which, under certain definite conditions, becomes available to the most "productively" working capitalist enterprises. It seems to me that this is still today the key to the problem. The vast growth in the size of the labor aristocracy apparently corresponds to the growth in the basis for surplus profits. At the present stage of the development, not only a few particularly favored enterprises, but almost all the large monopolistic concerns work under the conditions which make for surplus profit. On the other hand, the harmony of interests between the union bureaucracy and the large monopolistic combines is well known; you find some very good remarks on it already in Hilferding's *Finanzkapital*.[2] All this would make the hundreds and thousands of employees of the monopolistic key enterprises the true "mass basis" of the "collaborationist" labor groups.

The relation between the aristocracy and the rest of labor is not entirely that between active leadership and passive followers. The trend towards collaboration is fed from below as well as from above. The material benefits derived from the union policy is a very strong and very real tie. But what is the economic source out of which these benefits are being paid? Again the surplus profit? I don't know.

In any case, I think we know how the relation is in Nazi Germany. It is one of definite hostility towards the stratum of sub-leaders, foremen, trustees, etc. whom the Nazis have cleverly trained as a politically reliable and materially privileged "elite." This is why I said that the fascist *Gleichschaltung* [coordination] of labor has certainly not been successful. However, the opposition is not yet a political one, that is to say, not that of the class struggle.

It is a spontaneous, localized protest against harsh working conditions, speed up methods, long hours, bad food, etc.

In this country, the identity of the immediate interests between the union leadership and the organized workers is so great that the former may almost be characterized as the true representative of the latter. Moreover, in some striking cases, the collaborationist attitude of the workers seems to be even stronger than that of the unions. Take the famous Jack and Heintz factory in Cleveland (good article on it in the *New Republic* of Oct. 25), which is praised (also by the C[ommunist] P[arty]) as a paragon of the true relationships between workers and management. It is perhaps the most outstanding example of voluntary coordination of labor, and it shows how smoothly fascism can progress in a democratic environment.

I must apologize for the *Zusammenhangslosigkeit* [fragmentariness] of these brief remarks, but I can promise you that I shall continue to think about the problem and to send my notes. Of course I shall be glad to go through the whole paper and mark the passages which should be revised. I hope I can do this next week. The closer the war draws to its end, the more are we swamped with work, and the more am I anxious to return to real work and our common interests.

Best regards, also to your wife,
Cordially yours,
Herbert Marcuse

---

1 Marcuse is referring to Horkheimer's study of the "Sociology of Class Relations" discussed in Marcuse to Horkheimer, September 24, 1943, note 2 (page 247).
2 Rudolf Hilferding, *Das Finanzkapital: Eine Studie über die jüngste Entwicklung des Kapitalismus* (Vienna: 1910); translated, *Finance Capital: A Study of the Latest Phase of Capitalist Development*. London: Routledge & Kegan Paul, 1981.

May 22,1945
6600 Luzon Ave.
Washington 12, D.C.

Dear Horkheimer:

I have time and again postponed writing you about the *Philosophische Fragmente* because I was not ready to do it adequately.[1] I am still not ready, but I feel that I should at least describe to you my situation.

I have gone through the *Fragmente* twice. However, my reading was not continuous and concentrated enough: I was interrupted for days and even for weeks by office work which either took my evenings or tired me out into the evening. The result: there are too many passages which I don't understand, and too many ideas which I cannot follow up beyond the condensed and abbreviated form in which you give them. But I have to do it: I must be able to grasp the entirety behind the fragments before I can answer them. Therefore I have decided not to read them anymore here in Washington after office hours, but to take them along in my vacations where I can give them my whole time and attention.

You probably don't realize how I regret that we do not meet personally. As far as I am concerned, I did not even get to New York on business. We have now plenty of work for the War Crimes Commission, and the pressure is even greater than before. And the hope that you would come down here has not materialized.

You have received the preliminary report from Frankfurt. We expect more in the near future. Symbolism: the only big buildings which have not been damaged are the Hauptbahnhof, the main Synagogue and the I.G. Farben building. The university professors have so far not come into the open. We prohibit all political activity. Everywhere there is a return to the *Väter* who dominated the *selige* Weimar Republic: *Gespenstersonate*.[2]

How long are you going to be in New York? Maybe there will be an opportunity for me to get away for a couple of days.

With best regards to your wife,
Cordially yours,
Herbert Marcuse

---

1 *Philosophische Fragmente* (*Philosophical Fragments*) was the original title of Horkheimer and Adorno's text that became *Dialectic of Enlightenment* (the original title was included as a subtitle in its German publication, but left off in the 1972 English translation). Marcuse was initially going to be one of Horkheimer's collaborators on the project, but Adorno became his sole writing partner on the project and, as this letter indicates, Marcuse was totally immersed in his government war work and was not integrally involved in the book's production.
2 " . . . return to the *Fathers* who dominated the holy Weimar Republic: *Ghost Sonata*." The latter reference is to a play by August Strindberg (1908).

April 6, 1946
4609 Chevy Chase Blvd.
Washington 15, D.C.

Dear Horkheimer:

Your letter arrived the day after Pollock and his wife left. As always, there wasn't much time for a proper discussion. Nonetheless several themes were at least touched on and the necessity of discussing them further was once again all too clear.

As for me: an outside opportunity to do so may present itself soon enough. You will have heard that the State Department's Research and Intelligence Division has come under fierce attack for alleged communist tendencies. With this justification the Appropriations Committee has, for the time being, rejected new funding. Now the general horse-trading over the usual compromise begins, but quite possibly the Division will be dissolved on June 30.[1]

Actually I wouldn't exactly be sad were that to happen. What I, in recent years, have written and collected "off the job" has turned out to be the basis for a new book, about which Pollock will tell you. It is, naturally enough, centered on the problem of the "revolution that never happened." You will recall the drafts I wrote in Santa Monica on the transformation of language, on the function of scientific management, and on the structure of regimented experience. I want to develop these drafts into a portion of the book.[2]

How might all of this fit into your plans? Do you think that, in the near future – following or simultaneous with the projects on anti-semitism – there might be time for other projects? Have you considered continuing the *Zeitschrift* (something I would support enthusiastically)?[3] In any case: how is your health and how is life treating you physiologically?

Hoping to hear from you soon, and with best wishes and greetings, also to your wife.

Yours,
Herbert Marcuse[4]

---

1 The State Department's Research and Intelligence Division was indeed shut down, but Marcuse was transferred to the Central European Division of the State Department which he headed and where he worked until 1951.
2 Reflections on "the revolution that never happened" are found in the "33 Theses," written during 1946–7 (page 217f.), while the analyses of language, scientific management and regimented experience eventually were developed in *One-Dimensional Man*. The drafts Marcuse mentions here were not found in his archives.
3 Marcuse was urging Horkheimer to begin again with the publication of *Zeitschrift für Sozialforschung* and he eventually produced his "33 Theses" for inclusion in a special issue that would relaunch the journal with perspectives on the present situation, but the project never came to fruition.
4 Translated by Benjamin Gregg.

August 22, 1946
4609 Chevy Chase Blvd.
Washington 15, D.C.

Dear Horkheimer:

Many thanks for your letter.[1] To all the ominous signs of the times you count up, I could add many. But we know all that already, and have already lived through it all once before. Probably the wisest thing would be to develop or cultivate good relations with those members of the old new "elite" who now constitute the leadership of the Socialist Unity Party in Germany's Soviet Zone. An affidavit from that group could soon be quite useful. Yet one still has one's doubts! And in the end it's of no use anyway.

There is still a plan, however, to send me to Europe, but since that could still be put off for some time, I've decided to go to London for one or two weeks as a private individual. My mother, now over seventy and ailing, has invited me in the most urgent terms, and I feel I shouldn't postpone this trip much longer. My plan is to fly out of New York on September 21. I think I could arrange to travel from London to Paris (or Holland) if there's anything I could do for you there. Please let me know soon.

I am very pleased to hear negotiations are being conducted on resuming publication of the *Zeitschrift*. Of course unrestricted importation will hardly be possible in the foreseeable future, but I believe we can get official authorization. In any case, most important is that such materials are there, available and within reach – everything else will take care of itself.

In the meantime I have continued to collect the material we will need for our theoretical studies. It is already a rather peculiar collection. I would have very much liked to send you one or the other of these documents, but even though none is "classified," I wouldn't want to entrust any of them to the mail, as most of them are irreplaceable. Hopefully we will soon be able to tackle this material together.

The fact that all the nastiness of world politics has once again become concentrated on the Jews may be weak consolation to you in your work for the committee.[2]

With best wishes for a good vacation and cordial greetings to
you and your wife,
Yours,
Herbert Marcuse[3]

---

1 Horkheimer requested that Marcuse help him get a visa to visit Germany after the war. Civilian travel was limited and Horkheimer was trying to get a visit sponsored by government auspices. Marcuse attempted to get him permission to represent the U.S. government on a visit and was suggesting Horkheimer cultivate connections with the Socialist Unity Party in the Soviet zone, eventually to become the German Democratic Republic (DDR). Horkheimer received an invitation from Frankfurt University and began visiting Germany in 1948, returning the Institute of Social Research to Germany in 1950, while Marcuse continued to live and work in the U.S.

2 The Nuremberg War Crimes trials were unfolding at this time, revelations of the horrors of the concentration camps were widely discussed in the media, and Horkheimer and the Institute of Social Research were carrying out studies of anti-semitism.
3 Translated by Benjamin Gregg.

November 15, 1946
4609 Chevy Chase Blvd.
Washington 15, D.C.

Dear Horkheimer:

Thank you for your letter. The message is somewhat more promising than the one that preceded it; in the meantime I'm keeping all my fingers crossed. For superstitious reasons I don't want to go into detail about my proposals for the issue on Germany, but rather shall only say a few words toward explicating what I have in mind.[1]

The available material is comprehensive: economics, philosophy, political theory and praxis, law, "the re-orientation of culture," and so forth. Not only the official programs of the parties, but also debates internal to the parties, addresses to assemblies of functionaries, laws and statutes, critiques, philosophical pamphlets, and so on. Hence dividing the work among us shouldn't be difficult: we might choose, for each of the fields represented, a central problem as it appears in contemporary debates. For example in economics: competing perspectives on the forms of "de-concentration," limited or partial socialization, planning. Further: the role of the organized labor movement in boosting the economy. In literature: the endless resuscitation of the classics (the function of such resuscitation more generally). In philosophy: the pronouncements of Herr Jaspers.[2] Political theory: the "renewal" of Marxism by Social Democracy and Communism, etc. In just this way we could equally well identify other problems, for we could immediately trace them all back to a common core. When we are at that stage I shall look through the material and send you precise overviews and proposals.

As to the question of "external" collaborators: naturally I've never even considered Jean Wahl as a *contributor*: he is an impossible person and has nothing in common with us. I would suggest perhaps Merleau-Ponty, or one of the leading leftist existentialists, or Henri Lefevbre, Charles Bettelheim, Pierre Naville. Among the unknown younger scholars: Stefano, who has made an outstanding translation of Hegel. Among the Germans in Paris: Fritz Meyer. Toward increasing sales, we could win over the great Sartre for an essay. After reading his critical discussion of historical materialism in *Temps Modernes* I hardly think he would bring us into discredit.[3]

In England on the other hand I've not met anyone whom, in good conscience, I could name. Richard Löwenthal is dreadfully intelligent and unpleasant. Rudolf Schlesinger is much better but surely too much busy.[4]

Yet unfortunately these must remain concerns for a later time. How nice it would be were we at that stage already.

I hope to hear from you soon.

With cordial greetings, also to your wife,
Yours,
Herbert Marcuse[5]

---

1 Horkheimer had discussed with Marcuse the possibilities of recommencing publication of *Zeitschrift für Sozialforschung* with a special issue on Germany. Marcuse lists here material and topics that could be utilized and addressed.
2 German philosopher Karl Jaspers had spent the war in Switzerland and as one of the few major philosophers who had not supported National Socialism, he had much prestige in post-war German and indeed international intellectual circles.
3 Jean Wahl was a leading French existentialist who had written on Kierkegaard and Heidegger. Merleau-Ponty combined existentialism, phenomenology and Marxism, while Lefevbre, Bettelheim and Naville were leading Marxist intellectuals, Stefano was a Hegel scholar. "Fritz Meyer" probably refers to Hans Mayer who the Institute was supporting in Paris during the war and who later became a major German literary critic. Mayer had close connections to Horkheimer, exchanging many letters with him in the 1940s. Sartre, of course, was the leading French intellectual of the day who was coming closer to Marxism during this period.
4 Richard Löwenthal was a German political scientist in exile in England who wrote on totalitarianism, capitalism and socialism, while Rudolf Schlesinger was a German literary critic who had published books on Soviet literature and articles on the topic in the Institute journal.
5 Translated by Benjamin Gregg.

February 9, 1947
4609 Chevy Chase Blvd.
Washington 15, D.C.

Dear Horkheimer:

First of all my cordial greetings and best wishes for your birthday. I had hoped that this day in 1947 would already fall in a period of our collaboration, but I've had to postpone this hope once again. Several days ago I was in New York and had a thorough discussion with Pollock; he'll fill you in himself. To postpone any longer that which needs to be said strikes me as unacceptable both subjectively and objectively. That goes for the *Zeitschrift* as well. I regard the necessity of its reappearance as even more acute now than three months ago – with full consideration given to Löwenthal's counter arguments. I've done my own small part toward preparation: I (and, I fear, I alone) have prepared the reports we agreed on at our last meeting. These are really nothing but notes. But I am working on them further, and since their completion is still not in sight, I'll send you the first part as soon as it is typed up. Perhaps that will at the least get a discussion going.[1]

Unfortunately it will be interrupted, as I am supposed to go to Germany and Austria for three months on April 1.[2] Pollock and I agreed that I should still go. I would be grateful to you if, before my departure, you might let me know your views and plans.

I'd like to take this opportunity to ask another favor of you. When I left, you were kind enough to place several of my books under your personal protection. Among them, as I recall, were works by Eduard Bernstein and Trotsky, which I could now use for my studies. If you no longer need them, could you have Löwenthal bring them along? Should you want to get rid of the whole stack, I could of course relieve you of it now.

In hopes of hearing from you soon, and once again with the most cordial wishes and greetings, also for your wife, and from my wife.

Yours,
Herbert Marcuse[3]

---

1 Marcuse is referring here to the "33 Theses" which he completed in 1947 and which are published in this volume. Marcuse was correct that Horkheimer, Adorno and other Institute members had not written up possible contributions, though in a December 29, 1948 letter to Marcuse, Horkheimer suggested that he and Adorno were planning to write theses on the contemporary situation in the style of Marcuse's fragments and that republication of the Institute journal was again being contemplated – though nothing came of these thoughts.
2 During the visit that Marcuse mentions here, he visited his former philosophy teacher Martin Heidegger; see the exchange of letters between them on pages 263f.
3 Translated by Benjamin Gregg.

July 18, 1947
4609 Chevy Chase Blvd.
Washington 15, D.C.

Dear Horkheimer:

Many thanks for your letter and the invitation to come to California.

I of course accept gladly. But everything depends, stupidly enough, on the situation at the Office. Next week we will drive briefly to New Hampshire for a break. But I have to be back in Washington as soon as the beginning of the second week in August. At that time the British–American Conference on the Ruhr (for which we've done a lot of work) is to conclude and its resolutions are to be distributed to be worked on further. In any case I hope to come out at the end of August or at the beginning of September at the latest.[1] Please let me know if that would be convenient for you.

I've read your book.[2] At this point I'll only say that I agree with you completely. If only you could soon fully develop all of the perspectives you could only hint at there – especially those that worry me the most: that idea that reason, which has become total manipulation and power, even then remains reason, that the real horror of the system therefore lies more in rationality than in irrationality. This is of course what you *say* – but you still need to fill in all the steps for the reader – something no one else can and will do. I'd like to discuss this with you at length. The German situation is already at an advanced stage of the development you analyze: where negative rationality turns into positive irrationality.

Need I mention that I've spoken to dozens of people who have inquired about the *Zeitschrift*? Printed matter can now be imported into Germany again.

Hoping to see you again soon,
Yours,
Herbert Marcuse[3]

---

1 Marcuse visited Horkheimer in the Fall who wrote Löwenthal in an October 3, 1947 letter: "Marcuse's visit has been very pleasant so far. The theses he wrote as a possible program for the *Zeitschrift für Sozialforschung*, particularly the second part, contain some of the best formulations on these topics I have heard for a long time. Since the publication of the *Zeitschrift* with the aspirations and about the same volume of the old one would involve not only too much of our common time but also too great a risk, we considered the possibility of a smaller periodical which would be exclusively devoted to the critique of culture (i.e. of any work in the realm of the objective mind: books, periodicals, plays, movies, compositions etc.) . . . During the next few months each of us should probably write one article." Again, nothing came of this suggestion.

2 Marcuse is referring here to Horkheimer's *Eclipse of Reason* which he circulated to colleagues in 1946 for their comments; it was published in 1947. Marcuse evidently never commented in detail during this period on *Dialectic of Enlightenment*, which, however, he described to me during a December 1978 interview in La Jolla as "one of the authentic expressions of critical theory."

3 Translated by Benjamin Gregg.

October 17, 1947
4609 Chevy Chase Blvd.
Washington 15, D.C.

Dear Horkheimer:

I'd like to thank you particularly for the time in Los Angeles: it meant a lot to me and again gave me some hope for the future. I immediately began to work through and add to the theses, in the spirit of our discussion. Other works, inspired by our discussion, will follow.

Several days ago I received a letter from Germany informing me that one of my acquaintances – a former German sociologist who now has a position at an American college and who recently returned from work in Berlin for the Military Government – wants to establish a German–American journal of social research. Preparations were already well under way. Fortunately his German publisher asked me what I thought of his qualifications. I responded negatively: I said I considered the publication of such a journal in Germany today to be an undertaking of such great responsibility that it should not be left to someone who would only serve up warmed-over nonsense. I assume that settled the matter.

Also I got in touch again with Robert Schmid to find out something about the planned expert-missions. What's your opinion of the Speier Committee on Anti-Semitism in Germany?[1]

Together with this letter I am sending you *Dokumente der Menschenverachtung* [Documents of Contempt for Humanity] and Heidegger, *Vom Wesen der Wahrheit* [The Essence of Truth]. The latter belongs to you; please return the *Dokumente* after you've used them.

Hoping to hear from you soon, again with the most cordial thanks, and best wishes also from my wife, to you and your wife.

Yours,
Herbert Marcuse

Have you thought about drafting a *plan for an institute*?[2]

---

1 I could find no biographical references to Robert Schmid. The Speier Committee on Anti-Semitism was headed by Hans Speier, a German sociologist who had emigrated to the United States in 1932 and who had taught at the New School for Social Research and worked for the U.S. government in Washington from 1942–7.
2 Translated by Benjamin Gregg.

January 20, 1949
4609 Chevy Chase Blvd.
Washington, 15, D.C.

Dear Horkheimer:

Unfortunately your trip to Germany is still pending. Last week I asked again in the Pentagon: the telegram was sent around Christmas yet the answer hasn't arrived yet.[1] I don't want to press these people too hard and would suggest I wait another week until I'm back in touch with them. In the meantime I have, as Löwenthal surely has informed you, drawn up with him a short outline of your lecture on recent trends in social research, an outline the Pentagon requested of me. Of course it in no way commits you and probably will remain buried somewhere in the Pentagon's files: the goal was to show that the lecture fits in with the "Social Science Project" of OMGUS. Since we were in a great hurry I wasn't able to, nor did I want to, trouble you with this.

With envy I read over your studies and only wish I could take part in them. If your trip does not come to pass, we should then have, at least in the summer, a lengthy discussion! There's not much one can say in writing. I've read only half of Lukàcs's book on Hegel: I consider the destruction of legends to be very worthwhile.[2] For my part I've been occupied again mainly with Marxist theory – in connection with the lectures on dialectical materialism that in February I'll give again at the Russian Institute at Columbia University. I'm always coming up with ever more exciting things which, in connection with what I'm learning in the Office, are all the more exciting.[3] On the side I've written a critique of Lord Acton's *Essays on Freedom and Power* for the *American Historical Review,* and now hope to finally begin writing an essay on Vico that the *Journal of Philosophy* wants from me.[4]

Hoping to see you again soon, one way or another, and with the best of greetings to you and your wife, also from my wife.

Yours
Herbert Marcuse[5]

---

1 Marcuse was attempting to use his State Department connections to facilitate a passport for Horkheimer to travel to Germany to lecture at Frankfurt University.
2 Georg Lukàcs, *Der Junge Hegel*; translated *The Young Hegel.* London: Merlin Press, 1975.
3 Marcuse lectured at the Russian Institute at Columbia University in February 1949 and later in the 1950s; his March 30, 1949 letter to Horkheimer (page 259) indicates that he received an offer of a Senior Fellowship from the Russian

Institute to learn Russian and work on a study of Russian Marxism. The product
of this work and his time at Harvard was *Soviet Marxism*.
4 Marcuse's review of Acton's *Essay on Freedom and Power* was published in
American Historical Review, 54, 3 (April 1949), pp. 447–9, while the essay on
Vico was never published and is not found in the Marcuse archives, so was
presumably never written.
5 Translated by Benjamin Gregg.

———————

March 30, 1949
4609 Chevy Chase Blvd.
Washington 15, D.C.

Dear Horkheimer:

A new development has occurred, which involves so many problems that
I should like to report it to you for discussion and advice: I have been
offered a Senior Fellowship by the Russian Institute, Columbia University.
The grant, in the amount of $5,000, is for a period of two years, with no
other obligation than to learn the Russian language (which may be done
under the fellowship grant). The offer came as an outgrowth of my lectures.
Under the fellowship, I am to work on a study of Russian Marxism (from
the split of the Russian party to the latest manifestations of Stalinism) in
its interconnection with the transformation of Western society since the
beginning of the century. This study should be published as a book (not
necessarily under the auspices of the Russian Institute). The Institute
assumes no commitment or obligation after the completion of the two year
period; however, I was told that there is a good chance that they will be
able to place me in a fairly adequate academic position, since they have
excellent connections.

Thus far the facts. Here are some of the implications: I would have to
work in New York, since I am supposed to use the facilities of the Institute
and to participate in the staff discussions and seminars. I could in all
likelihood get one year leave of absence from the State Department, but
certainly not two years; I would therefore have to resign from the
Department after one year.

As you will see, the risk is considerable, especially in view of the fact that
my present position is a permanent one (which of course does not at all
include my being fired if the office is abolished, or also for other reasons).
There is also a very considerable cut in my income. On the other hand,
it seems to me that I (or let me say: we) have no right to turn down this
offer, which is probably the last I am going to get. None of us can take the
responsibility of continuing in such a function as my present one if he has

the opportunity to do work which may find favor before our heavenly tribunal. The proposed study under the fellowship would give me enough leeway to write the things which we want to write (at least to a very great extent, and in certain fields), and I count on our really working together on it. The technical arrangements can be easily made. I will have enough time to do at least part of the work with you out there.

The main hitch is of course, as always, the material basis. $5,000 would hardly be enough to sustain me under the new arrangement, especially since I am now also supporting my mother. Would you be willing to supplement the grant? I am fully aware of the financial situation, but I hope that you approve. I think I can promise you that the return, the finished product, will be to your credit, and that you will not regret it. The situation would, of course, be altogether different if you could now arrange for my full-time participation in yours and the common work; In this case, I would gladly turn down the offer and resign from my present position. However you may decide, the decision should no longer be postponed. To say that time is running short is an understatement.[1]

With best wishes and greetings to you and your wife, also from my wife,
Cordially yours,
Herbert Marcuse

---

1 Marcuse was appealing to Horkheimer for continued support which would make possible academic work. As it turned out, Marcuse's wife Sophie had cancer and he stayed in Washington, D.C. with his State Department position until she died in 1951, and then took up the Columbia University Russian Institute offer.

X

Martin Heidegger

† This exchange of letters between Marcuse and Heidegger was found in the Marcuse archives; the letters were translated by Richard Wolin, whom we thank for providing permission to publish his translations here.

HEIDEGGER AND
MARCUSE†

A Dialogue in Letters

MARCUSE TO HEIDEGGER, AUGUST 28, 1947

4609 Chevy Chase Blvd.
Washington 15, D.C.

Lieber Herr Heidegger,

I have thought for a long time about what you told me during my visit to Todtnauberg, and I would like to write to you about it quite openly.[1]

You told me that you fully dissociated yourself from the Nazi regime as of 1934, that in your lectures you made extremely critical remarks, and that you were observed by the Gestapo. I will not doubt your word. But the fact remains that in 1933 you identified yourself so strongly with the regime that today in the eyes of many you are considered as one of its strongest intellectual proponents.[2] Your own speeches, writings and treatises from this period are proof thereof. You have never publicly retracted them – not even after 1945. You have never publicly explained that you have arrived at judgments other than those which you expressed in 1933–34 and articulated in your writings. You remained in Germany after 1934, although you could have found a position abroad practically anywhere. You never publicly denounced any of the actions or ideologies of the regime. Because of these circumstances you are still today identified with the Nazi regime. Many of us have long awaited a statement from you, a statement that would clearly and finally free you from such identification, a statement that honestly expresses your current attitude about the events that have occurred. But you have never uttered such a statement – at least it has never emerged from the private sphere. I – and very many others – have admired you as a philosopher; from you we have learned an infinite amount. But we cannot make the separation between Heidegger the philosopher and Heidegger the man, for it contradicts your own philosophy. A philosopher can be deceived regarding political matters; in which case he will openly acknowledge his error. But he cannot be deceived about a regime that has killed millions of Jews – merely because they were Jews – that made terror into an everyday phenomenon, and that turned everything that pertains to the ideas of spirit, freedom and truth into its bloody opposite. A regime that in every respect imaginable was the deadly caricature of the western tradition that you yourself so forcefully explicated and justified. And if that regime was not the caricature of that tradition but its actual culmination – in this case, too, there could be no deception, for then you would have to indict and disavow this entire tradition.

Is this really the way you would like to be remembered in the history of ideas? Every attempt to combat this cosmic misunderstanding founders on the generally shared resistance to taking seriously a Nazi ideologue. Common sense (also among intellectuals), which bears witness to such resistance, refuses to view you as a philosopher, because philosophy and Nazism are irreconcilable. In this conviction common sense is justified. Once again: you (and we) can only combat the identification of your person and your work with Nazism (and thereby the dissolution of your philosophy) if you make a public avowal of your changed views.

This week I will send off a package to you. My friends have recommended strongly against it and have accused me of helping a man who identified with a regime that sent millions of my co-religionists to the gas chambers (in order to forestall misunderstandings, I would like to observe that I was not only an anti-Nazi because I was a Jew, but also would have been one from the very beginning on political, social and intellectual grounds, even had I been "100 per cent aryan"). Nothing can counter this argument. I excuse myself in the eyes of my own conscience, by saying that I am sending a package to a man from whom I learned philosophy from 1928 to 1932. I am myself aware that that is a poor excuse. The philosopher of 1933–34 cannot be completely different than the one prior to 1933; all the less so, insofar as you expressed and grounded your enthusiastic justification of the Nazi state in philosophical terms.

---

1 In a February 9, 1947 letter from Marcuse to Horkheimer (page 254), Marcuse mentions that he was planning a three-month visit to Germany and Austria,

beginning on April 1. During this trip, undertaken in part in conjunction with his activities with the State Department, Marcuse visited Heidegger in his Black Forest, Todtnauberg hut and exchanged letters with him after returning to the States.

2 On the controversies concerning Heidegger's relations to the Nazis, see Richard Wolin, editor, *The Heidegger Controversy: A Critical Reader*. New York: Columbia University, 1991.

HEIDEGGER TO MARCUSE, JANUARY 20, 1948

If I may infer from your letter that you are seriously concerned with [reaching] a correct judgment about my work and person, then your letter shows me precisely how difficult it is to converse with persons who have not been living in Germany since 1933 and who judge the beginning of the National Socialist movement from its end.

Regarding the main points of your letter, I would like to say the following:

1 Concerning 1933: I expected from National Socialism a spiritual renewal of life in its entirety, a reconciliation of social antagonisms and a deliverance of western Dasein from the dangers of communism. These convictions were expressed in my Rectoral Address (have you read this *in its entirety?*), in a lecture on "The Essence of Science" and in two speeches to students of [Freiburg] University. There was also an election appeal of approximately 25–30 lines, published in the [Freiburg] student newspaper. Today I regard a few of the sentences as misleading [*Entleisung*].

2 In 1934 I recognized my political error and resigned my rectorship in protest against the state and party. That no. 1 [i.e., Heidegger's Party activities] was exploited for propaganda purposes both here and abroad, and that no. 2 [his resignation] hushed up for equally propagandistic reasons, failed to come to my attention and cannot be held against me.

3 You are entirely correct that I failed to provide a public, readily comprehensible counter-declaration; it would have been the end of both me and my family. On this point, Jaspers said: that we remain alive is our guilt.

4 In my lectures and courses from 1933–44 I incorporated a standpoint that was so unequivocal that among those who were my students, none fell victim to Nazi ideology. My works from this period, if they ever appear, will testify to this fact.

5 An avowal after 1945 was for me impossible: the Nazi supporters

announced their change of allegiance in the most loathsome way; I, however, had nothing in common with them.

6 To the charges of dubious validity that you express "about a regime that murdered millions of Jews, that made terror into an everyday phenomenon, and that turned everything that pertains to the ideas of spirit, freedom and truth into its bloody opposite," I can merely add that if instead of "Jews" you had written "East Germans" [i.e., Germans of the eastern territories], then the same holds true for one of the allies, with the difference that everything that has occurred since 1945 has become public knowledge, while the bloody terror of the Nazis in point of fact had been kept a secret from the German people.

MARCUSE TO HEIDEGGER, MAY 12, 1948

4609 Chevy Chase Blvd.
Washington 15, D.C.

Lieber Herr Heidegger,

For a long time I wasn't sure as to whether I should answer your letter of January 20. You are right: a conversation with persons who have not been in Germany since 1933 is obviously very difficult. But I believe that the reason for this is not to be found in our lack of familiarity with the German situation under Nazism. We were very well aware of this situation – perhaps even better aware than people who were in Germany. The direct contact that I had with many of these people in 1947 convinced me of this. Nor can it be explained by the fact that we "judge the beginning of the National Socialist movement from its end." We knew, and I myself saw it too, that the beginning already contained the end. The difficulty of the conversation seems to me rather to be explained by the fact that people in Germany were exposed to a total perversion of all concepts and feelings, something which very many accepted only too readily. Otherwise, it would be impossible to explain the fact that a man like yourself, who was capable of understanding western philosophy like no other, were able to see in Nazism "a spiritual renewal of life in its entirety," a "redemption of occidental Dasein from the dangers of communism" (which however is itself an essential component of that Dasein!). This is not a political but instead an intellectual problem – I am tempted to say: a problem of cognition, of truth. You, the philosopher, have confused the liquidation of occidental Dasein with its renewal? Was this liquidation not already evident in every word of the "leaders," in every gesture and deed of the

SA, long before 1933?

However, I would like to treat only one portion of your letter, otherwise my silence could be interpreted as complicity.

You write that everything that I say about the extermination of the Jews applies just as much to the allies, if instead of "Jews" one were to insert "East Germans." With this sentence don't you stand outside of the dimension in which a conversation between men is even possible – outside of Logos? For only outside of the dimension of logic is it possible to explain, to relativize [*auszugleichen*], to "comprehend" a crime by saying that others would have done the same thing. Even further: how is it possible to equate the torture, the maiming and the annihilation of millions of men with the forcible relocation of population groups who suffered none of these outrages (apart perhaps from several exceptional instances)? From a contemporary perspective, there seems already to be a night and day difference in humanity and inhumanity in the difference between Nazi concentration camps and the deportations and internments of the post-war years. On the basis of your argument, if the allies had reserved Auschwitz and Buchenwald – and everything that transpired there – for the "East Germans" and the Nazis, then the account would be in order! If however the difference between inhumanity and humanity is reduced to this erroneous calculus, then this becomes the world historical guilt of the Nazi system, which has demonstrated to the world what, after more than 2000 years of western Dasein, men can do to their fellow men. It looks as though the seed has fallen upon fertile ground: perhaps we are still experiencing the continuation of what began in 1933. Whether you would still consider it to be a "renewal" I am not sure.

INDEX

absolutism, 70, 109, 113, 114, 116, 125

abundance/scarcity, 41, 61, 62, 63, 64, 84, 109, 171, 172

Academy for German Law, 78

Acheson, Dean, 26

Acton, Lord, 258 and n

administration, *see* domination

Adorno, T. W., 2, 36, 255 n; *Dialectic of Enlightenment*, 14, 16 n, 249 and n, 256 n; Horkheimer and, 12, 15–16, 234 n, 246 n; Husserl, 16 n; Marcuse and, 16 n; Marx, 34; "message in a bottle", 234 n; return to Germany, 31, 34

Aesthetic Dimension, The, 30, 200

aesthetics, *see* art

American Historical Review, 258, 259 n

American Jewish Committee, 240 n, 243 n

Anabaptists, 101

anarchy, 127, 225, 226

Anderson, Eugene, 20, 239, 240 n

anthropology, 103

anti-intellectualism, 144

anti-liberalism, 121

anti-rationalism, 121

anti-semitism, 90, 144, 240 n, 242 and n, 251, 252 n; Christianity and, 245; spearhead theory, 244 and n;

Speier committee, 257 and n

Antisthenes, 96

apparatus (term), 44

Aragon, Louis, 199–214; *Aurélian*, 29, 208–12; *Monde réel*, 209, 212; *Vie antérieure*, 209

Aristippus, 96

Aristotle, 14, 97, 99, 109

Arnold, Thurman, 7, 12 and n, 146 n

art, 29; avant-garde, 202, 207; form in, 204; function of, 168–9; Hitler and, 169; monopoly, 201, 202; National Socialism and, 89–92, 153, 169, 199–214; negating power of, 203, 212; politics and, 199–214; propaganda and, 168–9; reality and, 203, 214; revolutionary, 201; sensuality, 204; totalitarianism and, 199–214

Auschwitz, 267

Austria: Marcuse visits, 252, 255, 263 and n; social life, 194

authoritarianism, 41, 53, 55, 70, 121, 122, 123, 128, 154

automobiles, 47

avant-garde, 202, 207

Avedon Set, 235 and n

Averroism, 99, 100

axis (term), 180

backwardness, 80